EARLY HARFORD COUNTIANS

Individuals Living in Harford County, Maryland
in its Formative Years

Volume 3: Supplement

Henry C. Peden, Jr.

HERITAGE BOOKS
2008

HERITAGE BOOKS
AN IMPRINT OF HERITAGE BOOKS, INC.

Books, CDs, and more—Worldwide

For our listing of thousands of titles see our website
at
www.HeritageBooks.com

Published 2008 by
HERITAGE BOOKS, INC.
Publishing Division
100 Railroad Ave. #104
Westminster, Maryland 21157

Copyright © 1999 Henry C. Peden, Jr.

All rights reserved. No part of this book may be reproduced or transmitted in any form or by any means, electronic or mechanical, including photocopying, recording or by any information storage and retrieval system without written permission from the author, except for the inclusion of brief quotations in a review.

International Standard Book Numbers
Paperbound: 978-1-888265-90-3
Clothbound: 978-0-7884-7573-3

CONTENTS

Preface to Revised Edition v

Additions and Corrections to Early Harford Countians vi

Introduction x

Sources and Abbreviations xi

Map of Harford County Hundreds in 1783..viii

Early Harford Countians, Supplement 1

PREFACE TO REVISED EDITION

This set of three volumes is a revision to the original version of Harford Countians which was published as a single volume in 1993. We have divided the original into two volumes for reasons of economy and in the interests of completeness we have added a third volume (supplement) to include the 1775 Census for Harford County and the 1776 Census for Susquenna Hundred and Spesutia Lower Hundred. These were not included in the original version. In addition we have included additions and corrections which Mr. Peden has uncovered in the intervening years.

The Publisher
Westminster, Maryland
1999

ADDITIONS AND CORRECTIONS TO EARLY HARFORD COUNTIANS

All persons designated throughout the book as "presidential electors" (source G2) were actually voters, not electors, in the election of 1789.

Dr. John Archer's ledger numbers (source D) have been mixed up in the Introduction. "Ledger F" should be "Ledgers D and F" and "Ledger D" should be "Ledger B" in the reference description.

Two of the hundreds on the map of Harford County were named in error. Eden Hundred should be Bush River Upper Hundred, and Bush Creek Upper Hundred (which was labeled improperly anyway; there is no Bush Creek in Harford County) should be Eden Hundred.

p. 2 - ALBERT FAMILY. Philip Albert married Rachel Webb and they had nine children, three of whom were William Albert (1779-1856), Samuel Albert (1780-1847), and Philip Albert (1787-1838), all of whom lived in Union County, Kentucky. [Ref: Information provided by Margaret S. Bishop, of Jarrettsville, Maryland].

p. 18 - BAKER, Maurice. He was born on September 29, 1783 in Harford County, Maryland, married Margaret Waters on February 8, 1809 in Maysville, Kentucky, and died on December 25, 1855 in Scott County, Iowa. [Ref: Harry Wright Newman's *Anne Arundel Gentry*, Vol. 2, p. 431].

p. 87 - COOLEY, Richard. He married Rachel Lewis on November 6, 1788. [Ref: Harry Wright Newman's *Maryland Revolutionary Records*, p. 112].

p. 102 - CUSICK, Christopher. He was a Revolutionary War soldier who married Mary Cave on May 10, 1790 in Harford County, Maryland and died in December, 1831. His widow lived in Baltimore in 1845. [Ref: Virgil D. White's *Genealogical Abstracts of Revolutionary War Pension Files*, Vol. I, p. 856, citing pension file W3955].

p. 114 - DICK, David. The note that his "name looks like Du David Dick" on the 1776 tax list is actually a reference to "Dr. David Dick." [Ref: Harford County Land Records, 1793, Liber JLG, No. L, f. 208].

p. 128 - "Eden Hundred FAMILY" at the bottom of the second column should actually read "EDEN FAMILY."

p. 130 - ELLIOTT, Samuel. He married Catherine or Keziah Webb in the spring of 1777. [Ref: Revolutionary War Pension File R3306].

p. 150 - GARISON, Cunell[?]. This is Cornelius Garrison. The "Jon Garison" is John Garrison, father of Cornelius, James, Philip, Samuel, and Hannah who married William Baldwin. The "John Dingany" or "Young" listed with the Garrisons is "John Guyon." Cornelius Garrison's mother was Ann Guyon, wife of John Garrison. The Garrisons and the Guyons were all from Staten Island, New York, settled for a few years in Bucks County, Pennsylvania, and then came to Harford

County, Maryland about 1768 or so. Cornelius Garrison was born on February 22, 1737 and died on June 13, 1814, His wife Susannah was born on September 15, 1764 and died on November 2, 1815. [Ref: *Bible and Family Records of Harford County, Maryland Families*, Vol. IV, p. 96, and information provided by Margaret Smith Keigler, of Monkton, Maryland].

p. 153 - GARRISON, Anna. The Cornelius Garrison Family Bible states she was born on Tuesday, October 26, 1784, at 7 o'clock in the morning. [Ref: *Bible and Family Records of Harford County, Maryland Families*, Vol. IV, p. 96].

p. 153 - GARRISON, John. The Cornelius Garrison Family Bible states he was born on Sunday, March 26, 1786, at 25 minutes past seven in the afternoon, and died on July 12, 1854. [Ref: *Bible and Family Records of Harford County, Maryland Families*, Vol. IV, p. 96].

p. 153 - GARRISON, Mary. The Cornelius Garrison Family Bible states she was born on July 24, 1786 and departed this life on July 29, 1875, aged 89 years and 5 days. [Ref: *Bible and Family Records of Harford County, Maryland Families*, Vol. IV, p. 96].

p. 199 - HOLLAND FAMILY. Francis Holland Family Records state that Francis Holland married Hannah Matthews on November 8, 1770 and their children were: Francis Uty Holland (August 30, 1771 - May 15, 1818); John Holland (born May 4, 1773); Henrietta Holland (April 9, 1777 - October 11, 1801); Betty Holland (February 16, 1779 - August 12, 1804); Thomas Holland (born May 20, 1787); and, Robert William Holland (February 22, 1793 - June 3, 1866). [Ref: *Bible and Family Records of Harford County, Maryland Families*, Vol. III, p. 63].

p. 199 - HOLLAND FAMILY. The George Washington Holland Bible states Mrs. Ann Holland, consort of Archibald Holland, died on January 7, 1835, aged 51, and Mr. Archibald Holland died on January 9, 1866, in his 80th year. It further states that Archibald Holland was born on March 9, 1786 and Mrs. Ann Holland was born in the year 1774 [sic]. Also listed are Benjamin Holland (born June 7, 1773), Abraham Holland (born July 25, 1775), James Holland (born July 13, 1781), and Jesey Holland (born April 10, 1790). [Ref: *Bible and Family Records of Harford County, Maryland Families*, Vol. III, p. 65].

p. 205 - HOSHAL, Jesse. He married Mary Hurst on December 22, 1779. [Ref: Harry Wright Newman's *Maryland Revolutionary Records*, p. 116].

p. 207 - HOWE, John. The Howe and Nagle Bible states John Howe was born on January 11, 1784 and died on July 18, 1851, aged 67 years, 6 months and 7 days. [Ref: *Bible Records Collected by the William Paca Chapter of the Daughters of the American Revolution, Harford County, Maryland, circa 1958-1962*, Vol. I, p. 76].

p. 208 - HOWLETT FAMILY. Howlett Family Records list the following births: Mary Howlett (born September 23, 1781); Nancy Howlett (born May 7, 1783); Martha Howlett (born November 12, 1784, daughter of James and Catherine Howlett); Catherine Howlett (born June 23, 1785); James Howlett (born February 7, 1788); and, Matthew Howlett (born August 17, 1791). [Ref: *Bible and Family Records of Harford County, Maryland Families*, Vol. III, p. 67].

p. 243 - LEE, John. He married Martha Howlett on August 4, 1779. [Ref: Harry Wright Newman's *Maryland Revolutionary Records*, p. 117].

p. 243 - LEE, John. He married Martha Graham on March 13, 1789. [Ref: Revolutionary War Pension File W4477].

p. 279 - MEADS, Daniel. He was born in Harford County in 1783, married Martha Magee in 1805, served in the War of 1812, and died in Baltimore City on January 4, 1873, aged 90. [Ref: Information provided by Janice D. Harding, of Baltimore, Maryland].

p. 282 - MILES, Joshua. He married Jane Glenn on February 6, 1785. [Ref: Harry Wright Newman's *Maryland Revolutionary Records*, p. 119].

p. 352 - NEVILLE, William. The Ezekiel Cole Family Bible states that William Neville was born on January 7, 1783 and not 1785 as transcribed from his tombstone. [Ref: *Bible and Family Records of Harford County, Maryland Families*, Vol. IV, p. 89].

p. 370 - PENNINGTON, John. The John Pennington Family Bible states he was born on October 31, 1789, married Catherine Bishop in 1819, and died on October 10, 1875. [Ref: *Bible and Family Records of Harford County, Maryland Families*, Vol. IV, p. 100].

p. 410 - RUTLEDGE, Jehu. The Rutledge Family Bible states that Jehu Rutledge was born on September 20, 1789, married Priscilla Fitzpatrick on January 9, 1817, and died on December 16, 1859. [Ref: *Bible Records Collected by the William Paca Chapter of the Daughters of the American Revolution, Harford County, Maryland, circa 1958-1962*, Vol. II, p. 92].

p. 413 - SCALF, Henry. This is "Henry Scarff." The taxable "John Scalf" is his son "John Scarff" (born 1759). The taxable "Sammel Griffin" is Samuel Griffin who married Henry's daughter Sarah Scarff (born 1761) circa 1778. [Ref: Research by the author].

p. 421 - SHERIDINE, James. The Howe and Nagle Family Bible states that James Sheridan (Shirdine) was born in 1774, died on April 3, 1838, aged 64, and was the father of Sarah Howe (How) who was born in 1794. [Ref: *Bible Records Collected by the William Paca Chapter of the Daughters of the American Revolution, Harford County, Maryland, circa 1958-1962*, Vol. I, p. 76].

p. 446 - STUMP, John. The Williams and Neilson Family Bible states that John Stump married Cassandra Wilson on October 2, 1779. [Ref: *Bible and Family Bible Records of Harford County, Families*, Vol. III, p. 82, and Filing Case A, Maryland Historical Society].

p. 468 - TURNER, John. He married Anne Elizabeth Mariner on February 7, 1788. [Ref: Harry Wright Newman's *Maryland Revolutionary Records*, p. 124].

Volume III of *Early Harford Countians* contains information from the extant tax lists of 1775 for the hundreds of Harford County, viz., Deer Creek Upper, Deer Creek Lower, Bush River Upper, Bush River Lower, Susquehanna, Spesutia Upper, Spesutia Lower, and Gunpowder Lower. Also included are the 1776 tax lists for Spesutia Lower Hundred and Susquehanna Hundred which were not included in the first edition of my book. The original tax lists are in the Archives Division of The Historical Society of Harford County, 143 N. Main Street, P. O. Box 366, Bel Air, Maryland 21014-0366.

                                                             Henry C. Peden, Jr.
Bel Air, Maryland
February 14, 1999

INTRODUCTION TO ORIGINAL EDITION (Corrected)

Harford County was created from Baltimore County in 1773 and its first court was established in March 1774, in Harford Town (or Bush). Bel Air became the county seat in 1782.

In the first two decades following the creation of Harford County a great quantity of records of importance to local historians and genealogists was generated. These records are found today in the Harford County Courthouse, Library and Manuscript Division of the Historical Society of Harford County, Library and Manuscript Division of the Maryland Historical Society, Maryland State Archives, and in personal holdings of researchers and descendants. Some records have been abstracted and published, but contain errors, and a significant number of records have not been published.

This compilation was prepared with the intent of bringing together under one cover facts relating to individual Harford Countians from the creation of the county in 1773 through and including the first United States census of 1790. This book contains historical and genealogical information from the following sources: Tax List of 1774, Tax List of 1776, Tax List of 1778, Census of 1776, Property List of 1783, Medical Ledgers of Dr. John Archer from 1773 to 1790, Orphans Court Proceedings from 1778 to 1790, Family Bibles, Estate Administrations Index from 1774 to 1790, Genealogical Notes from the *Bulletin of the Historical Society of Harford County,* Gleanings from Walter W. Preston's *History of Harford County* and from C. Milton Wright's *Our Harford Heritage,* Births and Deaths from 1773 to 1790 in the Registers of St. John's and St. George's Parishes, Land Records Index from 1774 to 1790, Marriage Records from 1774 to 1790, Criminal Court Dockets from 1778 to 1788, List of Non-Associators and Non-Enrollers in 1775, Quaker Records of Deer Creek and Little Falls Monthly Meetings, Tombstone Inscriptions, Index to Wills Probated Between 1774 and 1790, County Court Minutes from 1783 to 1788, Committee of License Proceedings in 1775 and 1776, Certificates of Survey between 1773 and 1790, Presidential Electors in 1789, First U.S. Census of 1790, and Gleanings from *Revolutionary Patriots of Harford County, 1775-1783,* plus this compiler's own research and genealogical collections.

Virtually any person connected to an historical and/or genealogical event between 1773 and 1790 in Harford County has been included in this book. Since Harford County was created from Baltimore County, this book, although different in format, is somewhat of a continuation of those Harford County families described in *Baltimore County Families, 1659-1759,* by Robert W. Barnes. Therefore, it follows that the researcher will refer to Mr. Barnes' Baltimore County book for earlier Harford County genealogical information.

Following each entry is the source of information. These are identified by a letter or letter-number and are explained below:

(A)   Tax Lists of 1783: Property owners, heads of household, names of tracts, number of white inhabitants, single men, and paupers. (With all due respect to the publication of these lists by Bettie Carothers in 1978, the original lists were checked and many errors were detected in her book. Those mistakes have been corrected herein.)

(B)   Census of 1776: Families, individuals, slaves, hired hands, servants, and ages, plus their areas of residence, known as "hundreds." (Incomplete. One-half of this census is missing.) Extant lists were published in *Maryland Records, Vol. II*, by Gaius M. Brumbaugh (1915) and Bettie Carothers (n.d.) whose work has been reprinted by Family Line Publications.

(C)   Tax Lists of 1778: Taxables only (free white males aged 18 years and upwards, and slaves of all ages). (Copied by William Wilkins of Baltimore, Maryland, in 1959, but never published.)

(D)   Gleanings from the Medical Ledgers of Dr. John Archer: Ledger "D" & "F" (from 1779 to 1790) is coded "D1," and Ledger "B" (from 1773 to 1775) is coded "D2." (Original ledger "D" & "F" is in the Manuscripts Division of the Maryland Historical Society, and original ledger "B" is in the Manuscripts Division of the Historical Society of Harford County.)

(E)   Orphans Court Proceedings, 1778-1810: Only those events (primarily orphans, indentures, and dates of birth) mentioned between 1774 and 1790 were abstracted. Records are in the Harford County Courthouse. One should also consult *Abstracts of the Orphans Court Proceedings of Harford County, 1778-1800*, by Henry C. Peden, Jr. (1990).

(F)   Family Bible Records (collected by the DAR). Records are available at the Maryland Historical Society Library and the Library of the Historical Society of Harford County. One should also consult the *Inventory of Maryland Bible Records* published by the Genealogical Council of Maryland (1989).

(G)   The Historical Society of Harford County. Source "G1" is information from the Society's "Bulletin," including the genealogical notes of Jon Harlan Livezey. Source "G2" is a list of presidential voters of Harford County in 1789.

(H)   *History of Harford County*, by Walter W. Preston (1901).

(I)   Index to Estate Administrations, 1774-1790, and also supplemented with the names of the administrators. For more information one should consult *Heirs and Legatees of Harford County, 1774-1802*, by Henry C. Peden, Jr. (1989).

(J)   Births and Deaths from the Registers of St. John's and St. George's Parishes (only events between 1773 and 1790 were abstracted). For more information one should consult *St. John's and St. George's Parish Register, 1696-1851*, by Henry C. Peden, Jr. (1987) and *St. George's Parish Registers, 1689-1793*, by Bill and Martha Reamy (1988).

(K)   Criminal Court Dockets, 1778-1788 (Incomplete). The originals are maintained at the Maryland State Archives.

(L)   Index to land Records, 1774-1790: Grantors, grantees, and years of the conveyances (Harford County Courthouse).

(M)   Marriage Records, 1774-1790, held at the Harford County Courthouse. (Records are missing from 1774 to 1778, and 1786 to 1790). Information has been supplemented with marriage lists maintained in the Manuscript Division (MS.1999) of the Maryland Historical Society. Beware that the marriages published in Vol. VIII of *Publications of the Genealogical Society of Pennsylvania* (in 1923) contain many mistakes. A more accurate listing will be found in *Maryland Marriages, 1634-1777*, by Robert W. Barnes (1975), and *Maryland Marriages, 1778-1800*, by Robert W. Barnes

(1979).

(N) Non-Associators and Non-Enrollers, September 10, 1775: List maintained by the Manuscript Division (MS.1814) of the Maryland Historical Society.

(O) *Our Harford Heritage,* by C. Milton Wright (1967).

(P) Genealogical Collections of Henry C. Peden, Jr.

(Q) Quaker Records of Harford County: Source "Q1" relates to the Deer Creek Monthly Meeting. Source "Q2" relates to Little Falls Monthly Meeting. Records are on microfilm at the Maryland State Archives. One should also consult *The Little Falls Meeting of Friends, 1738-1988,* by Hunter C. Sutherland (The Historical Society of Harford County, 1988).

(R) *Revolutionary Patriots of Harford County, 1775-1783,* by Henry C. Peden, Jr. (1985). Only names of militiamen were gleaned from this book, so one should refer to it and Archives of Maryland, Vol. 18, for additional information for others who may have been in the Revolutionary War.

(S) First United States Census in 1790 (published in 1907).

(T) Tombstone Inscriptions: Dates of birth and death, and the places of burial. (Information gleaned from records in the Library of the Historical Society of Harford County.)

(U) Tax Lists of 1774: Taxables only (white males aged 18 years and upwards, plus servants and slaves of all ages). (Original lists are maintained in the Manuscript Division of the Historical Society of Harford County.)

(V) Tax Lists of 1776: Taxables only (white males aged 18 years and upwards, plus servants and slaves of all ages). Since the Census of 1776 is incomplete for Harford County, these tax lists were used to fill in for the hundreds that are missing. (Originals are maintained in the Manuscript Division of the Historical Society of Harford County.)

(W) Index to Wills Probated Between 1774 and 1790: Names of testators and years the wills were probated. Information was supplemented only with names of the executors and their relationships to the deceased, if stated. For a complete abstract of each will, one should consult *Harford County Wills, 1774-1800,* by Ralph H. Morgan, Jr. (1990).

(X) Committee of License Proceedings, 1775-1776. (Original records are maintained at the Maryland State Archives.)

(Y) County Court Minutes and Proceedings (Incomplete): Source "Y1" relates to the allowances ordered by the court in 1781; the original record is held by the Manuscripts Division (MS.1117) of the Maryland Historical Society. Source "Y2" relates to the court minutes from 1783 to 1788; the original records are held by the Maryland State Archives.

(Z) Certificates of Surveys, 1773-1790: Names of tracts and the persons for whom they were surveyed. These were gleaned from the survey books found in the Harford County Courthouse.

I trust that this listing of historical and genealogical events for the inhabitants of Harford County will serve as a useful source for those in search of elusive ancestors of long ago.

Henry C. Peden, Jr.
Bel Air, Maryland
January 1, 1993

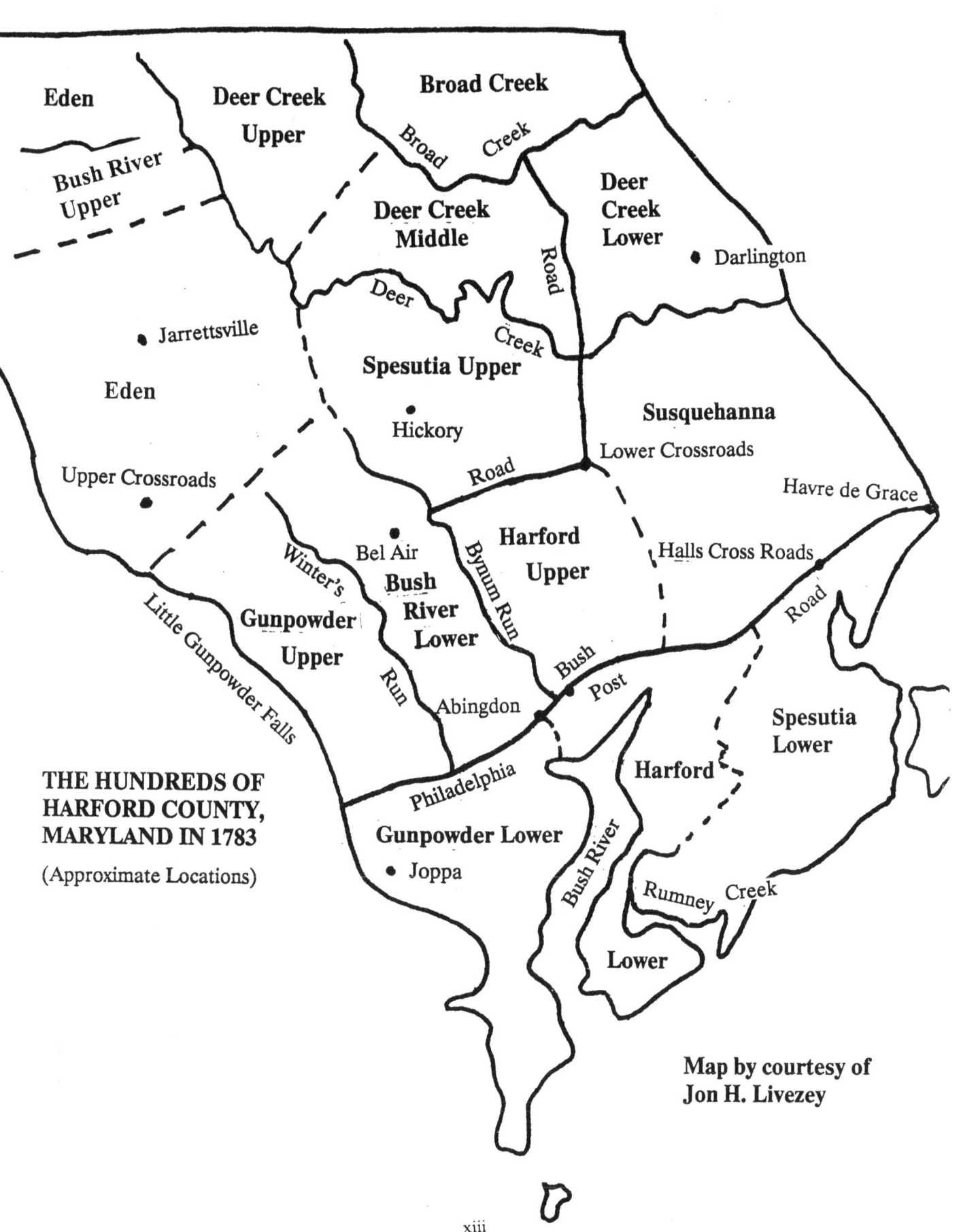

ADAMS, John. Taxable in Spesutia Lower Hundred, 1775.

ADY, Jonathan Jr. Taxable in Bush River Lower Hundred, 1775.

ADY, Jonathan Sr. Taxable in Bush River Lower Hundred, 1775.

ADY, William. Taxable in Bush River Lower Hundred, 1775, with taxables Daniel Wright and negro Dinah listed in his household.

AGARD, George. Taxable in Deer Creek Upper Hundred, 1775.

AKINS, Margret. Head of household in Bush River Upper Hundred, 1775, with taxable servant Edward Jameson (Jamson) listed in her household. See "Alexander Rogers," q.v.

AKINS, Samuel. Taxable in Deer Creek Lower Hundred, 1775.

ALBERT, Jacob. Taxable in Deer Creek Upper Hundred, 1775, with taxables Philip Albert (son) and Michael Albert (son) listed in his household.

ALBERT, Michael (son of Jacob). Taxable in household of his father Jacob Albert, Deer Creek Upper Hundred, 1775.

ALBERT, Philip (son of Jacob). Taxable in household of his father Jacob Albert, Deer Creek Upper Hundred, 1775.

ALENDER, John. Taxable in household of Nicholas Alender, Gunpowder Lower Hundred, 1775.

ALENDER, Nicholas. Taxable in Gunpowder Lower Hundred, 1775, with taxables John Alender and slaves Tral, Ned, Vilet, Gin, and Dina listed in his household.

ALEXANDER, James. Taxable in Deer Creek Upper Hundred, 1775.

ALEXANDER, Mathew. Taxable in Susquehanna Hundred, 1775, with taxable Walter Taylor listed in his household.

ALISON, Realph. Taxable on plantation of William Webb, Deer Creek Upper Hundred, 1775.

ALLASON, Alexander. Taxable in Bush River Upper Hundred, 1775.

ALLEN(?), Aaron [page torn]. Taxable in Bush River Lower Hundred, 1775.

ALLEN, Hugh. Taxable in Bush River Lower Hundred, 1775.

ALLEN, John. Taxable in Bush River Lower Hundred, 1775.

ALLEN, John. Taxable in Bush River Lower Hundred, 1775.

ALLEN, William. Taxable in household of Ann Stevenson, Spesutia Upper Hundred, 1775.

ALLENDER, William. Taxable in Deer Creek Upper Hundred, 1775, with taxable negro Grace listed in his household.

ALLET, John. Taxable in household of Andrew Wilson, Susquehanna Hundred, 1775.

ALLISON, James. Taxable in Spesutia Upper Hundred, 1775.

AMOS, James Jr. Taxable in Bush River Lower Hundred, 1775, with 5 taxables in his household, but only his name was given.

AMOS, John. Taxable in Bush River Upper Hundred, 1775.

AMOS, Maulden. Taxable in Bush River Lower Hundred, 1775, with taxable William Stewart listed in his household.

AMOS, Mordicai. Taxable in Bush River Lower Hundred, 1775, with taxable negroes Guy and Pegg listed in his household.

AMOS, Sarah. Head of household in Bush River Lower Hundred, 1775, with 3 taxables in her household, but only her name was given.

AMOS, William Jr. Taxable in Bush River Lower Hundred, 1775.

AMOS, William Sr. Taxable in Bush River Lower Hundred, 1775, with taxable negroes Cesar, Jean, Grace and Phillis listed in his household.

AMOSS, Aquila. Taxable in Bush River Upper Hundred, 1775, with taxable negro Mingo listed in his household.

AMOSS, Benjamin. Taxable in Bush River Upper Hundred, 1775, with taxable negro Charles listed in his household.

AMOSS, James. See "William Amoss," q.v.

AMOSS, James. Taxable in Bush River Upper Hundred, 1775, with taxables Joshua Amoss (son) and slaves Noah, James, Dana, and Hager listed in his household.

AMOSS, Joshua (son of James). Taxable in household of his father James Amoss, Bush River Upper Hundred, 1775.

AMOSS, Joshua (son of Joshua). Taxable in household of his father Joshua Amoss, Bush River Upper Hundred, 1775. See "William Amoss," q.v.

AMOSS, Joshua. Taxable in Bush River Upper Hundred, 1775, with taxables Joshua Amoss (son) and slaves Charles, Cesor, and Darby listed in his household.

AMOSS, Mordicka (son of Mordika). Taxable in household of his father Mordika Amoss, Bush River Upper Hundred, 1775.

AMOSS, Mordika. Taxable in Bush River Upper Hundred, 1775, with taxables Mordicka Amoss (son) and slaves Santy and ---- [illegible] listed in his household.

AMOSS, Nicklaus. Taxable in Bush River Upper

Hundred, 1775, with taxables Harry Reading (servant) and slaves Nero and Fany listed in his household.

AMOSS, Robert. Taxable in Bush River Upper Hundred, 1775, with taxable negro Gras listed in his household. See "Foster Stafard," q.v.

AMOSS, William (son of Joshua). Taxable in Bush River Upper Hundred, 1775. See "John Fowler," q.v.

AMOSS, William (son of James). Taxable in Bush River Upper Hundred, 1775, with taxable slave Dina listed in his household.

ANDERSON, Benjamin. See "William Anderson," q.v.

ANDERSON, Charles. Taxable in Susquehanna Hundred, 1775, with taxables Daniel Anderson and Richard Cannon listed in his household.

ANDERSON, Charles. Taxable in Susquehanna Hundred, 1776, with taxable Daniel Anderson listed in his household.

ANDERSON, Daniel Sr. Taxable in Susquehanna Hundred, 1775, with two taxable negroes in his household (no names given).

ANDERSON, Daniel. Taxable in household of Charles Anderson, Susquehanna Hundred, 1775.

ANDERSON, Daniel. Taxable in household of Charles Anderson, Susquehanna Hundred, 1776.

ANDERSON, Daniel. Taxable in Susquehanna Hundred, 1776, with taxable negroes Jenny and Ann listed in his household. See "Charles Anderson," q.v.

ANDERSON, George. Taxable in Deer Creek Lower Hundred, 1775.

ANDERSON, William (son of Benjamin). Taxable in Bush River Upper Hundred, 1775.

ANDERSON, William. Taxable in Bush River Lower Hundred, 1775, with taxable servant Daniel ---- (no last name given) listed in his household.

ANDERSON, William. Taxable in Bush River Upper Hundred, 1775.

ANDRES, Ephrem. Taxable in Susquehanna Hundred, 1776, with taxables Thomas Andres and negroes Jack, Frank, Will, Cate, Mary, Nann, and Pegg listed on his plantation.

ANDRES, Joshuha. Taxable in household of John Griffeth, Susquehanna Hundred, 1776.

ANDRES, Thomas. Taxable in household of Ephrem Andres, Susquehanna Hundred, 1776.

ANDREWS, Abraham. Taxable in Spesutia Upper Hundred, 1775, with taxable negro Sue listed in his household.

ANDREWS, Ephraim. See "Ephrem Andres," q.v.

ANDREWS, Ephraim. Taxable in Susquehanna Hundred, 1775, with taxables Thomas Andrews and negroes Jack, Will, Frank, Cate, Mary, Nan, Peg, and Defany listed in his household.

ANDREWS, John. Taxable in household of John Norris, Bush River Lower Hundred, 1775.

ANDREWS, Thomas. Taxable in household of Ephraim Andrews, Susquehanna Hundred, 1775.

ANNING, William. Taxable in Spesutia Lower Hundred, 1775, with taxable Michael Callahan listed in his household.

ANTEL, John. Taxable in Susquehanna Hundred, 1775.

ANTEL, John. Taxable in Susquehanna Hundred, 1776.

APPRENTICE ---- (no name given). Taxable in household of Elizabeth Gallion, Spesutia Lower Hundred, 1775.

ARCHER, John. Taxable in Spesutia Upper Hundred, 1775, with taxable negroes James, Anderson, Primos, Kate, and Dinnah listed in his household.

ARES, Jerimiah. Taxable in Bush River Upper Hundred, 1775.

ARLAT, Thomas. Taxable (servant) in the household of Benjamin Richardson, Deer Creek Upper Hundred, 1775.

ARMENT, Thomas. Taxable in Deer Creek Lower Hundred, 1775.

ARMSTRONG, David (son of Robert). Taxable in household of his father Robert Armstrong, Deer Creek Lower Hundred, 1775.

ARMSTRONG, James. Taxable in Spesutia Upper Hundred, 1775, with taxable negroes Jason and Flora listed in his household.

ARMSTRONG, John. Taxable in Bush River Lower Hundred, 1775.

ARMSTRONG, John. Taxable in Spesutia Lower Hundred, 1775.

ARMSTRONG, Joushshua. Taxable in Susquehanna Hundred, 1776, with taxable Sollommon Armstrong listed in his household.

ARMSTRONG, Robert (son of Robert). Taxable in household of his father Robert Armstrong, Deer Creek Lower Hundred, 1775.

ARMSTRONG, Robert. Taxable in Deer Creek Lower Hundred, 1775, with taxables Robert Armstrong (son) and David Armstrong (son) listed in his household.

ARMSTRONG, Shephard. Taxable in Bush River Lower Hundred, 1775, with taxable Joseph Jones listed in his household.

ARMSTRONG, Sollommon. Taxable in household of Joushshua Armstrong, Susquehanna Hundred, 1776.

ARNAL, William. Taxable in Deer Creek Lower Hundred, 1775.

ARNEL, Ephram. Taxable in Susquehanna Hundred, 1776.

ARNEL, William. Taxable in Susquehanna Hundred, 1776, with taxable William Crosgell listed in his household.

ARNOLD, Ephraim. Taxable in Susquehanna Hundred, 1775.

ARNOLD, William. Taxable in Susquehanna Hundred,

1775, with taxable Thomas Crodgill listed in his household.

ASHLEY, Thomas. Taxable in household of Josias Carvel Hall, Spesutia Lower Hundred, 1775.

ASHLEY, Thomas. Taxable on plantation of Dr. Josias Carvell Hall, Spesutia Lower Hundred, 1776.

ASHMORE, Samuel. Taxable in Bush River Upper Hundred, 1775, with taxable servant man ---- (no name given) listed in his household.

ASHMORE, William. See "Joseph Miller," q.v.

ASHMORE, William. Taxable in Deer Creek Upper Hundred, 1775, with taxable men Joseph McNemarer, John Gormen, Dinis Perkinson, and Patrick McHallan listed in his household.

ASPEL, John. Taxable in household of Henry Thomas, Jr., Spesutia Upper Hundred, 1775.

ASTEN, John. Taxable in household of Clement Lewis, Bush River Lower Hundred, 1775.

ASTIN, Joseph. Taxable in Bush River Lower Hundred, 1775.

ATKINSON, John. Taxable in Spesutia Lower Hundred, 1775.

AYERS, Jeremiah. See "Jerimiah Ares." q.v.

AYRES, Thomas. Taxable in Spesutia Lower Hundred, 1775, with taxable George Ford listed in his household.

AYRES, Thomas. Taxable in Spesutia Lower Hundred, 1776, with taxable George Todd in his household.

AYRS, Harry. Servant (and taxable) in household of William Bond (son of John), Bush River Lower Hundred, 1775.

A--M(?), Aaron. See "Aaron Allen(?)," q.v.

B----, James [page torn]. Taxable in Spesutia Upper Hundred, 1775.

BABE, Patrick. Taxable in Spesutia Lower Hundred, 1775.

BAIL, Adam. Taxable in household of James Everett, Bush River Lower Hundred, 1775.

BAILEY, Benjamin. Taxable in Susquehanna Hundred, 1775, with taxable John Hodges listed in his household.

BAILEY, Groumbrit. Taxable in Gunpowder Lower Hundred, 1775, with taxables James Bailey (son) and slave Dick listed in his household.

BAILEY, James (son of Groumbrit). Taxable in household of his father Groumbrit Bailey, Gunpowder Lower Hundred, 1775.

BAILEY, Jonas. Taxable in Susquehanna Hundred, 1775.

BAILEY, Joseph. Taxable in Susquehanna Hundred, 1775.

BAILEY, Nathaniel. Taxable in Susquehanna Hundred, 1775.

BAILEY, Nehemiah. Taxable in Spesutia Lower Hundred, 1775.

BAILEY, Samuel. Taxable in Susquehanna Hundred, 1775.

BAILEY, Thomas. Taxable in Susquehanna Hundred, 1775, with James Ford as his security.

BAKER, Charles. Taxable in Bush River Upper Hundred, 1775, with taxable servant John Morris listed in his household.

BAKER, Christon. Head of household in Spesutia Upper Hundred, 1775, with negroes Coff, Priss, Dinnah, and Sall in her household.

BAKER, John. Taxable in household of Theophilus Baker, Bush River Lower Hundred, 1775.

BAKER, Maurice. Taxable in Gunpowder Lower Hundred, 1775.

BAKER, Nicholas. Taxable in Susquehanna Hundred, 1775, with taxable John Frame listed in his household.

BAKER, Nickles. Taxable in Susquehanna Hundred, 1776, with taxable John Fram listed in his household.

BAKER, Theophilus. Taxable in Bush River Lower Hundred, 1775, with taxable John Baker listed in his household.

BAKER, William. Taxable in Gunpowder Lower Hundred, 1775. His name (among others) was listed on the back of the tax list.

BAKER, William. Taxable in Bush River Upper Hundred, 1775.

BALDERSON, Isiah. Taxable in Deer Creek Upper Hundred, 1775.

BALDERSON, Jacob. Taxable in Deer Creek Upper Hundred, 1775.

BALES, Daniel. Taxable in Susquehanna Hundred, 1776.

BALES, Jonas. Taxable in Susquehanna Hundred, 1776.

BALEY, Aqule. Taxable in household of Joseph Baley, Susquehanna Hundred, 1776.

BALEY, Benedick. Taxable in household of Joseph Baley, Susquehanna Hundred, 1776.

BALEY, Charles. Taxable in household of Joseph Baley, Susquehanna Hundred, 1776.

BALEY, Joseph. Taxable in household of Joseph Baley, Susquehanna Hundred, 1776., with taxables Charles Baley, Aqule Baley, and Benedick Baley listed in his household.

BALEY, Josias. Taxable in Susquehanna Hundred, 1776.

BALIS, Benjamin. Taxable in Susquehanna Hundred, 1776, with taxables Robert Balis and John Hodges listed in his household.

BALIS, Nathanel. Taxable in Susquehanna Hundred, 1776, with taxable Edward Sutton listed in his household.

BALIS, Robert. Taxable in household of Benjamin Balis, Susquehanna Hundred, 1776.

BALY, Alias(?). Taxable in household of Sammul Baly, Susquehanna Hundred, 1776.

BALY, Sammul. Taxable in Susquehanna Hundred, 1776, with taxable Alias(?) Baley listed in his household.

BANKHEAD, John. Taxable in Bush River Upper Hundred, 1775.

BANKHEAD, William. Taxable in Bush River Upper Hundred, 1775.

BANKS, Andrew. Taxable in Bush River Lower Hundred, 1775.

BANNING, James. Taxable in household of Daniel Durbin, Spesutia Lower Hundred, 1776.

BARCLAY, John. Taxable in Deer Creek Lower Hundred, 1775, with taxable negro Dick listed in his household.

BARNARD, James. Taxable in household of Samuel Lenhard, Deer Creek Upper Hundred, 1775.

BARNES, Bathia. Head of household in Susquehanna Hundred, 1775, with taxable negro Defany listed in her household.

BARNES, Gregory. Taxable in Susquehanna Hundred, 1775, with taxable negro Chloe listed in his household.

BARNES, James. Taxable in Susquehanna Hundred, 1775, with taxable Joseph Barnes listed in his household.

BARNES, Jobe Jr. Taxable in Deer Creek Lower Hundred, 1775.

BARNES, Jobe. Taxable in Deer Creek Lower Hundred, 1775, with taxable negroes Charles and Dinah listed in his household. See "Christopher Hall," q.v.

BARNES, John. Taxable in Spesutia Upper Hundred, 1775.

BARNES, Joseph. Taxable in household of James Barnes, Susquehanna Hundred, 1775.

BARNES, Joseph. Taxable in Spesutia Upper Hundred, 1775.

BARNES, Marthew. Taxable in household of Thomas Ellet, Bush River Upper Hundred, 1775.

BARNES, Ruth (widow). Head of household in Susquehanna Hundred, 1775, with taxable negro Leander listed in her household.

BARNES, William. Taxable in Spesutia Upper Hundred, 1775.

BARNET, Mark. Taxable in Deer Creek Lower Hundred, 1775.

BARNS, ---- (no first name given). Taxable in Spesutia Lower Hundred, 1775, with Thomas Fisher as his security.

BARNS, Benjamin. Taxable in household of James Barns, Susquehanna Hundred, 1776.

BARNS, Bennet. Taxable in Susquehanna Hundred, 1775.

BARNS, Bennet. Taxable in Susquehanna Hundred, 1776.

BARNS, Bethiah. Head of household in Susquehanna Hundred, 1776, wit taxable negro Dofney listed in her household.

BARNS, Elizabeth. Head of household in Susquehanna Hundred, 1776, with taxable negro Ned listed in her household.

BARNS, Gregrey. Taxable in Susquehanna Hundred, 1776, with taxable N. Cole listed in his household.

BARNS, James. Taxable in Susquehanna Hundred, 1776, with taxable Benjamin Barns listed in his household.

BARNS, John. Taxable in household of William Barns, Susquehanna Hundred, 1776.

BARNS, Joseph. Taxable in Susquehanna Hundred, 1776, with Nickles Baker as his security.

BARNS, Nehemiah. Taxable in Spesutia Lower Hundred, 1776.

BARNS, Thomas. Taxable in Bush River Lower Hundred, 1775.

BARNS, Thomas. Taxable in Bush River Lower Hundred, 1775.

BARNS, William. Taxable on the plantation of Amos Garrett, Spesutia Lower Hundred, 1775.

BARNS, William. Taxable in Susquehanna Hundred, 1776, with taxables John Barns, John Cotton and negro Tom listed in his household.

BARRETT, John. Taxable in Bush River Upper Hundred, 1775, with taxable negro Wench listed in his household.

BARROW(?), Henery. Taxable in Susquehanna Hundred, 1776.

BARTLEY, George. Taxable in Susquehanna Hundred, 1775.

BARTON, James. Taxable in Bush River Upper Hundred, 1775.

BARTON, John (son of John). Taxable in household of his father John Barton, Bush River Upper Hundred, 1775.

BARTON, John. Taxable in Bush River Upper Hundred, 1775, with taxable John Barton (son) and slaves Duke, Samson, Fan, and Moll listed in his household.

BARTON, William. Taxable in Deer Creek Upper Hundred, 1775.

BASKET, Richard. Taxable in Bush River Lower Hundred, 1775.

BATES, William. Taxable in household of Hugh Whiteford, Jr., Deer Creek Upper Hundred, 1775.

BATES(?), John. Taxable in Bush River Upper Hundred, 1775.

BATTON, John. Taxable in household of Charles Gilbert, Jr., Susquehanna Hundred, 1776.

BAVARD, James. Taxable in Deer Creek Upper Hundred, 1775.

BAXTER, Patrick. Taxable in household of William Chapel, Susquehanna Hundred, 1775.

BAY, Andrew. Taxable in Bush River Lower Hundred, 1775.

BAY, Hugh. Taxable in Bush River Lower Hundred, 1775.

BAY, Hugh. Taxable in household of William Bay, Bush River Lower Hundred, 1775.

BAY, William. Taxable in Bush River Lower Hundred, 1775, with taxable Hugh Bay listed in his household.

BAY(?), William. Taxable in Bush River Upper Hundred, 1775.

BAYLEY, Nehemiah. Taxable in Spesutia Lower Hundred, 1776.

BEAL, James. Taxable in household of James Ford (shumaker), Susquehanna Hundred, 1776.

BEALL, Joseph. Taxable (servant) in household of Samuel Calwell, Bush River Lower Hundred, 1775.

BEALL, Robert. Taxable in Bush River Upper Hundred, 1775.

BEATY, Archibald. Taxable in Spesutia Lower Hundred, 1775, with taxable slave Bale listed in his household.

BEATY, Archibald. Taxable in Spesutia Lower Hundred, 1776, with taxable Thomas Nelson listed in his household.

BEATY, William. Taxable in Bush River Upper Hundred, 1775, with taxable servant James Jakelin(?) listed in his household.

BEAVER, Charles. Taxable in Deer Creek Upper Hundred, 1775.

BEAVER, John. Taxable in Deer Creek Upper Hundred, 1775.

BECK, Caleb. Taxable in Spesutia Lower Hundred, 1775, with taxable Richard Jury listed in his household.

BECK, John. Taxable at Richard Dallam's Quarters at Romney, Spesutia Lower Hundred, 1775.

BECK, Mathew. Taxable in Gunpowder Lower Hundred, 1775.

BEDINGHAM (BODINGHAM?), Edward. Taxable in household of Joseph Brownley, Spesutia Upper Hundred, 1775.

BELL, David. Taxable in Bush River Upper Hundred, 1775.

BELL, John. Taxable in Bush River Upper Hundred, 1775.

BELSHUR, Mical. Taxable in household of James Mitchel (weaver), Susquehanna Hundred, 1776.

BENDAL, Joss. Taxable in household of Sarah McCarty, Susquehanna Hundred, 1775.

BENDON, Joseph. Taxable in household of Sarah Cartie, Spesutia Lower Hundred, 1776.

BENFIELD, David. Taxable in Bush River Lower Hundred, 1775, with taxables Charles Shepherd and Patrick Malen listed in his household.

BENINGTON, Henry. Taxable in Deer Creek Lower Hundred, 1775.

BENINGTON, William. Taxable in Deer Creek Lower Hundred, 1775.

BENNET, Benjamin. Taxable in Spesutia Lower Hundred, 1775.

BENNETT, Abm. Taxable in household of Peter Bennett, Spesutia Lower Hundred, 1775.

BENNETT, Peter. Taxable in Spesutia Lower Hundred, 1775, with taxables Abm. Bennett and slave Moll listed in his household.

BENNETT, Zebedee. Taxable in Spesutia Lower Hundred, 1775.

BENSHAFT, Paul. Taxable in Deer Creek Upper Hundred, 1775, with taxable Stophel Benshaft (son) listed in his household.

BENSHAFT, Stophel (son of Paul). Taxable in household of his father Paul Benshaft, Deer Creek Upper Hundred, 1775.

BENTLEY, Joshua. Taxable in Bush River Upper Hundred, 1775.

BERNARD, Richard. Taxable in Gunpowder Lower Hundred, 1775.

BERRY, Richard. Taxable on the plantation of Amos Garrett, Spesutia Lower Hundred, 1775.

BESSIE (BESSIC?), Edward. Taxable in Bush River Upper Hundred, 1775, with a taxable negro (no name given) listed in his household.

BEVARD, Charles. Taxable in Deer Creek Lower Hundred, 1775.

BIARDS, Ephram. Taxable in Susquehanna Hundred, 1776, with taxable "prentis boy Perrey" listed in his household.

BIARDS, James. Taxable in Susquehanna Hundred, 1776.

BIARS, Ephraim. Taxable in Susquehanna Hundred, 1775, with taxable James Perry listed in his household.

BIARS, James. Taxable in Susquehanna Hundred, 1775.

BIDDEL, Benjamin. Taxable in Bush River Upper Hundred, 1775, with taxable servant William Martin and slave ---- [illegible] listed in his household.

BIGGS, Nat. Taxable in household of John Day (son of Edward), Gunpowder Lower Hundred, 1775. [His name looks like "Nat. Biggh" on the 1775 tax list, but this is the "Nathaniel Bigs" listed in the 1778 tax list for Spesutia Lower Hundred and the "Nathaniel Biggs" listed in the 1790 census for Harford County].

BIGS, Thomas. Taxable in household of Samuel Griffith, Spesutia Lower Hundred, 1775.

BILLINGSLEY, Walter Jr. Taxable in Bush River Lower Hundred, 1775.

BILLINGSLEY, Walter. Taxable in Spesutia Upper Hundred, 1775, with taxable negroes Sambo, Joshua, Pugg, Feby, and Gin listed in his household.

BILLINGSLY, Charles. Taxable in Bush River Lower

Hundred, 1775.

BILLINGSLY, Francis. Taxable in Bush River Lower Hundred, 1775, with taxables John Cotman and Joseph Colony listed in his household.

BILLINGSLY, Jervis. Taxable in household of his mother Ruth Billingsly, Deer Creek Upper Hundred, 1775.

BILLINGSLY, Ruth. Head of household in Deer Creek Upper Hundred, 1775, with taxables Jervis Billingsly (son) and negro Rachel listed in her household.

BILLINGSLY, Sias. Taxable in Deer Creek Upper Hundred, 1775, with taxables Stephen Lockwood and Joseph Rogers (servants) listed in his household.

BIRCH, William. Taxable in the household of John Watkins, Spesutia Lower Hundred, 1775.

BISHOP, Robbert. Taxable in Gunpowder Lower Hundred, 1775, with taxable slaves Bolt, Nicholas, Dublin, Akhilles, Clo, Rose, and Mint listed in his household.

BLACK, George (son of Robert). Taxable in household of his father Robert Black, Bush River Upper Hundred, 1775.

BLACK, Robert (son of Robert). Taxable in household of his father Robert Black, Bush River Upper Hundred, 1775.

BLACK, Robert. Taxable in Bush River Upper Hundred, 1775, with taxables George Black (son) and Robert Black (son) listed in his household.

BLACK, Samuel. Taxable in Bush River Upper Hundred, 1775.

BLACKBURN, John. Taxable in Spesutia Upper Hundred, 1775.

BLACKBURN, John. Taxable in household of Robert Blackburn, Spesutia Upper Hundred, 1775.

BLACKBURN, Robert. Taxable in Spesutia Upper Hundred, 1775, with taxable John Blackburn listed in his household.

BLACKMAN, William. Taxable in household of John Riddall, Spesutia Lower Hundred, 1776.

BLACKMORE, William. Taxable in the household of John Riddal, Spesutia Lower Hundred, 1775.

BLACKSTONE, Elijah. Taxable in Gunpowder Lower Hundred, 1775, with taxable slave George listed in his household.

BLACKSTONE, Thomas. Taxable in Spesutia Lower Hundred, 1775.

BLAKE, John. Taxable in household of Alexander Cowen, Gunpowder Lower Hundred, 1775.

BLANCH, J. Taxable (servant) in household of James Hutcheson, Deer Creek Upper Hundred, 1775.

BLANCHARD, Peter. Taxable in Spesutia Lower Hundred, 1775.

BLANEY, Edward Sr. Taxable in Bush River Lower Hundred, 1775, with taxables John Blaney and Edward Blaney, Jr. listed in his household.

BLANY, James. Taxable in Bush River Upper Hundred, 1775.

BLOODWORTH, Timothy. Taxable in Spesutia Lower Hundred, 1775.

BLOYNEY, Thomas. Taxable in Bush River Upper Hundred, 1775.

BOADLEY, J, Beale. Taxable in Gunpowder Lower Hundred, 1775, with taxable slaves Jacob, Hamdon, Ciser, Fender, Feeb, and Pen listed in his household.

BOALEY, Thomas. Taxable in Susquehanna Hundred, 1775.

BOARDSMAN, William. Taxable in Spesutia Upper Hundred, 1775.

BODINGHAM (BEDINGHAM?), Edward. Taxable in household of Joseph Brownley, Spesutia Upper Hundred, 1775.

BODKIN, Robert. Taxable in Deer Creek Lower Hundred, 1775.

BOLES, Thomas. Taxable in Susquehanna Hundred, 1776.

BOLIN, Peto. Taxable in household of Mary Thompson, Susquehanna Hundred, 1776.

BONAR, Arther. Taxable in household of John Bonar, Susquehanna Hundred, 1776.

BONAR, John. Taxable in Susquehanna Hundred, 1776, with taxable Arther Bonar listed in his household.

BONAR, Mathew. Taxable in household of William Bonar, Susquehanna Hundred, 1776.

BONAR, William Jr. Taxable in Susquehanna Hundred, 1776, with taxables Peter Irons and Richard Thomson listed in his household.

BONAR, William. Taxable in Susquehanna Hundred, 1776, with taxable Mathew Bonar listed in his household.

BOND, Ann. Head of household in Bush River Lower Hundred, 1775, with taxables James Bond and negroes Dick, Duke, Henry, Doll, Flora, Pomp, Hannah, and Rachel listed in her household.

BOND, Buckler. Taxable in Bush River Lower Hundred, 1775, with taxable negroes Joe and Ned listed in his household.

BOND, Dannill. Taxable in Bush River Upper Hundred, 1775, with taxabale slaves John, Gee, and Dina listed in his household.

BOND, J----. See "Thomas Bond," q.v.

BOND, Jacob Jr. Taxable in household of Jacob Bond, Sr., Bush River Lower Hundred, 1775.

BOND, Jacob Sr. Taxable in Bush River Lower Hundred, 1775, with taxables Jacob Bond, Jr., John Sadler, John Cook, Elijah Joice, with Jacob Bond as his security), and negroes Toney, Phillis, Antony, Poll, Cate, Dinah, Samson, Cesar, Dinah, Roger, Honour, Prudy, and Charles, all listed in his household.

EARLY HARFORD COUNTIANS: Supplement

BOND, Jacob's Quarters. Gunpowder Lower Hundred, 1775, with taxable slaves Tom, Brista, Hannah, and Mumah listed at these quarters.

BOND, James. Taxable in household of Ann Bond, Bush River Lower Hundred, 1775.

BOND, John Jr. Taxable in Bush River Lower Hundred, 1775, with taxable servant Stephen Fell listed in his household.

BOND, John Sr. Taxable in Bush River Lower Hundred, 1775, with taxables Nathan Bond and negro Doll listed in his household.

BOND, Nathan. Taxable in household of John Bond, Sr., Bush River Lower Hundred, 1775.

BOND, Peter. Taxable in Bush River Lower Hundred, 1775, with taxables Peter Brannon and negroes Solomon, Adam, and Pugg listed in his household.

BOND, Samuel. Taxable in Bush River Lower Hundred, 1775.

BOND, Thomas (Jr. or Sr.?), son of J---- [illegible]. Taxable in Bush River Lower Hundred, 1775, with 9 taxables in his household, but only his name was given.

BOND, Thomas Jr. Taxable in Bush River Upper Hundred, 1775, with taxable servant John Price and negroes Grove, Ned, and Cate listed in his household.

BOND, Thomas Sr. Taxable in Bush River Lower Hundred, 1775, with taxable negroes Voluntine, Sam, Ben, Many, and Jenny listed in his household.

BOND, Thomas. See "Peter Miles," q.v.

BOND, William (son of John). Taxable in Bush River Lower Hundred, 1775, with taxable servant Harry Ayrs listed in his household.

BOND, William. Taxable at Benjamin Howard's Quarters, Gunpowder Lower Hundred, 1775.

BONER, Barnet. Taxable in Susquehanna Hundred, 1775, with taxable James Boner listed in his household.

BONER, James. Taxable in household of Barnet Boner, Susquehanna Hundred, 1775.

BONER, James. Taxable in household of William Williams, Susquehanna Hundred, 1775.

BONER, Mathew. Taxable in household of William Boner, Susquehanna Hundred, 1775.

BONER, William Jr. Taxable in Susquehanna Hundred, 1775, with taxables Peter Irons and Richard Thompson listed in his household.

BONER, William. Taxable in household of William Boner, Susquehanna Hundred, 1775.

BONER, William. Taxable in Susquehanna Hundred, 1775, with taxables Mathew Boner and William Boner listed in his household.

BOSSLEY(?), William. Taxable in Bush River Upper Hundred, 1775.

BOTH, Henry. Taxable in Bush River Lower Hundred, 1775.

BOTS, George. Taxable in Susquehanna Hundred, 1776.

BOTS, John. Taxable in Susquehanna Hundred, 1776, with taxable negro Bess listed in his household.

BOTTS, George. Taxable in Susquehanna Hundred, 1775.

BOTTS, Jacob. Taxable in Susquehanna Hundred, 1775. [The entry is written "Botts Jacob Wms. Security" which could be interpeted to mean Jacob Botts was William's security, or Jacob Botts was the taxable and ---- Williams was his security].

BOTTS, John. Taxable in Susquehanna Hundred, 1775, with taxable negro Bet listed in his household.

BOULDEN, William. Taxable in Bush River Lower Hundred, 1775, with taxable negro Antony listed in his household.

BOULSTER, William. Taxable on the plantation of Amos Garrett, Spesutia Lower Hundred, 1775.

BOVE, Thomas. Taxable in household of John McComas, Bush River Lower Hundred, 1775.

BOWMAN, Harden. Taxable in Susquehanna Hundred, 1775.

BOYD, William. Taxable in Bush River Lower Hundred, 1775.

BOYER, William. Taxable in Spesutia Lower Hundred, 1775. [The actual entry by the constable at the end of the tax list is strangely written as follows: "Wm. Boyer" (on the first line), "Jno. Cox for Jacob Giles" (on the next line), with a brace "}" connecting the two lines, and a straight line drawn to the right with the number "1" written at the end in the taxable column].

BRADFORD, George. Taxable in Spesutia Upper Hundred, 1775, with taxable negroes Cato, Ben, Dutches, and Nan listed in his household.

BRADFORD, William. Taxable in Bush River Lower Hundred, 1775, with taxable servant John Johnson listed in his household.

BRADFORD, William. Taxable in Spesutia Upper Hundred, 1775, with taxables Charles Neale, Joseph Scott, and negro Hannah listed in his household.

BRADY, Nicholas. Taxable in household of Jacob Forward, Spesutia Lower Hundred, 1775.

BRAKENRIGG, William. Taxable in Deer Creek Upper Hundred, 1775.

BRAKINGRIG, John. Taxable in Deer Creek Upper Hundred, 1775.

BRANNAN, Caleb. Taxable on plantation of Dr. Josias Carvell Hall, Spesutia Lower Hundred, 1776.

BRANNON, Patrick. Taxable in Susquehanna Hundred, 1775.

BRANNON, Peter. Taxable in household of Peter Bond, Bush River Lower Hundred, 1775.

BRANNON(?), Henery. Taxable in Susquehanna Hundred, 1776.

BRECKINRIDGE, John. See "John Brakingrig," q.v.

BRECKINRIDGE, William. See "John Brakenrigg," q.v.

BRENHEIN, Caleb. Taxable in household of Josias Carvel Hall, Spesutia Lower Hundred, 1775.

BREWER, Jacob. Taxable in household of James Brewer, Susquehanna Hundred, 1776.

BREWER, James. Taxable in Susquehanna Hundred, 1775, with taxable son-in-law Jacob Pennin listed in his household.

BREWER, James. Taxable in Susquehanna Hundred, 1776, with taxable Jacob Brewer listed in his household.

BRIAN, John. Taxable in Deer Creek Lower Hundred, 1775, with Robert Cook as his security.

BRIARLY, Robert. Taxable in Bush River Upper Hundred, 1775, with taxables Joseph ---- (no last name given) and negroes Nan and Eag listed in his household. [Although this would be 4 taxables altogether, the constable only wrote in 3. Also, Joseph ---- was Joseph Wood, a servant, as shown in another tax list].

BRICE, James. Taxable in Deer Creek Lower Hundred, 1775, with taxable man Owen Corkron (servant) listed in his household.

BRICE, Thomas. Taxable in Deer Creek Upper Hundred, 1775, with taxable man Mart Carter (servant) listed in his household.

BRIDGE, James. Taxable in Bush River Lower Hundred, 1775.

BROADRICK, William. Taxable in Bush River Lower Hundred, 1775.

BROOKS, John. Taxable in Spesutia Upper Hundred, 1775.

BROOKS, John. Taxable in Bush River Upper Hundred, 1775.

BROWN, Daniel Jr. Taxable in Gunpowder Lower Hundred, 1775, with taxable slave Jo listed in his household.

BROWN, David. Taxable in Bush River Upper Hundred, 1775.

BROWN, Freeborn. Taxable in Spesutia Lower Hundred, 1775, with taxable slaves Jack, Maria, Jack 2nd, Voll, Jane, Barbara, and Dutchess listed in his household.

BROWN, Freeborn. Taxable in Susquehanna Hundred, 1776, with taxable negroes Ollerver and Dinah listed in his household.

BROWN, James. See "Francis Garland," q.v.

BROWN, James. Taxable in Spesutia Lower Hundred, 1775, with taxable Brian Curry listed in his household.

BROWN, James. Taxable in the household of William Reading, Spesutia Lower Hundred, 1775.

BROWN, James. Taxable in Bush River Upper Hundred, 1775.

BROWN, James. Taxable in Spesutia Lower Hundred, 1776.

BROWN, John. Taxable in Bush River Lower Hundred, 1775.

BROWN, John. Taxable in Spesutia Lower Hundred, 1775.

BROWN, John. Taxable in Spesutia Lower Hundred, 1775, with taxable slaves Caff, Toney, Cumbo, Sam, Fann, Mary, and Old Toney listed in his household.

BROWN, John. Taxable in Bush River Upper Hundred, 1775.

BROWN, John. Taxable in Spesutia Lower Hundred, 1776, with taxable negroes Sam, Fann, Moll, Combo, Cuff, and Toney listed in his household.

BROWN, Perregrin. Taxable in Gunpowder Lower Hundred, 1775.

BROWN, Robert. Taxable in Spesutia Lower Hundred, 1775, with taxable slave Violet listed in his household.

BROWN, Salomon. Taxable in Bush River Upper Hundred, 1775.

BROWN, Samuel. Taxable in Bush River Lower Hundred, 1775.

BROWN, Sarah Jr. Head of household in Spesutia Lower Hundred, 1776, with taxable negroes Murrier and Dutchesses listed in her household.

BROWN, Sarah. Head of household in Spesutia Lower Hundred, 1776, with taxable negroes Jack, Jack Jr., Jean, and Murrier listed in her household.

BROWN, Thomas. Taxable at Jacob Giles' Quarters at Romney, Spesutia Lower Hundred, 1775.

BROWN, Thomas. Taxable in Deer Creek Upper Hundred, 1775.

BROWN, William. Taxable in Bush River Lower Hundred, 1775.

BROWNING, Thomas. Taxable in Spesutia Lower Hundred, 1775.

BROWNING, Thomas. Taxable in Spesutia Lower Hundred, 1776. See "William Jeffery," q.v.

BROWNLEY, Joseph. Taxable in Spesutia Upper Hundred, 1775, with taxables Jacob Zeatch (Yeatch?), Edward Bedingham (Bodingham?), and negro Dinah listed in his household.

BRUCE, John. Taxable in Deer Creek Lower Hundred, 1775, with taxable man John Richey (servant) listed in his household.

BRUCEBANKS, Abraham. Taxable in Spesutia Lower Hundred, 1775.

BRUCEBANKS, Edward (son of Abraham). Taxable in Spesutia Lower Hundred, 1775.

BRUCEBANKS, Edward Horton. Taxable in Spesutia Lower Hundred, 1775.

BRUCEBANKS, Edward Orton. Taxable in Spesutia Lower Hundred, 1776.

EARLY HARFORD COUNTIANS: **Supplement**

BRUCEBANKS, Edward. Taxable in Spesutia Lower Hundred, 1776.

BRYARLY, Hugh. Taxable in Bush River Upper Hundred, 1775. [The constable indicated three taxables in his household, but only named Hugh Bryarly].

BRYERTON, Henry (son of John). Taxable in household of his father John Bryerton, Bush River Upper Hundred, 1775.

BRYERTON, John. Taxable in Bush River Upper Hundred, 1775, with taxable Henry Bryerton (son) listed in his household.

BUCHANAN, William's Quarters. Gunpowder Lower Hundred, 1775, with taxables Thomas Hunt, John Gough, and slaves Wil, Charles, Mol, and Modey listed at these quarters.

BUCKINGHAM, Thomas. Taxable in Bush River Upper Hundred, 1775.

BUCKLER, Daniel. Taxable in household of Daniel Durbin, Spesutia Lower Hundred, 1776.

BUCKLEY, Daniel. Taxable at Richard Dallam's Quarters at Swan Creek, Spesutia Lower Hundred, 1775.

BUCKLEY, John. Taxable in Bush River Lower Hundred, 1775.

BUCKLEY, John. Taxable in Spesutia Lower Hundred, 1775.

BULL, Edmond. Taxable in Spesutia Upper Hundred, 1775, with taxable negroes Bell, Lonnon, Tom, and Nell listed in his household. See "Jacob Bull," q.v.

BULL, Edward (son of Jacob). Taxable in Bush River Lower Hundred, 1775, with a taxable servant named George Oeal [sic] listed in his household.

BULL, Jacob (son of Edmond). Taxable in Spesutia Upper Hundred, 1775.

BULL, Jacob Jr. Taxable in household of Jacob Bull, Sr. Bush River Lower Hundred, 1775.

BULL, Jacob Sr. Taxable in Bush River Lower Hundred, 1775, with taxables Jacob Bull, Jr., and negroes Bob, Oliver, Cesar, and Hagar listed in his household.

BULL, William Sr. Taxable in Bush River Lower Hundred, 1775, with taxable negroes Pomp, Toney, Phillis, and Ben listed in his household.

BULL, William. Taxable in Bush River Lower Hundred, 1775.

BURK, Thomas. Taxable in Deer Creek Upper Hundred, 1775.

BURNINGHAM, ---- (no first name given). Taxable in household of Manessith Finney, Deer Creek Upper Hundred, 1775.

BURNS, Patrick. Taxable in Deer Creek Upper Hundred, 1775.

BURNSIDE, Marthew. Taxable in Bush River Upper Hundred, 1775.

BUSEY, Susanna. Head of household in Bush River Lower Hundred, 1775, with 2 taxables in her household (no names given).

BUSH, William. Taxable in household of Jacob Giles, Susquehanna Hundred, 1775.

BUSSEY, Thomas. Taxable in Bush River Lower Hundred, 1775, with taxable negro Daff listed in his household.

BUTLER, Joseph. Taxable in Spesutia Upper Hundred, 1775, with taxable negroes Sagg and Gin listed in his household.

BUTLER, Patrick. Taxable in household of Joseph Woolsy, Spesutia Upper Hundred, 1775.

BUTTERS, James. Taxable in Gunpowder Lower Hundred, 1775. See "James Wheeler," q.v.

BYFOOT, Jarman. Taxable in Bush River Lower Hundred, 1775.

BYFOOT, Moses. Taxable in Bush River Lower Hundred, 1775.

CADY, John. Taxable at Thomas Frisby Henderson's Quarters, Spesutia Lower Hundred, 1775.

CALLAHAN, Michael. Taxable in household of William Anning, Spesutia Lower Hundred, 1775.

CALLENDER, John. Taxable in Spesutia Upper Hundred, 1775.

CALLENDER, Robert. Taxable in Spesutia Upper Hundred, 1775.

CALLWELL, John. Taxable in Deer Creek Upper Hundred, 1775.

CALWELL, David. Taxable in household of James Cox, Bush River Lower Hundred, 1775.

CALWELL, Samuel. Taxable in Bush River Lower Hundred, 1775, with taxable servants Joseph Beall and Hugh Melone listed in his household.

CAMMAL, James. Taxable in Bush River Upper Hundred, 1775.

CAMMELL, John Jr. Taxable in Bush River Upper Hundred, 1775.

CAMP, James. Taxable in Bush River Lower Hundred, 1775.

CAMPBELL, Daniel. Taxable in Spesutia Lower Hundred, 1775, with taxable Jeremiah Gelons listed in his household.

CAMPBELL, Daniel. Taxable in Spesutia Lower Hundred, 1776, with taxable Jeremiah Collings listed in his household.

CAMPBELL, James. Taxable in Deer Creek Upper Hundred, 1775.

CAMPTON, Robin. Taxable in Susquehanna Hundred, 1776, with Richard Cruse possibly as his security since it indicates one taxable, not two, in this household.

CANNABEL, Mical. Taxable on plantation of Jacob Giles, Susquehanna Hundred, 1776.

CANNADAY, Robert. Taxable in Deer Creek Upper Hundred, 1775, with two taxable men William ---- and ----[illegible], apparently servants, listed in his household.

CANNON, Richard. Taxable in household of Charles Anderson, Susquehanna Hundred, 1775.

CANNON, Robert. Taxable in Bush River Upper Hundred, 1775.

CANT, ---- [illegible]. Taxable in Susquehanna Hundred, 1775.

CAPEN, Rowlan. Taxable (servant) in household of Edward Norris, Deer Creek Upper Hundred, 1775.

CAR, Michal. Taxable in Bush River Lower Hundred, 1775.

CAR, Nason. Taxable in Spesutia Upper Hundred, 1775.

CARKER, Patrick. Taxable in the household of Edward Carvel Tolley, Spesutia Lower Hundred, 1775.

CARLILE, John. Taxable in Spesutia Lower Hundred, 1775, with taxable John Kight (Right?) listed in his household.

CARLILE, John. Taxable in Spesutia Lower Hundred, 1776, with taxable Jeremiah Dalley listed in his household.

CARLILE, Mary. Head of household in Bush River Lower Hundred, 1775, with taxable negroes Ja--- [page torn], Marmur, Cook, and Fanny listed in her household.

CARLILE, Robert. Taxable in Bush River Lower Hundred, 1775.

CARLILE, William? [illegible]. Taxable in Bush River Lower Hundred, 1775.

CARRAL(?), John. Taxable on plantation of William Webb, Deer Creek Upper Hundred, 1775.

CARREL, John. Taxable in Susquehanna Hundred, 1776, with Jane Cole as his security.

CARROL, John. Taxable in household of Jan Cole (widow), Susquehanna Hundred, 1775.

CARROL, Peter. Taxable in Bush River Upper Hundred, 1775.

CARROLL, Elizabeth. Head of household in Bush River Lower Hundred, 1775, with 3 taxables in her household (no names given).

CARROLL, James. Taxable in Bush River Lower Hundred, 1775, with taxable negro Sall listed in his household.

CARROLL, James. Taxable in Bush River Lower Hundred, 1775.

CARROLL, John. Taxable in Bush River Lower Hundred, 1775.

CARSON, John. Taxable in Bush River Lower Hundred, 1775.

CARTER, Mart. Taxable (servant) in household of Thomas Brice, Deer Creek Upper Hundred, 1775.

CARTIE, John. Taxable in Bush River Upper Hundred, 1775, with taxable Lues Corbit listed in his household.

CARTIE, Sarah. Head of household in Spesutia Lower Hundred, 1776, with taxable Joseph Bendon listed in her household.

CASTLEDINE, John. Taxable at Luke Griffith's Quarters, Spesutia Lower Hundred, 1776.

CASTLEDRINE, John. Taxable at Luke Griffin's Quarters, Spesutia Lower Hundred, 1775.

CAVENOUGH, Patrick. Taxable in Bush River Upper Hundred, 1775.

CEELY, John. Taxable in Susquehanna Hundred, 1776.

CELLY, Charles. Taxable (servant) in the household of Aquila Clark, Bush River Upper Hundred, 1775.

CELLY, William. Taxable in household of Thomas Hutchens, Bush River Lower Hundred, 1775.

CHALK, George. Taxable in Bush River Upper Hundred, 1775.

CHALK, Gorg (George). Taxable in Bush River Upper Hundred, 1775, with taxable negro Jacob listed in his household.

CHALK, John. Taxable in Bush River Upper Hundred, 1775.

CHALK, Joshua. Taxable in Bush River Upper Hundred, 1775, with taxables servant Thomas ---- (no last name given) and slave Gras listed in his household.

CHALK, Mary (widow). Head of household in Bush River Upper Hundred, 1775, with taxable slaves Sam and Jane listed in her household.

CHALK, Tuder. Taxable in Bush River Upper Hundred, 1775 [The constable actually spelled the name "Chauk" even though all others by that name were listed as "Chalk"].

CHAMBERS, Thomas. Taxable in Spesutia Upper Hundred, 1775.

CHAMBERS, William. Taxable in Gunpowder Lower Hundred, 1775.

CHANCEY, Benjamin. Taxable in household of George Chancey, Sr., Spesutia Lower Hundred, 1775.

CHANCEY, George Jr. Taxable in Spesutia Lower Hundred, 1775, with taxable slaves Simon, Sharper, Moll, and Dinah listed in his household.

CHANCEY, George Sr. Taxable in Spesutia Lower Hundred, 1775, with taxables Benjamin Chancey and slaves Dongo, Rose, Tom, and Hannah listed in his household.

CHANCEY, James. Taxable in Spesutia Lower Hundred, 1775, with taxable slave Pat listed in his household.

CHANCEY, John. Taxable in Spesutia Lower Hundred, 1775, with taxable slaves Priss and Pug listed in his household.

CHANDLEY, William. Taxable in Spesutia Lower Hundred, 1775, with taxable William Duzan listed in his household.

EARLY HARFORD COUNTIANS: Supplement

CHANEY, Burgess. Taxable in Bush River Lower Hundred, 1775, with taxables Greenbury Chaney and negroes Da--- [page torn], Nell, Grace, and Denal listed in his household.

CHANEY, Greenbury. Taxable in household of Burgess Chaney, Bush River Lower Hundred, 1775.

CHANEY, Richard. See "Thomas Chaney" and "Richard Cheney," q.v.

CHANEY, Thomas. Taxable in Spesutia Lower Hundred, 1775, with Richard Chaney as his security.

CHANLEY, James. Taxable in Susquehanna Hundred, 1776.

CHAPEL, William. Taxable in Susquehanna Hundred, 1775, with taxables Edward Wall, Patrick Baxter, Charles Wright, and negroes Phoebe and Esther listed in his household.

CHARRETT, William. Taxable in Bush River Upper Hundred, 1775.

CHENEY, Richard. Taxable in Spesutia Lower Hundred, 1775.

CHERRY, James. Taxable in Bush River Upper Hundred, 1775.

CHESNEY, Richard. Taxable in Susquehanna Hundred, 1776.

CHEW, Richard. Taxable in household of John Jolley, Deer Creek Lower Hundred, 1775.

CHEW, Thomas. Taxable in Deer Creek Lower Hundred, 1775, with taxable negroes Judy, Suck, and Holaday listed in his household.

CHILDS, George. Taxable on the plantation of Amos Garrett, Spesutia Lower Hundred, 1775.

CHINA, Richard. Taxable in Spesutia Lower Hundred, 1776, with taxable Thomas China listed in his household.

CHINA, Thomas. Taxable in household of Richard China, Spesutia Lower Hundred, 1776.

CHISHOLM, Thomas. Taxable in Susquehanna Hundred, 1776, with taxable Thomas Young listed in his household.

CHISHOLME, Thomas. Taxable in household of Josias Carvel Hall, Spesutia Lower Hundred, 1775.

CHRISTIE, Gabriel. Taxable in Spesutia Lower Hundred, 1775.

CHRISTIE, Gabriel. Taxable in Spesutia Lower Hundred, 1776.

CHURNMAN, John. Taxable in household of Henry Vansickleton, Spesutia Lower Hundred, 1776.

CINNAMON, John. Taxable in the household of Henry Vansickleton, Spesutia Lower Hundred, 1775.

CLARK, Aquila. Taxable in Bush River Upper Hundred, 1775, with taxable sercant Charles Celly listed in his household.

CLARK, David. Taxable in Spesutia Upper Hundred, 1775, with taxable negroes Coffy and Judy listed in his household.

CLARK, James. See "James Clerk," q.v.

CLARK, James. Taxable in Spesutia Upper Hundred, 1775, with taxable James Hews listed in his household.

CLARK, John (reverend). Head of household in Bush River Upper Hundred, 1775, with taxable Partrick Murfey listed in his household. [The constable mistakenly counted the reverend as a taxable, but clergymen were exempt from paying taxes].

CLARK, John (schoolmaster). Taxable in Spesutia Lower Hundred, 1775. [His name appeared at the end of the alphabetical tax list and at the end of, or perhaps even a part of, the entry on William Young's household. The constable did not draw a line to separate them].

CLARK, John (schoolmaster). Taxable in Susquehanna Hundred, 1776, with John Hathhorne as his security.

CLARK, John. See "Allexander Turner," q.v.

CLARK, John. Taxable in household of Eleven Ingram, Gunpowder Lower Hundred, 1775.

CLARK, John. Taxable in Susquehanna Hundred, 1775.

CLARK, Larrance. Taxable in Spesutia Upper Hundred, 1775, with taxable negro Abraham listed in his household.

CLARK, Robert. See "Robert Clerk," q.v.

CLARK, Robert. Taxable in Bush River Upper Hundred, 1775.

CLARK, Sillina. Head of household in Spesutia Upper Hundred, 1775, with taxable negro Jack listed in her household.

CLARK, Thomas. Taxable in Spesutia Upper Hundred, 1775.

CLARK, Thomas. Taxable in household of Joseph Husbands, Susquehanna Hundred, 1776.

CLARK, William (son of William). Taxable in Spesutia Upper Hundred, 1775 his father William Clark, Spesutia Upper Hundred, 1775.

CLARK, William. See "Robert Clerk," q.v.

CLARK, William. Taxable in Spesutia Upper Hundred, 1775, with taxables William Clark (son) and negroes Joshua, Toby, and Jenny listed in his household.

CLEMEN, Christopher. Taxable in household of Thomas Wright, Bush River Lower Hundred, 1775.

CLEMONS, John. Taxable in Bush River Upper Hundred, 1775.

CLEMONS, Partrick. Taxable in Bush River Upper Hundred, 1775.

CLEMONS, Samuel. Taxable in household of Underwood Guiton, Bush River Lower Hundred, 1775.

CLENDENON, James. Taxable in Spesutia Upper Hundred, 1775, with taxables Richard Gill and Alexander Stevenson listed in his household.

CLERK, James. Taxable in Deer Creek Upper Hundred,

1775, with negro Suck listed in his household.
CLERK, Robert Jr. Taxable in Deer Creek Upper Hundred, 1775.
CLERK, Robert Sr. Taxable in Deer Creek Upper Hundred, 1775, with taxables William Clerk (son) and negroes Pug and Dinah listed in his household.
CLERK, William. Taxable in household of Robert Clerk, Sr., Deer Creek Upper Hundred, 1775.
CLOSE, George. Taxable in Susquehanna Hundred, 1775.
CLOSE, George. Taxable in Susquehanna Hundred, 1776.
COAL, Phillip. Taxable in Deer Creek Lower Hundred, 1775, with taxable negro Ben listed in his household.
COAL, Robert. Taxable in household of Benjamin Norris, Bush River Lower Hundred, 1775.
COAL, Samuel. Taxable in Deer Creek Lower Hundred, 1775.
COAL, Skipwith (son of William). Taxable in Deer Creek Lower Hundred, 1775.
COAL, Skipwith. Taxable in Deer Creek Lower Hundred, 1775, with taxable negroes Jack, London, George, and Sig listed in his household.
COAL, William (carpenter). Taxable in Deer Creek Lower Hundred, 1775, with taxables John Michel and Harice Spotter listed in his household.
COAL, William. Taxable in household of Winston Dallam, Deer Creek Lower Hundred, 1775.
COAL, William. Taxable in Deer Creek Lower Hundred, 1775, with taxables negroes James, Sam, Ceaser, Jenney, and Bett listed in his household.
COALE, William. Taxable in Spesutia Upper Hundred, 1775, with taxable John Cole [sic] and John Duly listed in his household.
COCKERTON, John. Taxable in Gunpowder Lower Hundred, 1775.
COEN, John. Taxable in Susquehanna Hundred, 1776. [The actual entry is written "Coen, John, Wm. Cowen" and indicates one taxable, not two, in this household; perhaps John was the son of William].
COEN, Thomas. Taxable in Susquehanna Hundred, 1776, with John Mahhan as his security.
COLDRIG, William. Taxable in Susquehanna Hundred, 1776.
COLE, Ephraim. Taxable in Susquehanna Hundred, 1775.
COLE, Ephrem. Taxable in Susquehanna Hundred, 1776.
COLE, James. Taxable in Susquehanna Hundred, 1775, with taxable John Savage listed in his household.
COLE, James. Taxable in Susquehanna Hundred, 1776.
COLE, Jan (widow). Head of household in Susquehanna Hundred, 1775, with taxable John Carrol listed in her household.
COLE, Jane. See "John Carrel," q.v.

COLE, John. Taxable in household of William Coale, Spesutia Upper Hundred, 1775.
COLE, N. Taxable in household of Gregrey Barns, Susquehanna Hundred, 1776.
COLE, Skipwith. See "Skipwith Coal," q.v.
COLEMAN, Charles. Taxable in Bush River Lower Hundred, 1775.
COLEMAN, George. Taxable in Bush River Lower Hundred, 1775.
COLEMAN, Michael. Taxable in the household of William Loney, Spesutia Lower Hundred, 1775.
COLEMAN, Michael. Taxable in household of William Loney, Spesutia Lower Hundred, 1776.
COLLINGS, Jeremiah. Taxable in Spesutia Lower Hundred, 1776 Daniel Campbell, Spesutia Lower Hundred, 1776.
COLLINS, Isaac. Taxable in Spesutia Lower Hundred, 1775.
COLLINS, Jacob. Taxable in household of Moses Collins, Spesutia Lower Hundred, 1775.
COLLINS, John. Taxable in household of William Collins, Spesutia Lower Hundred, 1775.
COLLINS, John. Taxable in household of Baltus Fie, Spesutia Lower Hundred, 1775.
COLLINS, John. Taxable in household of Josias William Dallam, Spesutia Lower Hundred, 1775.
COLLINS, John. Taxable in household of Baltus Fie, Spesutia Lower Hundred, 1776.
COLLINS, John. Taxable in household of Henry Vansickleton, Spesutia Lower Hundred, 1776.
COLLINS, Moses. Taxable in Spesutia Lower Hundred, 1775, with taxables Jacob Collins, Samuel Collins, and William Irons listed in his household.
COLLINS, Robert. Taxable in Bush River Lower Hundred, 1775.
COLLINS, Robert. Taxable in Bush River Upper Hundred, 1775.
COLLINS, Samuel. Taxable in household of Moses Collins, Spesutia Lower Hundred, 1775.
COLLINS, William. Taxable in Spesutia Lower Hundred, 1775, with taxable John Collins listed in his household.
COLLINS, William. Taxable in Spesutia Lower Hundred, 1776.
COLONY, Joseph. Taxable in household of Francis Billingsly, Bush River Lower Hundred, 1775.
COLTREY(?), Thomas. Taxable in Susquehanna Hundred, 1776.
COMBEST, Israel. Taxable in Spesutia Lower Hundred, 1776.
COMBEST, Jacob Jr. Taxable in Spesutia Lower Hundred, 1775, with taxable James Dunny listed in his household.
COMBEST, Jacob Sr. Taxable in Spesutia Lower

Hundred, 1775.
COMBEST, Jacob Sr. Taxable in Spesutia Lower Hundred, 1776.
COMBEST, Utiae. Taxable in Spesutia Lower Hundred, 1775.
COMEN, Phillip. Taxable in Susquehanna Hundred, 1776, with taxable Sammuel Comens listed in his household. [The names are spelled differently on the tax list and only one taxable, not two, is indicated; the constable apparently made errors in this enumeration].
COMMENS, John. Taxable in Susquehanna Hundred, 1776.
COMMENS, Paul. Taxable in Susquehanna Hundred, 1776.
CONARD, Edward. Taxable in Bush River Lower Hundred, 1775.
CONDROM, John Jr. Taxable in Bush River Upper Hundred, 1775, with taxable William Condrom listed in his household.
CONDROM, William. Taxable in household of John Condrom, Jr., Bush River Upper Hundred, 1775.
CONLEY, John. Taxable in Spesutia Lower Hundred, 1775.
CONN, John. Taxable in household of Robert Conn, Bush River Lower Hundred, 1775.
CONN, Robert. Taxable in Bush River Lower Hundred, 1775, with taxable John Conn listed in his household.
CONNALLY, John. Taxable on the plantation of Amos Garrett, Spesutia Lower Hundred, 1775.
CONNELLY, Wiliam. Taxable in Deer Creek Upper Hundred, 1775, with Samuel Morgan as his security.
CONNER, James. Taxable in household of William Ensor, Gunpowder Lower Hundred, 1775.
CONNS, William. Taxable in Bush River Lower Hundred, 1775.
CONOVER, Jacob Sr. Taxable in Bush River Lower Hundred, 1775, with taxable Jacob Conover, Jr. listed in his household.
CONOWAY, Michael. Taxable in Spesutia Lower Hundred, 1775.
CONROD, Edward. Taxable in Bush River Lower Hundred, 1775.
COOK, John Jr. Taxable in Bush River Upper Hundred, 1775.
COOK, John. Taxable in household of Jacob Bond, Sr., Bush River Lower Hundred, 1775.
COOK, John. Taxable in Bush River Upper Hundred, 1775. [The constable entered his name on the tax list and then lined it out; no reason given].
COOK, Robert. See "John Brian," q.v.
COOK, Robert. Taxable in Deer Creek Lower Hundred, 1775.
COOLEY, John. Taxable in Susquehanna Hundred, 1775.
COOLEY, Richard. Taxable in Bush River Upper Hundred, 1775, with taxable William Cooley (son) listed in his household.
COOLEY, William (son of Richard). Taxable in household of his father Richard Cooley, Bush River Upper Hundred, 1775.
COOP, Richard. Taxable in Bush River Upper Hundred, 1775.
COOPER, Henry. Taxable in Spesutia Upper Hundred, 1775, with taxables Nathanel Cooper (son) and negroes Jim, Jacob, and Priss listed in his household.
COOPER, James. Taxable in Deer Creek Upper Hundred, 1775, with Samuel Morgan as his security.
COOPER, Nathanel (son of Henry). Taxable in household of his father Henry Cooper, Spesutia Upper Hundred, 1775.
COOPER, William. Taxable in household of James Giles, Spesutia Lower Hundred, 1775.
COOPER, William. Taxable in Spesutia Upper Hundred, 1775.
COPELAND, John. Taxable in Spesutia Lower Hundred, 1775, taxable negroes Grace, Jefro, and Cloe listed in his household. Taxable in Spesutia Lower Hundred, 1775.
COPLAND, George. Taxable in Spesutia Lower Hundred, 1775, with taxable slaves Ned, Sall, Harry, and Vingo listed in his household.
CORBIT, James. Taxable in household of his father William Corbit, Bush River Upper Hundred, 1775.
CORBIT, Lewis. Taxable in Bush River Upper Hundred, 1775.
CORBIT, Lues (Lewis). Taxable in household of John Cartie, Bush River Upper Hundred, 1775.
CORBIT, Samuel. Taxable in household of his father William Corbit, Bush River Upper Hundred, 1775.
CORBIT, William. Taxable in Bush River Upper Hundred, 1775, with taxables James Corbit (son) and Samuel Corbit (son) listed in his household.
CORD, Amos. See "Timothy Murphy," q.v.
CORD, Amos. Taxable in Spesutia Lower Hundred, 1775.
CORD, Amos. Taxable in Spesutia Lower Hundred, 1776, with taxable William Hamby listed in his household.
CORD, Ashberry. Taxable in Spesutia Lower Hundred, 1776, with taxable negro Jeffery listed in his household.
CORD, Rodger. Taxable in household of William Welch, Susquehanna Hundred, 1776.
CORD, Roger. Taxable in Susquehanna Hundred, 1775.
CORHON, James. Taxable in Bush River Upper Hundred, 1775.
CORKER, Patrick. Taxable on plantation of Edward Carvel Tolley, Spesutia Lower Hundred, 1776.
CORKRON, Owen. Taxable (servant) in household of

James Brice, Deer Creek Lower Hundred, 1775.

CORNEY, Peter. Taxable in Bush River Lower Hundred, 1775.

COSEBURY, James. Taxable in household of John Hannah, Spesutia Upper Hundred, 1775.

COSTLET, John. Taxable in Gunpowder Lower Hundred, 1775, with taxable Thomas Costlet listed in his household.

COSTLET, Thomas. Taxable in household of John Costlet, Gunpowder Lower Hundred, 1775.

COTMAN, John. Taxable in household of Francis Billingsly, Bush River Lower Hundred, 1775.

COTTER, Edward. Taxable on plantation of Josias William Dallam, Spesutia Lower Hundred, 1776.

COTTEY, Edward. Taxable in household of Josias William Dallam, Spesutia Lower Hundred, 1775.

COTTON, John. Taxable in household of William Barns, Susquehanna Hundred, 1776.

COTTREY(?), Thomas. Taxable in Susquehanna Hundred, 1776.

COURTNEY, Thomas. Taxable in Susquehanna Hundred, 1775.

COWAN, Edward. Taxable in Susquehanna Hundred, with John Cowan as his security.

COWAN, John. See "Edward Cowan," q.v.

COWAN, Thomas. Taxable in Susquehanna Hundred, 1775, with John Mahon as his security.

COWAN, William Jr. Taxable in Susquehanna Hundred, 1775.

COWEN, Alexander. Taxable in Gunpowder Lower Hundred, 1775, with taxables John Blake, servants George ---- and Charles ---- (no last names given) and slaves Mudlin, Cash, Lucy, and Suke listed in his household.

COWEN, John (son of Mark). Taxable in Spesutia Lower Hundred, 1776.

COWEN, John. Taxable in Spesutia Lower Hundred, 1775, with taxable Mark Cowen listed in his household.

COWEN, Mark. See "John Cowen," q.v.

COWEN, Mark. Taxable in household of John Cowen, Spesutia Lower Hundred, 1775.

COWEN, William. Taxable in Susquehanna Hundred, 1776. See "John Coen," q.v.

COWLEY, Thomas. Taxable on plantation of Aquila Hall, Spesutia Lower Hundred, 1775.

COWLEY, Thomas. Taxable in Spesutia Lower Hundred, 1776.

COX, Charles. Taxable in household of Josias William Dallam, Spesutia Lower Hundred, 1775.

COX, Charles. Taxable on plantation of Josias William Dallam, Spesutia Lower Hundred, 1776.

COX, James. Taxable in Bush River Lower Hundred, 1775, with taxable David Calwell listed in his household.

COX, John. See "John Power" and "William Boyer," q.v.

COX, John. Taxable in Susquehanna Hundred, 1775.

COX, John. Taxable in Susquehanna Hundred, 1776.

COX, William Jr. Taxable in Susquehanna Hundred, 1775.

COX, William Jr. Taxable in Susquehanna Hundred, 1776.

COX, William. Taxable in Susquehanna Hundred, 1775.

COX, William. Taxable in Susquehanna Hundred, 1776, with taxable Charles Wright listed in his household.

CRAFORD, James (son of Mordica). Taxable in household of his father Mordica Craford, Deer Creek Lower Hundred, 1775.

CRAFORD, Mordica. Taxable in Deer Creek Lower Hundred, 1775, with taxable James Craford (son) and negro Jenney listed in his household.

CRAFORD, Robert. Taxable in Deer Creek Lower Hundred, 1775, with taxable man Barnaby Dougherty (servant) listed in his household.

CRAGE, John. Taxable in household of Andra Meak, Susquehanna Hundred, 1776.

CRAGGIN, Thomas. Taxable in household of William Smith, Gunpowder Lower Hundred, 1775.

CRAITON, W--- [illegible]. Taxable in Susquehanna Hundred, 1775.

CRALE, Philip. Taxable in Deer Creek Upper Hundred, 1775.

CRATA, David. Taxable in household of Baker Rigdon, Deer Creek Upper Hundred, 1775.

CRATAIN, James. Taxable in Bush River Upper Hundred, 1775.

CRATON, James. Taxable in household of John Craton, Spesutia Upper Hundred, 1775.

CRATON, John. Taxable in household of John Craton, Spesutia Upper Hundred, 1775.

CRATON, John. Taxable in Spesutia Upper Hundred, 1775, with taxables James Craton, John Craton, and negroes Jim, Rache, and Rose listed in his household.

CRATON, John. Taxable in Bush River Upper Hundred, 1775.

CRAWFORD, Alexander. Taxable in Spesutia Upper Hundred, 1775.

CRAWFORD, James. Taxable on plantation of William Webb, Deer Creek Upper Hundred, 1775.

CREIGHTON, Patrick. Taxable in Susquehanna Hundred, 1775, with taxables William Nowlan and negro Moll listed in his household.

CREITON, John. Taxable in Bush River Upper Hundred, 1775. [The constable entered his name on the teaxc list and then lined it out; no reason given].

CRESWELL, James. Taxable in household of William Creswell, Susquehanna Hundred, 1775.

CRESWELL, James. Taxable in household of William

EARLY HARFORD COUNTIANS: Supplement

Creswell, Susquehanna Hundred, 1776.

CRESWELL, Robert (wheelwright). See "William Creswell," q.v.

CRESWELL, Robert. Taxable in household of William Creswell, Susquehanna Hundred, 1775.

CRESWELL, Robert. Taxable in household of William Creswell, Susquehanna Hundred, 1776.

CRESWELL, William. Taxable in Susquehanna Hundred, 1775, with taxables James Creswell, Robert Creswell, and negroes Jack and Mariah listed in his household.

CRESWELL, William. Taxable in Susquehanna Hundred, 1776, with taxables Robert Creswell, James Creswell, Robert Creswell, and negroes Jack and Merer listed in his household. [Robert Creswell was listed twice; another tax list indicated one Robert was a wheelwright].

CRODGILL, Thomas. Taxable in household of William Arnold, Susquehanna Hundred, 1775.

CROMMELL, James. Taxable in household of Elizabeth Gallion, Spesutia Lower Hundred, 1776.

CROOKS, Henry. Taxable in Deer Creek Upper Hundred, 1775, with taxables William Crooks, Thomas Crooks, and negro Phillis listed in his household.

CROOKS, Thomas. Taxable in household of Henry Crooks, Deer Creek Upper Hundred, 1775.

CROOKS, William. Taxable in household of Henry Crooks, Deer Creek Upper Hundred, 1775.

CROSBEY, Richard. Taxable in Deer Creek Lower Hundred, 1775.

CROSGELL, William. Taxable in household of William Arnel, Susquehanna Hundred, 1776.

CROUCH, John. Taxable in household of George Ford, Spesutia Lower Hundred, 1775.

CROUCH, Stephen. Taxable in Spesutia Lower Hundred, 1775, with William Osborn, Jr. as his security.

CROWELL, Marthews. Taxable in Bush River Upper Hundred, 1775.

CRUISE, John. Taxable in Susquehanna Hundred, 1775, with taxable George Woolt listed in his household.

CRUISE, Richard. Taxable in Susquehanna Hundred, 1775, with taxable James Wills listed in his household.

CRUSE, Richard. Taxable in Susquehanna Hundred, 1776. See "Robin Campton," q.v.

CRUSSON, John. Taxable in Susquehanna Hundred, 1776, with taxable George Wood listed in his household.

CUBING, Barney. Taxable (servant) in household of John Rutlage, Bush River Upper Hundred, 1775.

CULVER, Benjamin. Taxable in Susquehanna Hundred, 1775.

CULVER, Benjamin. Taxable in Susquehanna Hundred, 1776.

CULVER, Robert. Taxable in Susquehanna Hundred, 1775, with taxables Hugh McIntosh and negro Mariah listed in his household.

CULVER, Robert. Taxable in Susquehanna Hundred, 1776, with taxables Hugh McAntos and negro Merer listed in his household.

CUMBERLAND FORGE. Taxable negroes Dandee, Marcus, Annabaal, Jack, Andrew, Demitres, Black John, Cupit, -?-nkey Tom, Carpenter Tom, and James listed at this forge. [The constable listed 11 taxables at this forge, one name after another with no comma's, so the last name might refer to Tom James, carpenter].

CUMMINS, John. Taxable in Susquehanna Hundred, 1775.

CUMMINS, Paul. Taxable in Susquehanna Hundred, 1775.

CUMMINS, Philip. Taxable in Susquehanna Hundred, 1775, with taxable Samuel Cummins listed in his household.

CUMMINS, Samuel. Taxable in Susquehanna Hundred, 1775 Philip Cummins, Susquehanna Hundred, 1775.

CUNNINGHAM, Clotworthy. Taxable in Gunpowder Lower Hundred, 1775, with taxable George Cunningham listed in his household.

CUNNINGHAM, George. Taxable in household of Clotworthy Cunningham, Gunpowder Lower Hundred, 1775.

CUNNINGHAM, James. Taxable in Bush River Lower Hundred, 1775.

CUNNINGHAM, Jonathan. Taxable in Bush River Upper Hundred, 1775.

CUNNINGHAM, Thomas (son of Thomas). Taxable in household of his father Thomas Cunningham, Bush River Upper Hundred, 1775.

CUNNINGHAM, Thomas. Taxable in Bush River Upper Hundred, 1775, with taxable Thomas Cunningham (son) listed in his household.

CUNNINGHAM, William. Taxable in Bush River Upper Hundred, 1775.

CURK, Garratt. Taxable in household of George Ford, Spesutia Lower Hundred, 1775.

CURKWOOD, Robert. Taxable in Bush River Upper Hundred, 1775. [The constable not only misspelled the name (which was actually Robert Kirkwood), he listed the name among the "T's" on the tax list].

CURRY, Brian. Taxable in household of James Brown, Spesutia Lower Hundred, 1775.

CURRY, James. Taxable in Bush River Upper Hundred, 1775.

CURRY, Thomas. Taxable in household of John Skaff, Bush River Lower Hundred, 1775.

CUTHBERT, William. Taxable in Bush River Lower Hundred, 1775.

DALAM, John. Taxable in household of his brother Richard Dalam (Dallam), Deer Creek Lower Hundred, 1775.

DALAM, Richard. Taxable in Deer Creek Lower Hundred, 1775, with taxable John Dalam (brother) and negroes Ben, Fan, and Dal listed in his household.

DALEY, William. Taxable in Gunpowder Lower Hundred, 1775.

DALLAM, John. See "Richard Dallam," q.v.

DALLAM, Josias William. Taxable in Spesutia Lower Hundred, 1775, with taxables John Collins, Charles Cox, Edward Cottey, and slaves Tower, Ceaser, Pitt, Adam, Cromwell, Sipp, Bob, Lew, and Beck listed in his household.

DALLAM, Josias William. Taxable in Spesutia Lower Hundred, 1776, with taxables Charles Cox, Edward Cotter, John Donn, and negroes Crommell, Sitop, Tower, Bobb, Adam, Caeser, Mobber, Patt, Lew, Beck, and Orange listed on his plantation.

DALLAM, Josias. See "Thomas Walker," q.v.

DALLAM, Richard. See "Richard Dalam," q.v.

DALLAM, Richard's Quarters. Spesutie Lower Hundred, 1775, with taxables Peter Duzan, John Perry, Daniel Buckley, John Don, and slaves Dick, Peter, and Laury (all at Swan Creek) and taxables John Beck and slaves Cato, Morey, Dan, Sall, and Hannah (all at Romney), listed at these quarters.

DALLAM, Winston. Taxable in Deer Creek Lower Hundred, 1775, with taxable William Coal listed in his household.

DALLEY, Jeremiah. Taxable in household of John Carlile, Spesutia Lower Hundred, 1776.

DALY, John. Taxable in Bush River Upper Hundred, 1775.

DANDLEY (DANDBY?), Jeremiah. Taxable in Gunpowder Lower Hundred, 1775.

DARBEY, Robert. Taxable in Deer Creek Lower Hundred, 1775.

DAUGHERTY, George. Taxable in Spesutia Lower Hundred, 1775, with taxables Samuel Daughtery and slave Sarah listed in his household.

DAUGHERTY, Michael. Taxable in Deer Creek Upper Hundred, 1775.

DAUGHERTY, Samuel. Taxable in household of George Daugherty, Spesutia Lower Hundred, 1775.

DAUGHERTY, Samuel. Taxable in Spesutia Upper Hundred, 1775, with taxable negro Dick listed in his household.

DAUGHERTY, William. Taxable in Spesutia Lower Hundred, 1775.

DAUGHERTY, William. Taxable in Spesutia Lower Hundred, 1776.

DAUL, John. Taxable in Bush River Upper Hundred, 1775, with taxable negro Dina listed in his household.

DAVENSON, John. Taxable in Susquehanna Hundred, 1776.

DAVIDGE, John. Taxable in Spesutia Lower Hundred, 1775, with William Hall as his security.

DAVIS, David. Taxable in Bush River Upper Hundred, 1775, with taxable Thomas Davis (son) listed in his household. See "William Logan," q.v.

DAVIS, Elizabeth. Head of household in Bush River Lower Hundred, 1775, with taxable negroes Joe, Phillis, and Tamer listed in her household.

DAVIS, Jacob. Taxable in Bush River Upper Hundred, 1775.

DAVIS, Jacob. Taxable at Zacheus Onion's Quarters, Bush River Upper Hundred, 1775.

DAVIS, John (reverend). Head of household in Bush River Upper Hundred, 1775, with taxables John Turner and negro Bine listed in his household.

DAVIS, John. Taxable in Bush River Upper Hundred, 1775. [The constable wrote the name followed by "Ck." (possible abbreviation for "clerk"), but then drew a line through it].

DAVIS, Joseph. Taxable in Deer Creek Upper Hundred, 1775.

DAVIS, Thomas (son of David). Taxable in household of his father David Davis, Bush River Upper Hundred, 1775.

DAVISS, Isaac. Taxable in Susquehanna Hundred, 1775.

DAWNEY, Thomas Jr. Taxable in Gunpowder Lower Hundred, 1775.

DAWS, Benjamin. Taxable in household of Isaac Daws, Bush River Lower Hundred, 1775.

DAWS, Isaac. Taxable in Bush River Lower Hundred, 1775, with taxables Benjamin Daws and negro Jeremiah listed in his household.

DAWSEY, Mathew. Taxable in household of Isaac Tulock, Spesutia Lower Hundred, 1776.

DAWSON, Cristefur (Christopher). Taxable in Bush River Upper Hundred, 1775.

DAWSON, John. Taxable in Susquehanna Hundred, 1775.

DAY, John (son of Edward). Taxable in Gunpowder Lower Hundred, 1775, with taxables John Day (son), Nat. Biggs, and slaves Peter, Jim, Fie, Nan, and Chan listed in his household.

DAY, John (son of John). Taxable in household of his father John Day (son of Edward), Gunpowder Lower Hundred, 1775.

DAY, Nick. Taxable in household of James Tusty(?), Bush River Upper Hundred, 1775.

DAY, Sammuell. Taxable in Bush River Upper Hundred, 1775.

DAY, Samuel. Taxable in Bush River Lower Hundred, 1775.

DEACON, Francis. Taxable in Spesutia Lower Hundred,

1775.

DEAKON, William. Taxable on plantation of Jacob Giles, Jr., Susquehanna Hundred, 1776.

DEALE, James. Taxable in Bush River Lower Hundred, 1775, with taxable Aquilla Durham listed in his household.

DEARMOTT, John. Taxable in household of Mary Dearmott, Bush River Lower Hundred, 1775.

DEARMOTT, Mary. Head of household in Bush River Lower Hundred, 1775, with taxable John Dearmott listed in her household.

DEARMOTT, Thomas. Taxable in Bush River Lower Hundred, 1775.

DEATH, James. Taxable in Susquehanna Hundred, 1775, with taxable negro Nell listed in his household.

DEATH, James. Taxable in Susquehanna Hundred, 1776, with taxable negro Nel listed in his household.

DEATON, William. Taxable at Jacob Giles, Jr.'s Quarters, Spesutia Lower Hundred, 1776.

DEAVER, Aqualia. Taxable in Deer Creek Upper Hundred, 1775.

DEAVER, David. Taxable in Susquehanna Hundred, 1776.

DEAVER, Hugh. See "Hugh Devver," q.v.

DEAVER, James. Taxable on the plantation of Amos Garrett, Spesutia Lower Hundred, 1775.

DEAVER, James. Taxable in Deer Creek Upper Hundred, 1775.

DEAVER, James. Taxable in Spesutia Lower Hundred, 1776.

DEAVER, John. Taxable in Spesutia Lower Hundred, 1776.

DEAVER, Micajah. Taxable in Spesutia Lower Hundred, 1775. See "Thomas Deaver," q.v.

DEAVER, Micajah. Taxable in Spesutia Lower Hundred, 1776.

DEAVER, Richard Jr. Taxable in Deer Creek Upper Hundred, 1775.

DEAVER, Richard Sr. Taxable in Deer Creek Upper Hundred, 1775.

DEAVER, Thomas. Taxable in Spesutia Lower Hundred, 1775, with Micajah Deaver as his security.

DEBRULAR, Benjamin. Taxable in Gunpowder Lower Hundred, 1775.

DEBRULAR, George. Taxable in Gunpowder Lower Hundred, 1775.

DEBRULAR, James. Taxable in Gunpowder Lower Hundred, 1775.

DEBRULAR, Micajah. Taxable in Gunpowder Lower Hundred, 1775.

DEBRULAR, Uphan(?). Taxable in Gunpowder Lower Hundred, 1775, with taxable slave Phillis listed in her household.

DEBRULAR, William. Taxable in Gunpowder Lower Hundred, 1775, with taxable slave Ben listed in his household.

DEBRULER, John. Taxable in Spesutia Upper Hundred, 1775.

DEIEY, William. Taxable in household of Jacob Lemmon, Susquehanna Hundred, 1775.

DELANY, Isaac. Taxable in Spesutia Lower Hundred, 1776.

DEMORSE (DEMOREE?), John. Taxable in Bush River Upper Hundred, 1775, with taxable Dannill Dorty, Jr. listed in his household.

DENBO, John. Taxable in Spesutia Upper Hundred, 1775.

DENNEY, Oliver. Taxable in household of Jonathan White, Spesutia Lower Hundred, 1776.

DENNEY, Simon. Taxable in Spesutia Upper Hundred, 1775.

DENNEY, Thomas. Taxable in Spesutia Upper Hundred, 1775, with taxable servant John --- (no last name given) listed in his household.

DENNISON, James. Taxable on the plantation of Amos Garrett, Spesutia Lower Hundred, 1775.

DENNISON, James. Taxable on plantation of Amos Garrett, Spesutia Lower Hundred, 1776.

DENNY, James. Taxable in Deer Creek Upper Hundred, 1775, with taxable Walter Denny (son) listed in his household.

DENNY, Walter (son of James). Taxable in household of his father James Denny, Deer Creek Upper Hundred, 1775.

DENTON, William. Taxable in the household of Reuben Sutton, Spesutia Lower Hundred, 1775.

DERBIN, Thomas. Taxable in Gunpowder Lower Hundred, 1775.

DERFORD, Charles. Taxable in Gunpowder Lower Hundred, 1775. His name (among others) was listed on the back of the tax list.

DEVEN, Hugh. Taxable in Susquehanna Hundred, 1776.

DEVIN, John. Taxable in Gunpowder Lower Hundred, 1775. His name (among others) was listed on the back of the tax list.

DEVVER, Hugh. Taxable in Deer Creek Lower Hundred, 1775.

DIEMER, John. Taxable in Spesutia Lower Hundred, 1775, with taxable slaves Welton, Mory, Violet, Nan, and Alexander listed in his household. See "William Mooberry, Jr.," q.v.

DIGBY, John. Taxable in Deer Creek Upper Hundred, 1775.

DIGMAN, Patrick. Taxable in Bush River Lower Hundred, 1775.

DILLING, Larrance. Taxable in Susquehanna Hundred, 1776.

DILLON, George. Taxable in Susquehanna Hundred,

1775.

DILLON, Lawrence. Taxable in Susquehanna Hundred, 1775.

DILLON, Roger. Taxable in Susquehanna Hundred, 1775, with Jacob Lemmon as his security.

DINES, Frank. Taxable in Bush River Upper Hundred, 1775.

DINNAM, Ceaser. Taxable in Susquehanna Hundred, 1775.

DITTO, William. Taxable in Bush River Upper Hundred, 1775, with taxable negroes Mint and Thomas listed in his household.

DIVEN, William. Taxable in Gunpowder Lower Hundred, 1775, with Thomas Mill, security(?). [small writing, difficult to read].

DIXSON, David. Taxable in Spesutia Upper Hundred, 1775.

DOBBINS, James. Taxable in Spesutia Upper Hundred, 1775.

DOCKKET, John. Taxable in household of Robert Mils [sic], Susquehanna Hundred, 1776.

DOMINICK, Nathannile. Taxable in household of Ann Johnson (widow), Deer Creek Upper Hundred, 1775.

DON, John. Taxable at Richard Dallam's Quarters at Swan Creek, Spesutia Lower Hundred, 1775.

DONAHEY, John. Taxable in Deer Creek Upper Hundred, 1775.

DONAVON, Richard. Taxable on the plantation of Amos Garrett, Spesutia Lower Hundred, 1775.

DONLEY, Michael. Taxable in Spesutia Upper Hundred, 1775.

DONN, John. Taxable on plantation of Josias William Dallam, Spesutia Lower Hundred, 1776.

DONNILEY, Francis. Taxable in Spesutia Upper Hundred, 1775.

DONOHU, Daniel (mason). Taxable in Susquehanna Hundred, 1776.

DONOLDSON, James. Taxable in Bush River Lower Hundred, 1775.

DONOVEN, Daniel. Taxable in household of Daniel Donoven, Susquehanna Hundred, 1776.

DONOVEN, Daniel. Taxable in Susquehanna Hundred, 1776, with taxables Daniel Donoven, Jacob Donoven, and Thomas Donoven listed in his household.

DONOVEN, Jacob. Taxable in household of Daniel Donoven, Susquehanna Hundred, 1776.

DONOVEN, Phillip. Taxable in Susquehanna Hundred, 1775, with taxable James Townsend listed in his household.

DONOVEN, Thomas. Taxable in household of Daniel Donoven, Susquehanna Hundred, 1776.

DONOVEN, William. Taxable in Susquehanna Hundred, 1775.

DONOVEN, William. Taxable in Susquehanna Hundred, 1776.

DOOLEY, Samuel. Taxable in Spesutia Lower Hundred, 1776, with taxable negroes Sall and Mosa listed in his household.

DORBEY, Michael. Taxable in household of Henry Vansickleton, Spesutia Lower Hundred, 1776.

DORRAN, Hugh. Taxable in Bush River Upper Hundred, 1775, with taxable Patrick Dorran (son) and negroes Dill and Hannah listed in his household.

DORRAN, Patrick (son of Hugh). Taxable in household of his father Hugh Dorran, Bush River Upper Hundred, 1775.

DORSEY, Frisby. Taxable in household of Greenberry Dorsey, Spesutia Lower Hundred, 1775.

DORSEY, Frisby. Taxable in household of Greenberry Dorsey, Spesutia Lower Hundred, 1776.

DORSEY, Greenberry. Taxable in Spesutia Lower Hundred, 1775, with taxables Frisby Dorsey, Jacob Duran, and slaves Dick, Ceaser, Jim, Hannah, Sue, and Patt listed in his household.

DORSEY, Greenberry. Taxable in Spesutia Lower Hundred, 1776, with taxables Frisby Dorsey and negroes Dick, Caesar, Jim, Hannah, Sue, and Patt listed in his household. See "William Smith," q.v.

DORSEY, Mathew. Taxable in Gunpowder Lower Hundred, 1775.

DORTY, Dannill Jr. Taxable in household of John Demorse (Demoree?), Bush River Upper Hundred, 1775.

DOUGHERTY, Barnaby. Taxable (servant) in household of Robert Craford, Deer Creek Lower Hundred, 1775.

DOUGHERTY, George. Taxable in Spesutia Lower Hundred, 1776, with taxables Samuel Dougherty and negro Sall listed in his household.

DOUGHERTY, Samuel. Taxable in household of George Dougherty, Spesutia Lower Hundred, 1776.

DOWLEY, Edward. Taxable in the household of Edward Carvel Tolley, Spesutia Lower Hundred, 1775.

DOWNING, Francis. Taxable in Deer Creek Lower Hundred, 1775, with taxable William Downing and negroes York, Ollever, Abraham, and Hannah listed in his household.

DOWNING, William. Taxable in household of Francis Downing, Deer Creek Lower Hundred, 1775.

DOWNS, Thomas. Taxable in Gunpowder Lower Hundred, 1775.

DOWNS, William. See "Negro ----," q.v.

DOWNS, William. Taxable in Bush River Lower Hundred, 1775.

DRANON, John. Taxable in Bush River Lower Hundred, 1775.

DRAPER, John. Taxable "at Mrs. Hall's" in Spesutia Lower Hundred, 1775.

DREW, George. Taxable in Spesutia Lower Hundred,

1775, with taxable Lewis Pedlar listed in his household.

DREW, James. Taxable in Spesutia Lower Hundred, 1775.

DUBLIN, John. Taxable in household of Peter Fort, Susquehanna Hundred, 1775.

DUGLESS, Daniel (molato). Taxable in Bush River Lower Hundred, 1775 (listed with his wife Sarah Dugless; James Matthews, security), Bush River Lower Hundred, 1775.

DUGLESS, Sarah. Wife of Daniel Dugless (molato), Bush River Lower Hundred, 1775.

DULANY, Isaac. Taxable in Spesutia Lower Hundred, 1775.

DULY, John. Taxable in household of William Coale, Spesutia Upper Hundred, 1775.

DUNN, Thomas. Taxable in the household of William Reading, Spesutia Lower Hundred, 1775.

DUNNY, James. Taxable in household of Jacob Combest, Jr., Spesutia Lower Hundred, 1775.

DURAN, Jacob. Taxable in household of Greenberry Dorsey, Spesutia Lower Hundred, 1775.

DURBIN, Daniel. Taxable in Susquehanna Hundred, 1775, with taxable negro Poll listed in his household.

DURBIN, Daniel. Taxable in Spesutia Lower Hundred, 1776, with taxables James Banning, Daniel Buckler, and negroes Sam, Pool, and Lowrey listed in his household.

DURBIN, Francis. Taxable in Susquehanna Hundred, 1775.

DURBIN, Francis. Taxable in Susquehanna Hundred, 1776.

DURBIN, Samuel. Taxable in household of Jacob Giles, Jr., Susquehanna Hundred, 1775.

DURBIN, Thomas. Taxable in household of John Periman, Susquehanna Hundred, 1775.

DURBIN, Thomas. Taxable in household of John Peremon, Susquehanna Hundred, 1776.

DURHAM, Aquilla. Taxable in household of James Deale, Bush River Lower Hundred, 1775.

DURHAM, David. Taxable in Bush River Upper Hundred, 1775, with taxable negro Peg listed in his household.

DURHAM, Ellender. Head of household in Bush River Lower Hundred, 1775, with taxable negroes Hamond, Marai, Phebe, Diels, Fanny, Tom, and Phillis listed in her household.

DURHAM, J--- [page torn]. Taxable in Gunpowder Lower Hundred, 1775.

DURHAM, James. Taxable in Bush River Lower Hundred, 1775.

DURHAM, John (son of Joshua). Taxable in Bush River Lower Hundred, 1775.

DURHAM, Joshua. Taxable in Bush River Lower Hundred, 1775, with taxable servant Dick ---- (no last name given) listed in his household.

DURHAM, Mordicai. Taxable in Bush River Lower Hundred, 1775.

DURHAM, Samuel. Taxable in Bush River Lower Hundred, 1775, with taxable negro Jean listed in his household.

DUYR, Darby. Taxable (servant) in household of James Mathers, Bush River Lower Hundred, 1775.

DUZAN, Alexander. Taxable in Spesutia Lower Hundred, 1775.

DUZAN, Alexander. Taxable in Spesutia Lower Hundred, 1775, with taxable Isaac Duzan (and Peter Duzan as his security).

DUZAN, Alexander. Taxable on plantation of Amos Garrett, Spesutia Lower Hundred, 1776.

DUZAN, Isaac. Taxable in household of Alexander Duzan, Spesutia Lower Hundred, 1775.

DUZAN, John. Taxable in Spesutia Lower Hundred, 1775, with taxable James Humes listed in his household.

DUZAN, John. Taxable in Spesutia Lower Hundred, 1776.

DUZAN, Peter. See "Alexander Duzan," q.v.

DUZAN, Peter. Taxable at Richard Dallam's Quarters at Swan Creek, Spesutia Lower Hundred, 1775.

EAGON, Samson. Taxable in Bush River Upper Hundred, 1775, with taxable Patrick Marthew listed in his household.

EARS, Stephan. Taxable in Bush River Upper Hundred, 1775 [He is listed after the "W's" at the end of the tax list].

EATON, William. See "John Flyn," q.v.

EATON, William. Taxable in Spesutia Lower Hundred, 1775.

EAVENS, David. Taxable in Bush River Upper Hundred, 1775.

EAVENS, Eaven. Taxable in Bush River Upper Hundred, 1775, with taxable Griffe Eavens listed in his household.

EAVENS, Griffe. Taxable in household of Eaven Eavens, Bush River Upper Hundred, 1775.

EAVINS, William. Taxable in household of Joseph Stiles, Spesutia Upper Hundred, 1775.

EDWARDS, James. Taxable in Susquehanna Hundred, 1776.

EDWARDS, Joseph. Taxable in household of Rachael Gallion, Spesutia Lower Hundred, 1775.

ELDER, Robert. Taxable in Bush River Upper Hundred, 1775.

ELLETT, Thomas. Taxable in Bush River Upper Hundred, 1775, with taxables William Norrid, Marthew Barnes, and William Worrilow listed in his household.

ELLIOTT, Samuel (son of William). Taxable in Deer Creek Upper Hundred, 1775.

ELLIOTT, William. See "Samuel Elliott," q.v.

ELLIS, John. Taxable in Spesutia Upper Hundred, 1775, with taxable negro Polador listed in his household.

ELLIS, John. Taxable in household of Phillip Quinlan, Spesutia Upper Hundred, 1775.

ELLIS, William. Taxable in Deer Creek Lower Hundred, 1775, with John Morgan as his security.

ELY, Hugh. Taxable in Deer Creek Lower Hundred, 1775.

ELY, Mahlon. Taxable in Deer Creek Lower Hundred, 1775.

ELY, Thomas (son of Thomas). Taxable in household of his father Thomas Ely, Deer Creek Lower Hundred, 1775.

ELY, Thomas. Taxable in Deer Creek Lower Hundred, 1775, with taxable Thomas Ely (son) listed in his household.

ENGLAND, George. Taxable in Bush River Upper Hundred, 1775.

ENGLAND, Joseph. Taxable in Bush River Upper Hundred, 1775.

ENGLAND, Robert. Taxable in Bush River Upper Hundred, 1775.

ENLOWES, Henry. Taxable in Bush River Upper Hundred, 1775, with taxable Thomas Nuth listed in his household.

ENSOR, Thomas. Taxable in Bush River Upper Hundred, 1775, with taxable James Hobs listed in his household.

ENSOR, William. Taxable in Gunpowder Lower Hundred, 1775, with taxables James Conner and slave Rosa listed in his household.

EVANS, Edward. Taxable in Spesutia Lower Hundred, 1775.

EVANS, Evan. See "Eaven Eavens," q.v.

EVANS, Evan. Taxable on the plantation of Amos Garrett, Spesutia Lower Hundred, 1775.

EVANS, Evan. Taxable in Spesutia Lower Hundred, 1776.

EVANS, William. Taxable in Spesutia Lower Hundred, 1775.

EVANS, William. Taxable in Spesutia Lower Hundred, 1776.

EVENS, John. Taxable in Susquehanna Hundred, 1776.

EVEREST, Benjamin. Taxable on plantation of George Ford, Spesutia Lower Hundred, 1776.

EVEREST, John. Taxable in household of Thomas Everest, Spesutia Lower Hundred, 1775.

EVEREST, John. Taxable in household of Thomas Everest, Spesutia Lower Hundred, 1776.

EVEREST, Joseph. Taxable in Spesutia Lower Hundred, 1775, with taxable slaves Basiel and Rachael listed in his household.

EVEREST, Joseph. Taxable in Spesutia Lower Hundred, 1776, with taxable negroes Basiel and Rachael listed in his household.

EVEREST, Thomas. Taxable in Spesutia Lower Hundred, 1775, with taxables John Everest, Nathan Tomson, and slave Fann listed in his household.

EVEREST, Thomas. Taxable in Spesutia Lower Hundred, 1776, with taxables John Everest, Nathan Thompson, and negro Fann listed in his household.

EVERETT, James. Taxable in household of Samuel Everett, Bush River Lower Hundred, 1775.

EVERETT, James. Taxable in Bush River Lower Hundred, 1775, with taxable James Hunt listed in his household.

EVERETT, James. Taxable in Bush River Lower Hundred, 1775, with taxable servant John ---- (no last name given), John Wakelin and Adam Bail listed in his household.

EVERETT, Samuel. Taxable in Bush River Lower Hundred, 1775, with taxable James Everett listed in his household.

EVERIST, Benjamin. Taxable in household of Thomas Peregrin Frisby, Spesutia Lower Hundred, 1775.

EVERITT, John. Taxable in Bush River Upper Hundred, 1775.

EVET, William. Taxable in Susquehanna Hundred, 1776.

EVIT, Andrew. Taxable in Spesutia Lower Hundred, 1775, with George Garrettson as his security.

EVIT, William. Taxable in Susquehanna Hundred, 1775.

EVITT, Richard. Taxable in Bush River Upper Hundred, 1775.

EW, William. Taxable in household of Basil Smith, Gunpowder Lower Hundred, 1775.

EWING, Alexander. Taxable in Bush River Lower Hundred, 1775.

EWING, William. Taxable in Bush River Lower Hundred, 1775.

FARISH, Grigs. Taxable in Spesutia Upper Hundred, 1775.

FARMER, John. Taxable in Susquehanna Hundred, 1776.

FAWSETT, Jonathan. Taxable in Spesutia Lower Hundred, 1776.

FEALY, John. Taxable in Bush River Upper Hundred, 1775.

FELL, Stephen. Taxable (servant) in household of John Bond, Jr., Bush River Lower Hundred, 1775.

FERGUSON, Andy. Taxable in Susquehanna Hundred, 1775.

FIE, Baltus. Taxable in Spesutia Lower Hundred, 1775, with taxables Joseph Hewns and John Collins listed in his household.

FIE, Baltus. Taxable in Spesutia Lower Hundred, 1776,

with taxable Joseph Jones and John Collins listed in his household. See "James Fitsgarrell," q.v.

FIELDS, Joseph. Taxable on the plantation of Amos Garrett, Spesutia Lower Hundred, 1775.

FIELDS, Joseph. Taxable on plantation of Amos Garrett, Spesutia Lower Hundred, 1776.

FINLEY, Joseph. Taxable in Gunpowder Lower Hundred, 1775.

FINLY, James. Taxable in Bush River Upper Hundred, 1775, with taxable negro Wench listed in his household.

FINNEY, John. Taxable in Deer Creek Upper Hundred, 1775.

FINNEY, Manessith. Taxable in Deer Creek Upper Hundred, 1775, with taxable ---- Burningham (no first name given) listed in his household. [The actual entry states "Finney, Manessith Burningham ... 2" which indicates two taxables, probably Mr. Finney and an unnamed man servant].

FISHER, James. Taxable in Deer Creek Lower Hundred, 1775, with taxables John Linch and negro Toney listed in his household.

FISHER, Thomas. See "---- Barns," q.v.

FISHER, Thomas. Taxable in Spesutia Lower Hundred, 1775, with taxables Isaac Whitaker and Hezekiah Whitaker listed in his household.

FISHER, William Jr. Taxable in Deer Creek Upper Hundred, 1775, with taxables negroes Pet and Dull listed in his household.

FISHER, William. See "John Johnson (free negro)," q.v.

FISHER, William. Taxable in Deer Creek Lower Hundred, 1775, with taxable negroes Dick, Jack, and Beck listed in his household.

FITsGARRELL, Thomas. Taxable in Spesutia Lower Hundred, 1776.

FITSGARRELL, James. Taxable in Spesutia Lower Hundred, 1776, with Baltus Fie as his security.

FITSGARRELL, Michael. Taxable on plantation of George Ford, Spesutia Lower Hundred, 1776.

FITSIMMONS, Patrick. Taxable at Jacob Forward's Quarters, Spesutia Lower Hundred, 1776.

FITSJARROLD, Garrett. Taxable in the household of James McCrackin, Spesutia Lower Hundred, 1775.

FITSJARROLD, James. Taxable on the plantation of Amos Garrett, Spesutia Lower Hundred, 1775.

FITSJARRORD, Thomas. Taxable in Spesutia Lower Hundred, 1775.

FITZPATRICK, Michael. See "Michal Pichpatrik" and "George Ford" and "Benjamin Ford," q.v.

FLANAGAN, John. Taxable in Bush River Lower Hundred, 1775.

FLATT, John. Taxable in Deer Creek Upper Hundred, 1775.

FLEAHART, Joshua. Taxable in Bush River Upper Hundred, 1775.

FLEETWOOD, Benjamin. Taxable in Susquehanna Hundred, 1776, with taxable Joseph Willmurton listed in his household.

FLYN, John. Taxable in Spesutia Lower Hundred, 1775, with William Eaton as his security.

FONT, Peter. Taxable in the household of William Loney, Spesutia Lower Hundred, 1775.

FONT, Peter. Taxable in household of William Loney, Spesutia Lower Hundred, 1776.

FORD, Alexander. Taxable in household of George Ford, Spesutia Lower Hundred, 1776.

FORD, Benjamin. Taxable in Spesutia Lower Hundred, 1775, with taxable slaves Ned, Harry, Jim, Jupiter, Herculees, Priss, and Hannah, and included at the end of the list is taxable "Michl. Pichpatrik." [Note: This is actually "Michael Fitzpatrick." See comments under "George Ford," q.v.]

FORD, Benjamin. Taxable in household of George Ford, Spesutia Lower Hundred, 1776.

FORD, George. Taxable in household of Thomas Ayres, Spesutia Lower Hundred, 1775.

FORD, George. Taxable in Spesutia Lower Hundred, 1775, with taxables John Crouch, Garratt Curk, and slaves George, Ceaser, Jacob, Nan, Sarah, Peg, and Toney listed in his household. Included at the end of the list is taxable "Michal Pichpatrik Jr." [Note: In spite of what it appears, this is actually "Michael Fitzpatrick" and the "Jr." is barely discernible on the 1775 tax list. However, there was another person by this same name listed in the household of Benjamin Ford and his name does not have a "Jr." behind it].

FORD, George. Taxable in Spesutia Lower Hundred, 1776, with taxables Benjamin Ford, Alexander, Ford, Michael Fitsgarrell, Michael Plunket, Benjamin Everest, and negroes Caeser, George, Jacob, Jupiter, Ned, Herculees, Jim, Jerry, Andrew, Pompy, Isaac, Margaret, Nann, Sall, Jenny, Priss, and Hannah listed on his plantation.

FORD, James (shumaker). Taxable in Susquehanna Hundred, 1776, with taxable James Beal listed in his household.

FORD, James. See "Thomas Bailey," q.v.

FORD, James. Taxable in Spesutia Lower Hundred, 1775.

FORD, James. Taxable in Spesutia Lower Hundred, 1776.

FORD, John. Taxable in Bush River Lower Hundred, 1775.

FORD, John. Taxable in Gunpowder Lower Hundred, 1775.

FORD, Patrick. Taxable (servant) in household of Moses McComas, Bush River Lower Hundred, 1775.

FORD, Thomas. Taxable in Bush River Lower Hundred,

1775.

FORD, Thomas. Taxable in Susquehanna Hundred, 1775.

FORD, Thomas. Taxable in Spesutia Lower Hundred, 1775.

FORD, Thomas. Taxable in Spesutia Lower Hundred, 1776.

FORD, William Sr. Taxable in Bush River Lower Hundred, 1775, with taxable William Ford, Jr. listed in his household.

FORGHTNER, Robert. Taxable in the household of Michael Kennard, Spesutia Lower Hundred, 1775.

FORGONSON, Andraw. Taxable in Susquehanna Hundred, 1776.

FORT, Francis. Taxable in Susquehanna Hundred, 1775.

FORT, Peter. Taxable in Susquehanna Hundred, 1775, with taxable John Dublin listed in his household.

FORT, Peter. Taxable in Susquehanna Hundred, 1776, with taxables John Ore and Walter Taylor listed in his household.

FORWARD, Jacob. Taxable in Spesutia Lower Hundred, 1775, with taxables William Jefferies, Nicholas Brady, Warner Ludwick, and slave Nan listed in his household.

FORWARD, Jacob's Quarters. Spesutia Lower Hundred, 1776, with taxables Osmond Lunan, Patrick Fitsimmons, and negro Nann listed at these quarters.

FORWOOD, John (son of Samuel). Taxable in household of his father Samuel Forwood, Spesutia Upper Hundred, 1775.

FORWOOD, Joseph. Taxable in Spesutia Upper Hundred, 1775.

FORWOOD, Samuel. Taxable in Spesutia Upper Hundred, 1775, with taxables John Forwood (son), William Murphy, and negro Bell listed in his household.

FOSTER, Fedilas. Taxable in Deer Creek Lower Hundred, 1775.

FOSTER, Jese [sic]. Taxable in household of his father Thomas Foster, Deer Creek Upper Hundred, 1775.

FOSTER, Samel [sic] Jr. Taxable in Bush River Upper Hundred, 1775.

FOSTER, Thomas. Taxable in Deer Creek Upper Hundred, 1775, with taxable Jese [sic] Foster (son) and negroes Vilet and John listed in his household.

FOWLER, John. Taxable in Bush River Upper Hundred, 1775. [His name was written in the space between William Amoss (of Joshua) and Aquila Amoss, but he was not counted as a taxable in either household and no indication was given as to why he was placed there out of alphabetical order].

FOWLER, Patrick. Taxable in Susquehanna Hundred, 1775.

FOWLER, Patrick. Taxable in Susquehanna Hundred, 1776.

FOWLER, Samuel. Taxable in Spesutia Lower Hundred, 1775.

FOWLER, Samuel. Taxable in Spesutia Lower Hundred, 1776.

FOWLER, William Peregrine. Taxable in Spesutia Lower Hundred, 1776.

FOWLER, William Perry. Taxable in Spesutia Lower Hundred, 1775.

FOX, Thomas. Taxable in household of Thomas Presbury, Gunpowder Lower Hundred, 1775.

FRACIS, Joshua. Taxable in Bush River Lower Hundred, 1775.

FRALEY, Daniel. Taxable in Bush River Lower Hundred, 1775.

FRAM, John. Taxable in household of Nickles Baker, Susquehanna Hundred, 1776. See "Joseph Barns," q.v.

FRAME, John. Taxable in household of Nicholas Baker, Susquehanna Hundred, 1775.

FRANCIS, Joshua. Taxable in Bush River Lower Hundred, 1775.

FRAZIER, Samuel (ditcher). Taxable in Spesutia Lower Hundred, 1775.

FREEMAN, Edward. Taxable in Bush River Lower Hundred, 1775, with Nathaniel West as his security.

FREEN, Richard. Taxable in Bush River Upper Hundred, 1775.

FREW, Allexander. Taxable in Deer Creek Upper Hundred, 1775.

FREW, James. Taxable in Bush River Upper Hundred, 1775.

FRIER, Isaac. Taxable in Spesutia Upper Hundred, 1775.

FRISBY, Thomas Peregrin. Taxable in Spesutia Lower Hundred, 1775, with taxables Benjamin Everist and slaves Andrew, Jim, and Nan listed in his household.

FRISBY, Thomas Peregrine. Taxable in Spesutia Lower Hundred, 1776, with taxable negroes Jam, Andrew, and Ann listed in his household.

FULTON, John. Taxable in Bush River Lower Hundred, 1775, with taxable "son Wm." listed in his household.

FULTON, William. Taxable in household of his father John Fulton, Bush River Lower Hundred, 1775.

FYE, Godferry. Taxable in Deer Creek Upper Hundred, 1775.

G---- [blank], William. Taxable in Bush River Lower Hundred, 1775.

GADDESS, William. Taxable in Bush River Upper Hundred, 1775.

GALE, William. Taxable in Gunpowder Lower Hundred, 1775, with taxables John Kern and negro Jenny listed in his household.

GALLION, Elizabeth. Head of household in Spesutie Lower Hundred, 1775, with taxables Michael Truelove, slave Bet, and an unnamed apprentice listed on her plantation.

GALLION, Elizabeth. Head of household in Spesutia Lower Hundred, 1776, with taxables Mr. ---- Truebouer (first name blank), James Crommell, and negro Bett listed in her household.

GALLION, Gregory (son of Joseph). Taxable in household of his father Joseph Gallion, Deer Creek Lower Hundred, 1775.

GALLION, James. Taxable in Susquehanna Hundred, 1775, with taxable Thomas Gallion listed in his household.

GALLION, John (son of Joseph). Taxable in household of his father Joseph Gallion, Deer Creek Lower Hundred, 1775.

GALLION, Joseph. Taxable in Deer Creek Lower Hundred, 1775, with taxables Grrgeory Gallion (son) and John Gallion (son) listed in his household.

GALLION, Nathan. Taxable in household of Phebe Gallion, Spesutia Lower Hundred, 1775.

GALLION, Phebe. Head of household in Spesutie Lower Hundred, 1775, with taxables Nathan Gallion and slaves Jupiter, Bob, and Dinah listed on her plantation.

GALLION, Rachael. Head of household in Spesutie Lower Hundred, 1775, with taxable Joseph Edwards listed in her household. [The constable had originally written her last name as "Garretson," crossed it out, and then wrote in "Gallion"]. See "Francis Pitt," q.v.

GALLION, Samuel. Taxable in Spesutia Lower Hundred, 1775.

GALLION, Thomas. Taxable in household of James Gallion, Susquehanna Hundred, 1775.

GALLON, James. Taxable in Susquehanna Hundred, 1776, with taxable Thomas Gallon listed in his household.

GALLON, John. Taxable in Susquehanna Hundred, 1776.

GALLON, Samuel. Taxable in Susquehanna Hundred, 1776.

GALLON, Thomas. Taxable in household of James Gallon, Susquehanna Hundred, 1776.

GARDNER, John. Taxable in Gunpowder Lower Hundred, 1775. His name (among others) was listed on the back of the tax list.

GARLAND, Francis. Taxable in Spesutia Lower Hundred, 1775, with taxable slave Ruth (and James Brown as his security).

GARLAND, Francis. Taxable in Spesutia Lower Hundred, 1776.

GARRETSON, Freeborn. Taxable in household of Richard Garretson, Spesutia Lower Hundred, 1775.

GARRETSON, Freeborn. Taxable in Spesutia Lower Hundred, 1775, with taxable slave Ann listed in his housheold).

GARRETSON, Garret (New Park). Taxable in Spesutia Lower Hundred, 1775, with taxables William Green, Peter Murphy, and slaves Cuff and Silvia listed in his household.

GARRETSON, Garrett (son of Edward). Taxable in Spesutia Lower Hundred, 1775.

GARRETSON, George. Taxable in Bush River Lower Hundred, 1775, with taxables James Walker and negro Kate listed in his household.

GARRETSON, George. Taxable in Spesutia Lower Hundred, 1775, with taxable slaves Duke, Maria, Sedippo, Jeremiah, and Dinah listed in his household.

GARRETSON, Goldsmith. Taxable in Spesutia Lower Hundred, 1775, with taxable slave Davy listed in his household.

GARRETSON, John. Taxable in Spesutia Lower Hundred, 1775, with taxable slave Dido listed in his household.

GARRETSON, Rachel. See "Rachael Gallion," q.v.

GARRETSON, Richard. Taxable in Spesutia Lower Hundred, 1775, with taxables Freeborn Garretson and slaves Combow and Moll listed in his household.

GARRETT, Amos. Taxable in Spesutia Lower Hundred, 1775, with taxables John Hanson, John Walker, William Barns, John Connally, John Howell, Thomas Simpers, Nathan Swain, Gabriel Swain, Joseph Fields, Richard Berry, James Deaver, Richard Harrison, Horatio Harrison, Jacob Wooley, John McDowell, Thomas Young, James Fitsjarrold, James Dennison, Evan Evans, Samuel Tush, George Childs, William Westfield, John Marnham, Launcelot Taylor, Charles White, Richard Donavon, Thomas Huggins, George Nipper, William Boulster, and slaves Limbrick, Tom, Saunty, Jerry, Oval, Will, George, Pompy, Cuff, Dutchess, Perina, Esther, Dinah, Jack, Jacob, and Patience, all listed under Amos Garrett's name in the tax list. In addition, taxables Richard Peirce and slaves Duke, Sam, Tiney, and Eve were listed at Amos Garrett's Quarters.

GARRETT, Amos. Taxable in Spesutia Lower Hundred, 1776, with taxables Isaac Penrose, John Hanson, Alexander Duzan, John Walker, Joseph Fields, Gabriel Swain, Richard Pierce, James Dennison, Usher Tracey, and negroes Saunty, Oval, Pompy, George, Tom, Jerry, Dick, Jack, Jacob, Will, Limbrick, Dutchess, Esther, Perina, Patience, Duke, Sam, Femy, and Jemey listed on his plantation.

GARRETT, John. Taxable in Bush River Lower Hundred, 1775.

GARRETT, Mrs. See "Walter Tolley," q.v.

GARRETTSON, Freeborn. Taxable in household of Richard Garrettson, Spesutia Lower Hundred, 1776.

GARRETTSON, Garrett (son of James). Taxable in Spesutia Lower Hundred, 1776, with taxables William

Green and negroes Cuff and Silvia listed in his household.

GARRETTSON, George. See "Andrew Evit," q.v.

GARRETTSON, James. See "Garrett Garrettson," q.v.

GARRETTSON, John. Taxable in Spesutia Lower Hundred, 1776, with taxable negro Dinah listed in his household.

GARRETTSON, Martha. Head of household in Spesutia Lower Hundred, 1776, with taxable negroes Duke, Dupea, Jemina and Dinah listed in her household.

GARRETTSON, Richard. Taxable in Spesutia Lower Hundred, 1776, with taxables Freeborn Garrettson and negroes Moll and Combo listed in his household.

GARRISON, Cornelius. Taxable in household of John Garrison, Bush River Lower Hundred, 1775.

GARRISON, James. Taxable in household of John Garrison, Bush River Lower Hundred, 1775.

GARRISON, John. Taxable in Bush River Lower Hundred, 1775, with taxables Cornelius Garrison, James Garrison, and Philip Garrison).

GARRISON, Philip. Taxable in household of John Garrison, Bush River Lower Hundred, 1775.

GASH, Thomas. Taxable at William Paca's Quarters, Spesutia Lower Hundred, 1775.

GASH, Thomas. Taxable in Spesutia Lower Hundred, 1776, with taxable negroes Dick, David, Ben, Saul, Priss, Dinah, Jemima, Cate, Murrier, Agnus, Mary, Moll, Sall, and Poll listed on his plantation.

GASH, Thomas's Quarters. Spesutia Upper Hundred, 1775, with taxable negroes Cato and Norsay listed at these quarters.

GATTISON, John. Taxable in Susquehanna Hundred, 1775.

GELONS, Jeremiah. Taxable in household of Daniel Campbell, Spesutia Lower Hundred, 1775.

GIANT, Isaac. Taxable in Spesutia Lower Hundred, 1775, with Benedict Hall and Carvel Hall as his securities.

GIBB, John. Taxable in Spesutia Upper Hundred, 1775.

GIBBONS, Joseph. See "Joseph Gibons," q.v.

GIBONS, Joseph. Taxable in Deer Creek Upper Hundred, 1775.

GIBSON, Frank. Taxable in Bush River Upper Hundred, 1775.

GIBSON, John. Taxable in Bush River Upper Hundred, 1775.

GILBERT, Aquilla. Taxable in household of Micah Gilbert, Susquehanna Hundred, 1776.

GILBERT, Charles Jr. Taxable in Susquehanna Hundred, 1775.

GILBERT, Charles Jr. Taxable in Susquehanna Hundred, 1776, with taxable John Batton listed in his household.

GILBERT, Charles. Taxable in Susquehanna Hundred, 1775, with taxables Michael Gilbert, Robert Haire, and negroes Bimah, Judie, Rachael, and Joe listed in his household.

GILBERT, Charles. Taxable in Susquehanna Hundred, 1776, with taxables Robert Kerr and negro Binar listed in his household. See "Michel Gilbert," q.v.

GILBERT, James. Taxable in Susquehanna Hundred, 1775, with Thomas Gilbert as his security.

GILBERT, James. Taxable in Susquehanna Hundred, 1776, with Thomas Gilbert as his security.

GILBERT, Martin Taylor. Taxable in Susquehanna Hundred, 1775.

GILBERT, Micah. Taxable in Susquehanna Hundred, 1775, with taxable negro Peg listed in his household.

GILBERT, Micah. Taxable in Susquehanna Hundred, 1776, with taxables Aquilla Gilbert and negro Peg listed in his household.

GILBERT, Mical (son of Thomas). Taxable in Susquehanna Hundred, 1776.

GILBERT, Michael (son of Thomas). Taxable in Susquehanna Hundred, 1775.

GILBERT, Michael. Taxable in Susquehanna Hundred, 1775, with taxable negro Grace listed in his household. See "Charles Gilbert," q.v.

GILBERT, Michal. Taxable in Susquehanna Hundred, 1776, with taxable negroes Grace and Melkey listed in his household.

GILBERT, Michel (son of Charles). Taxable in Susquehanna Hundred, 1776, with taxable negroes Joe and Rachel listed in his household.

GILBERT, Michel Jr. Taxable in Spesutia Upper Hundred, 1775.

GILBERT, Parker. Taxable in Susquehanna Hundred, 1775.

GILBERT, Parker. Taxable in Susquehanna Hundred, 1776, with taxable Taylor Gilbert listed in his household.

GILBERT, Samuel. Taxable in Susquehanna Hundred, 1775.

GILBERT, Samuel. Taxable in Susquehanna Hundred, 1776.

GILBERT, Taylor. See "Martin Taylor Gilbert," q.v.

GILBERT, Taylor. Taxable in household of Parker Gilbert, Susquehanna Hundred, 1776.

GILBERT, Thomas. See "Michael Gilbert" and "James Gilbert," q.v.

GILBERT, Thomas. See "James Gilbert," q.v.

GILE, James. Taxable in Spesutia Lower Hundred, 1775, with taxables Thomas Harrington, Edward Kaine, William Cooper, James Hurley, and slaves Jerry, London, Mingo, Manner, and Jemmy listed in his household.

GILES & SMITH's Rock Run Plantation. Susquehanna Hundred, 1776, with taxables David Hampton and negroes Catto, Nero, Poladore, Cesaro, Tom, Pompey, Ceser, Young Tom, and Sepeo listed "at Rock Run Plantashon."

GILES, Jacob Jr. Taxable in Susquehanna Hundred, 1775, with taxables Samuel Durbin, John Lovel, Robert Williams, and negroes Daniel, Jane, Cato, and Chloe listed in his household.

GILES, Jacob Jr. Taxable in Susquehanna Hundred, 1776, with taxables William Deakon, John Lovel, Robert Rees, and negroes Daniel, Joe, Cato, Will, Rachel, and Lue listed on his plantation.

GILES, Jacob Jr.'s Quarters. Spesutia Lower Hundred, 1776, with taxables William Deaton and negroes Daniel, Cato, and Joe listed at these quarters.

GILES, Jacob. See "William Boyer," q.v.

GILES, Jacob. Taxable in Susquehanna Hundred, 1775, with taxables Charles Plaster, Daniel Williams, Tompain Lithhill, James Janaer, William Bush, and negroes Valentine, Ben, Herculees, Davy, Duke, Pompey, Cato, Bess, Anna, Filulbes, and Hagar listed in his household.

GILES, Jacob. Taxable in Susquehanna Hundred, 1776, with taxables Mical Cannabel and Charles Lutterfeild and negroes Vollentine, Tom, Pain, Ben, Duke, Pompey, Bes, Fillis, Grace, Will, and Harkellees listed on his plantation.

GILES, Jacob's Mill (Bush). Spesutie Lower Hundred, 1775, with taxables John Wilkinson, Thomas Williams, Charles Huffield, and John Robinson listed at his mill in Bush (aka Harford Town).

GILES, Jacob's Quarters (Romney). Spesutie Lower Hundred, 1775, with taxables Thomas Brown, Jonas Stevenson, Isaac Jennings, and slaves James, Peter, and Lot listed at his quarters at Romney.

GILES, Thomas. Taxable in Spesutia Lower Hundred, 1776, with taxables Daniel Williams and negroes James, Cato, David, and Sam listed in his household.

GILL, Richard. Taxable in household of James Clendenon, Spesutia Upper Hundred, 1775.

GILLASPEY, Charles. Taxable in Bush River Lower Hundred, 1775, with taxable John Gillaspey listed in his household.

GILLASPEY, John. Taxable in household of Charles Gillaspey, Bush River Lower Hundred, 1775.

GILTON, Andrew. Taxable in household of Robert Hawkins, Jr., Deer Creek Upper Hundred, 1775.

GINNIS, William. See "Robert Glenn," q.v.

GISAM, John. Taxable in Bush River Lower Hundred, 1775.

GITON, John Jr. Taxable in Bush River Upper Hundred, 1775.

GITTINGS, Asel's Quarters. Gunpowder Lower Hundred, 1775, with taxables William Saunders and slaves Cesar, Jack, and Dinah listed at these quarters.

GLADDEN, John. Taxable (servant) in household of Robert McNair, Deer Creek Upper Hundred, 1775.

GLADING, Jacob. Taxable in Bush River Upper Hundred, 1775.

GLASS (GLASCO?), Charles. Taxable in Spesutia Lower Hundred, 1775. [His last name on the tax list is dark and very smudged].

GLENN, Robert. Taxable in Bush River Upper Hundred, 1775, with taxable William Jinnis (Ginnis?) listed in his household.

GODSGRACE, William. Taxable at Clark Young's Quarters, Spesutia Lower Hundred, 1775.

GOLDSMITH, Winston. Taxable in Bush River Lower Hundred, 1775, with James Scott as his security.

GORDEN, James. Taxable in Deer Creek Lower Hundred, 1775.

GORDEN, William. Taxable in Bush River Lower Hundred, 1775.

GORDON, Alexander. Taxable in household of James Gordon, Spesutia Lower Hundred, 1775.

GORDON, Alexander. Taxable in Spesutia Lower Hundred, 1776.

GORDON, James. Taxable in Spesutia Lower Hundred, 1775, with taxable Alexander Gordon listed in his household.

GORDON, James. Taxable in household of Joseph Gordon, Spesutia Lower Hundred, 1776.

GORDON, John. Taxable in Spesutia Lower Hundred, 1775.

GORDON, Joseph. Taxable in Spesutia Lower Hundred, 1776, with taxable James Gordon listed in his household.

GORDON, Robert. Taxable in Deer Creek Upper Hundred, 1775, with taxable Samuel Poake listed in his household.

GORE, Micheal. Taxable in household of James Kanaday, Spesutia Upper Hundred, 1775.

GORMEN, John. Taxable in household of William Ashmore, Deer Creek Upper Hundred, 1775.

GORRAL, Issabelle. Head of household in Susquehanna Hundred, 1776, with taxables John Gorral, William Gorral, Joseph Gorral, and Thomas Gorral listed in her household.

GORRAL, John. Taxable in household of Issabelle Gorral, Susquehanna Hundred, 1776.

GORRAL, Joseph. Taxable in household of Issabelle Gorral, Susquehanna Hundred, 1776.

GORRAL, Thomas. Taxable in household of Issabelle Gorral, Susquehanna Hundred, 1776.

GORRAL, William. Taxable in household of Issabelle Gorral, Susquehanna Hundred, 1776.

GORREL, Isabella (widow). Head of household in Susquehanna Hundred, 1775, with taxables Thomas Gorrel and John Gorrel listed in her household.

GORREL, John. Taxable in household of Isabella Gorrel, Susquehanna Hundred, 1775.

GORREL, Joseph. Taxable in Susquehanna Hundred, 1775, with Robert Gorrel as his security.

GORREL, Robert. Taxable in Susquehanna Hundred, 1775. See "Joseph Gorrel," q.v.

GORREL, Thomas. Taxable in household of Isabella Gorrel, Susquehanna Hundred, 1775.

GORREL, William. Taxable in Susquehanna Hundred, 1775.

GOTT, Samuel. Taxable in Gunpowder Lower Hundred, 1775, with taxable slave Boner listed in his household.

GOUGH, John. Taxable at William Buchanan's Quarters, Gunpowder Lower Hundred, 1775.

GOVER, Elizabeth (widow). Head of household in Deer Creek Lower Hundred, 1775, with taxables Gidions Gover and negroes Lingas, James, Tower, Will, Dinah, and Nan listed in her household.

GOVER, Gidions. Taxable in household of his mother Elizabeth Gover, Deer Creek Lower Hundred, 1775.

GOVER, Philip. Taxable in Susquehanna Hundred, 1775, with taxable negroes Darbe, Mounan, Daniel, Jeffry, Sabra, Sarah, Judie, and Dinah listed in his household.

GOVER, Philip. Taxable in Susquehanna Hundred, 1776, with taxable negroes Darbey, Montsleer, Daniel, Jeffery, Sary, Judy, Dinar, Sabra, Sal, and Lundon listed on his plantation.

GOVER, Samuel. Taxable in Deer Creek Lower Hundred, 1775, with taxable negro Toney listed in his household.

GRACE, Aaron. Taxable in Spesutia Lower Hundred, 1775.

GRACE, Aaron. Taxable in Spesutia Lower Hundred, 1776.

GRAFTON, Danniel. Taxable in household of Alexander Thompson, Spesutia Upper Hundred, 1775.

GRAFTON, Samuel. Taxable in Spesutia Upper Hundred, 1775.

GRAFTON, Sarah. Head of household in Spesutia Upper Hundred, 1775, with taxable negroes Tom and Cate listed in her household.

GRAFTON, William. See "Robert Jewl," q.v.

GRAFTON, William. Taxable in Spesutia Upper Hundred, 1775.

GRANT, Jame. Taxable in Susquehanna Hundred, 1775.

GRANT, James. Taxable in household of Robert Mils [sic], Susquehanna Hundred, 1776.

GRAY, John. Taxable in Spesutia Lower Hundred, 1775.

GRAY, John. Taxable in Bush River Upper Hundred, 1775, with two taxable servant men (no names given) listed in his household.

GREEN, Benjamin. Taxable in Spesutia Upper Hundred, 1775, with taxable negroes Rachel and Luce listed in his household.

GREEN, Bennit. Taxable in Bush River Upper Hundred, 1775.

GREEN, Henry. Taxable in household of John Green, Bush River Lower Hundred, 1775.

GREEN, Henry. Taxable in Spesutia Upper Hundred, 1775, with taxable negroes Addam, Well, Luce, Jone, and Lotto listed in his household.

GREEN, John. Taxable in Bush River Lower Hundred, 1775, with taxables Henry Green and negroes James and Sarah listed in his household.

GREEN, Lenard. Taxable in Spesutia Upper Hundred, 1775, with taxable negro Will listed in his household.

GREEN, Richard. Taxable in Bush River Upper Hundred, 1775.

GREEN, William. Taxable in household of Garret Garretson, Spesutia Lower Hundred, 1775.

GREEN, William. Taxable in household of Garrett Garrettson (son of James), Spesutia Lower Hundred, 1776.

GREENLAND, Richard. Taxable in Susquehanna Hundred, 1775.

GREENLAND, Richard. Taxable in Susquehanna Hundred, 1776.

GREY, John. Included in Gunpowder Lower Hundred tax list in 1775, but his name was scratched off the list [no reason given].

GRIFFETH, John. Taxable in Susquehanna Hundred, 1776, weth taxables James West (Jr.?), Joshuha Andres, and negro Fellis listed in his household.

GRIFFEY, Evan. Taxable in Deer Creek Lower Hundred, 1775.

GRIFFIN, Luke's Quarters. Spesutie Lower Hundred, 1775, with taxables John Castledrine and slaves Will and Margaret listed at these quarters.

GRIFFITH, Luke's Quarters. Spesutia Lower Hundred, 1776, with taxables John Castledine and negroes Will and Margaret listed at these quarters.

GRIFFITH, Mary. Head of household in Spesutia Lower Hundred, 1775, with taxables Sauce or Samie(?) ---- (no last name given, possibly a slave named Sauce or a son named Samie?) and slaves Sall and Nell. [Note: The actual entry is written with Mary Griffith on the first line, the name Sauce or Samie (?) ... 1 (on the next line), followed by Slave Sall ... 1 (on the next line), and Slave Nell ... 1 (on the last line); thus, a total of 3 taxables].

GRIFFITH, Samie(?). See "Mary Griffith," q.v.

GRIFFITH, Samuel. Taxable in Spesutia Lower Hundred, 1775, with taxables John Major, Thomas Bigs, and slaves Phillis, Jack, Will, Hannah, Abigail, and Esther listed in his household.

GRIFFITH, Samuel. Taxable in Spesutia Lower Hundred, 1776, with taxables John Major and negroes Nell,

Jane, Phillis, Hannah, Esther, David, Jack or Jacob [sic], Caeser, Abigail, Damphies, and Bill listed on his plantation.

GUITON, Isaac. Taxable in Spesutia Upper Hundred, 1775.

GUITON, Underwood. Taxable in Bush River Lower Hundred, 1775, with taxables Samuel Clemons and John Jackson listed in his household.

GUNREY, Godfrey. Taxable in household of Lambert Wilmer, Gunpowder Lower Hundred, 1775.

GUSPEY, Henry. Taxable in Deer Creek Lower Hundred, 1775, with taxables Thomas Welch and negro Hannah listed in his household.

GUYTON, John Jr. See "John Giton, Jr.," q.v.

GWINN, Will (negro). Taxable on plantation of William Hall, Spesutia Lower Hundred, 1776.

HACKET, Richard. Taxable in Gunpowder Lower Hundred, 1775.

HADABUCK, John. Taxable in Spesutia Lower Hundred, 1775.

HADDEYWAY, Richard. Taxable in Susquehanna Hundred, 1776.

HAILEY, William. Taxable in Spesutia Lower Hundred, 1775, with William Murphy as his security.

HAILEY, William. Taxable in household of William Murphey, Spesutia Lower Hundred, 1776.

HAIRE, Robert. Taxable in household of Charles Gilbert, Susquehanna Hundred, 1775.

HAIRHURST, James Jr. Taxable in household of James Hairhurst, Sr., Bush River Lower Hundred, 1775.

HAIRHURST, James Sr. Taxable in Bush River Lower Hundred, 1775, with taxable James Hairhurst, Jr. listed in his household.

HALEY, Daniel (son of John). Taxable in household of his father John Haley, Deer Creek Upper Hundred, 1775.

HALEY, John. Taxable in Deer Creek Upper Hundred, 1775, with taxable Daniel Haley (son) listed in his household.

HALL, Aquila Jr. Taxable in Spesutia Upper Hundred, 1775, with taxable negroes Hannah and London listed in his household.

HALL, Aquila. Taxable in Spesutia Lower Hundred, 1775, with taxable Thomas Cowley and slaves Phill, Pegg, Oringe, Leah, Ned, Michael, George, Jacob, Peter, Leander, Hercules, Cudgo, Toney, Saunty, Ned, Old Dinah, Hannah, Fann, Hagar, LIttle Dinah, Rachel, Sarah's Rachael, Manuel, and Dic listed on his plantation.

HALL, Aquila's Quarters. Spesutia Lower Hundred, 1776. Quarters listed twice in a row on this tax list: first with taxable negroes Phill and Peg, and second with taxable negroes Orange, Ned, Mike, George, Jacob, and Lear.

HALL, Benedict Edward. Taxable in Spesutia Lower Hundred, 1775, with taxable slaves Morey, Maria, Pollipus, Lucy, Hester, Peg, and Maud listed in his household.

HALL, Benedict Edward. Taxable in Spesutia Lower Hundred, 1776, with taxable negroes Polipus, Mana, Lucey, Mora, Esther, Pegg, and Maud listed in his household.

HALL, Benedict. See "Isaac Giant," q.v.

HALL, Carvel. See "Isaac Giant," q.v.

HALL, Christopher. Taxable in Deer Creek Lower Hundred, 1775, with Jobe Barnes as his security.

HALL, E. See "Francis Standley," q.v.

HALL, Edward. Taxable in Spesutia Lower Hundred, 1775, with taxables David Nicolet and slaves Sampson, Moll, and Kate listed in his household.

HALL, Hannah. Head of household in Spesutia Lower Hundred, 1775, with taxable slaves Sam, James, George, Augustus, Stepney, Hector, Leander, Cloe, Luraner, Dorinder, Hannah, Silence, Jane, Patience, Dinah, Darcus, Judy, Sarah, Phillis, and Emmy listed on her plantation. Hannah Hall was also security for taxable Stephen Taylor (who was listed separate from the above).

HALL, Hannah. Head of household in Spesutia Lower Hundred, 1776, with taxable negroes Rachael, Montross, Leander, Sam, George, Sarah, Chloe, Hannah, Jane, Judiah, Dinah, Lynita, Silence, Amey, Phillis, Lew, Darcus, Patience, Cynthia, Augustus, and Hector listed on her plantation.

HALL, Isaac. Taxable in Gunpowder Lower Hundred, 1775. His name (among others) was listed on the back of the tax list.

HALL, John (captain). Taxable in Spesutia Lower Hundred, 1775, with taxables Francis Scroge and slaves Primus, Jacob, Stepney, Sharper, Fill, Judith, Beck, Milcah, Abigail, Perry, Bacchus, Cuff, and Sukey listed on his plantation.

HALL, John Beadle. Taxable in Spesutia Lower Hundred, 1775.

HALL, John Bedle. Taxable in Susquehanna Hundred, 1776, with taxable negroes Bes, Cuff, and Jack listed in his household.

HALL, Josias Carvel. Taxable in Spesutia Lower Hundred, 1775, with taxables Thomas Chisholme, Thomas Ashley, Caleb Brenhein, and slaves Jacob, Montros, Juba, Prye, Jeany, and Charity listed in his household.

HALL, Josias Carvell (doctor). Taxable in Spesutia Lower Hundred, 1776, with taxables Caleb Brannan, Thomas Ashley, and negroes Jacob, Stephney, Juley, Priss, Teeney, and Charity listed on his plantation.

HALL, Josias. Taxable in Susquehanna Hundred, 1775 [The tax list indicated 2 taxables in this household, but only named one. The actual entry stated "Hall, Josias & 1 Tax ... 2"].

HALL, Josias. Taxable in Susquehanna Hundred, 1776, with taxables Owen McCarty and negroes Dimcort, Crafet, and Hannah listed in his household.

HALL, Mordicai. Taxable in Bush River Lower Hundred, 1775.

HALL, Mrs. See "John Draper," q.v.

HALL, Thomas. Taxable in Spesutia Upper Hundred, 1775. See "Negro Emanuel," q.v.

HALL, William. See "John Davidge," q.v.

HALL, William. See "Samuel Jenkins," q.v.

HALL, William. Taxable in Spesutia Lower Hundred, 1775, with taxable slaves Aby, Zeb, Jimguin, Abraham, Will, Bill, Dick, Mick, Peg, Dinah, Sarah, Maria, and Fanny listed on his plantation.

HALL, William. Taxable in Spesutia Lower Hundred, 1776, with taxable negroes Jimmey, Abey, Abraham, Will Gwinn, Will, Bill, Dick, and Mike listed on his plantation.

HALLOW, Timothy. Taxable in household of Jacob Lemmon, Susquehanna Hundred, 1775.

HAMBEL, Archabel. Taxable in Bush River Upper Hundred, 1775.

HAMBLETON, Edward. Taxable in Bush River Lower Hundred, 1775.

HAMBLETON, Jonathan. Taxable in Deer Creek Lower Hundred, 1775.

HAMBY, William. Taxable in household of Amos Cord, Spesutia Lower Hundred, 1776.

HAMPTON, David. Taxable at Giles & Smith's Rock Run Plantation, Susquehanna Hundred, 1776.

HANEY, Patrick. Taxable in Susquehanna Hundred, 1775.

HANNAH, Alexander Taxable in Susquehanna Hundred, 1775.

HANNAH, Alexander. Taxable in Susquehanna Hundred, 1775 [The name was entered on the tax list and then was lined out; no reason was given].

HANNAH, John. Taxable in Spesutia Upper Hundred, 1775, with taxable James Cosebury listed in his household.

HANNAH, John. Taxable in Bush River Upper Hundred, 1775.

HANNAH, Patrick. Taxable in Susquehanna Hundred, 1775.

HANNEN (HANNER?), Robert. Taxable in household of Joseph Thomas, Bush River Upper Hundred, 1775.

HANNOR, Micheal. Taxable in Spesutia Upper Hundred, 1775, with taxable negroes Rich, James, Ceaser, Bett, Cloe, Gin, and Fan listed in his household.

HANSON, Benjamin. Taxable in Spesutia Lower Hundred, 1775, with taxables Samuel Hanson and slaves Jack, Nell, Hagur, Dinah, and Pug listed in his household.

HANSON, Edward. Taxable in Spesutia Upper Hundred, 1775, with taxable negro Dinnah listed in his household.

HANSON, Hollis. Taxable at Thomas Harrison's Quarters, Susquehanna Hundred, 1775.

HANSON, Hollis. Taxable in the household of John Hanson, Jr., Spesutia Lower Hundred, 1775.

HANSON, Jacob. Taxable in household of James Worker, Susquehanna Hundred, 1776.

HANSON, John Jr. Taxable in Spesutia Lower Hundred, 1775, with taxable Hollis Hanson listed in his household, with John Hanson, Sr. as security.

HANSON, John Sr. Taxable in Spesutia Lower Hundred, 1775, with taxable slaves Hannah and Ceaser listed in his household. See "John Hanson, Jr.," q.v.

HANSON, John. Taxable on the plantation of Amos Garrett, Spesutia Lower Hundred, 1775.

HANSON, John. Taxable on plantation of Amos Garrett, Spesutia Lower Hundred, 1776.

HANSON, Samuel. Taxable in the household of Benjamin Hanson, Spesutia Lower Hundred, 1775.

HANSON, Samuel. Taxable at Rev. William West's Quarters, Spesutia Lower Hundred, 1776.

HARBET, Benjamin. Taxable in Susquehanna Hundred, 1775, with taxables Benjamin Harbet and George Savage listed in his household.

HARBET, Benjamin. Taxable in household of Benjamin Harbet, Susquehanna Hundred, 1776.

HARBET, Benjamin. Taxable in Susquehanna Hundred, 1776, with taxables Benjamin Harbet and George Sevege listed in his household.

HARDIN, John. Taxable in household of Balcher Michael, Susquehanna Hundred, 1775.

HARE, Joseph. Taxable in Deer Creek Upper Hundred, 1775.

HARGASS, Stephen. Taxable in Susquehanna Hundred, 1775.

HARGROVE, Richard. Taxable in Spesutia Upper Hundred, 1775, with taxables William Hargrove and negro Aleck listed in his household.

HARGROVE, Richard. Taxable in Susquehanna Hundred, 1776.

HARGROVE, William. Taxable in household of Richard Hargrove, Spesutia Upper Hundred, 1775.

HARPER, Francis (son of Francis). Taxable in household of his father Francis Harper, Deer Creek Upper Hundred, 1775.

HARPER, Francis. Taxable in Deer Creek Upper Hundred, 1775, with taxable Francis Harper (son) listed in his household.

HARPER, George. Taxable in Bush River Upper Hundred, 1775.

HARPER, Samuel. Taxable in Bush River Upper

EARLY HARFORD COUNTIANS: Supplement

Hundred, 1775.

HARRINGTON, Thomas. Taxable in household of James Giles, Spesutia Lower Hundred, 1775.

HARRIS, Daniel. Taxable in Deer Creek Lower Hundred, 1775, with Martha Smith as his security.

HARRIS, James (blacksmith). Taxable in Spesutia Upper Hundred, 1775.

HARRIS, James (storekeeper). Taxable in Spesutia Upper Hundred, 1775.

HARRIS, Joseph. Taxable at Thomas Harrison's Quarters, Susquehanna Hundred, 1775.

HARRIS, Joseph. Taxable at Thomas Harrison's Quarters, Susquehanna Hundred, 1776.

HARRIS, Robert. Taxable in Bush River Upper Hundred, 1775.

HARRIS, Samuel. Deer Creek Lower Hundred, 1775, with taxable negroes Tower and Faney listed on his plantation. [The actual entry stated "Hopkins, Saml. Taxes Negroes Tower, Faney," and indicated 2 taxables, not 3, so Samuel was not counted; no reason given].

HARRIS, Samuel. Taxable in household of Geddean Pervale, Susquehanna Hundred, 1776.

HARRIS, William. Taxable in Spesutia Upper Hundred, 1775.

HARRIS(?), Nathan. Taxable in the household of John Wood, Spesutia Lower Hundred, 1775.

HARRISON, Horatio. Taxable on the plantation of Amos Garrett, Spesutia Lower Hundred, 1775.

HARRISON, Richard. Taxable on the plantation of Amos Garrett, Spesutia Lower Hundred, 1775.

HARRISON, Thomas' Quarters. Susquehanna Hundred, 1775, with taxables Joseph Harris, Hollis Hanson, and negroes Peter, Ragoo, Jack, Sawney, Wapping, Perry, George, Jacob, Ambo, Dydo, and Ned listed at these quarters.

HARRISON, Thomas' Quarters. Susquehanna Hundred, 1776, with taxables Joseph Harris and negroes Raggue, Orras, Ned, George, Jacob, Annaboe, Rachel, Peter, Jack, Soney, Jere, Whopen, and Dido listed at these quarters. [The constable indicated these taxables were "Lat Harrason Thomos Quarter"].

HARROD, Henry. Taxable in household of Nathaniel Rigbie, Deer Creek Lower Hundred, 1775.

HARRY, David. Taxable in Bush River Lower Hundred, 1775.

HART, John (schoolmaster). Taxable in Susquehanna Hundred, 1775.

HART, Ouy (Aug?). Taxable man in the household of Joseph Stokes, Deer Creek Upper Hundred, 1775.

HART, Robert. Taxable in Spesutia Upper Hundred, 1775, with James Mores as his security.

HART, William. Taxable in Deer Creek Upper Hundred, 1775.

HARTLEY, Joseph. Taxable in Bush River Lower Hundred, 1775, with taxable Giles Hodges listed in his household.

HARTON, John. Taxable in household of James Mitchel (weaver), Susquehanna Hundred, 1776.

HASLET, Moses (doctor). Taxable in Gunpowder Lower Hundred, 1775, with taxable slave Hanibol listed in his household.

HATHHORN, John. Taxable in Susquehanna Hundred, 1776.

HATHHORNE, John. See "John Clark (schoolmaster)," q.v.

HAVELL, Joseph. Taxable in Gunpowder Lower Hundred, 1775. His name (among others) was listed on the back of the tax list.

HAWKINS, Geregory. Taxable in Deer Creek Upper Hundred, 1775.

HAWKINS, Jeremiah. Taxable in Deer Creek Upper Hundred, 1775.

HAWKINS, John. Taxable in Deer Creek Lower Hundred, 1775, with taxable negroes James, Cuff, and Moll listed in his household.

HAWKINS, Richard. Taxable in Susquehanna Hundred, 1775.

HAWKINS, Richard. Taxable in Deer Creek Lower Hundred, 1775.

HAWKINS, Richard. Taxable in Susquehanna Hundred, 1776.

HAWKINS, Robert Jr. Taxable in Deer Creek Upper Hundred, 1775, with taxable Andrew Gilton listed in his household. [His name was listed among the "R's" instead of the "H's" on the tax list].

HAWKINS, Robert. Taxable in Susquehanna Hundred, 1775, with taxable negro Chloe listed in his household.

HAWKINS, Robert. Taxable in Deer Creek Upper Hundred, 1775, with taxable man ---- McGilton (servant, no first name given) listed in his household.

HAWKINS, Robert. Taxable in Susquehanna Hundred, 1776, with taxable negro Clem listed in his household.

HAWKINS, Samuel. Taxable in Deer Creek Lower Hundred, 1775.

HAWKINS, Thomas. Taxable in Deer Creek Lower Hundred, 1775, with taxable negro Peter listed in his household.

HAWKINS, Thomas. Taxable in Deer Creek Upper Hundred, 1775.

HAWKINS, William. Taxable in Susquehanna Hundred, 1775, with taxable Francis Musgrove listed in his household.

HAWKINS, William. Taxable in Susquehanna Hundred, 1776, with taxable Francis Muskgrove listed in his household.

HAWTHORN, John. Taxable in Susquehanna Hundred, 1775.

HAY, John. Taxable in Gunpowder Lower Hundred, 1775. His name (among others) was listed on the back of the tax list.

HAYS, John Jr. Taxable in Bush River Lower Hundred, 1775, with taxable negro Hannah listed in his household.

HAYS, John Sr. Taxable in Spesutia Upper Hundred, 1775, with taxable negroes Araco, Gin, and Sall listed in his household. Taxable in Spesutia Upper Hundred, 1775.

HEARN, James. Taxable in Spesutia Lower Hundred, 1776.

HEATTON, Jeremiah. Taxable in Deer Creek Upper Hundred, 1775.

HEEPES (HUPES?), Robert. Taxable in Bush River Upper Hundred, 1775, with taxable Robert Heepes (Hupes?), Jr. listed in his household.

HENDERSIDES, William. Taxable in Bush River Lower Hundred, 1775.

HENDERSON, Phillip. Taxable in Spesutia Upper Hundred, 1775, with taxable Aaron White and negro Ammey listed in his household.

HENDERSON, Thomas Frisby's Quarters. Spesutia Lower Hundred, 1775, with taxables John Hall Hughes, John Cady, and slaves Toney, Peter, and Mint listed at these quarters.

HENLEY, Patrick. Taxable in Bush River Lower Hundred, 1775.

HENLEY, Peter (schoolmaster). Taxable in Spesutia Upper Hundred, 1775.

HENSON, Jacob. Taxable in household of James Walker, Susquehanna Hundred, 1775.

HERBERT, Benjamin. See "Benjamin Harbet," q.v.

HERBERT, Benjamin. See "Benjamin Harbet," q.v.

HERBERT, Richard. Taxable in household of Daniel Norris (son of Edward), Bush River Lower Hundred, 1775.

HERBERT, Richard. Taxable in Spesutia Upper Hundred, 1775.

HEWET, William. Taxable in household of Jacob Lemmon, Susquehanna Hundred, 1775.

HEWNS, Joseph. Taxable in household of Baltus Fie, Spesutia Lower Hundred, 1775.

HEWS, James. Taxable in household of James Clark, Spesutia Upper Hundred, 1775.

HICKS, James. Taxable in Bush River Lower Hundred, 1775.

HILL, Alexander. Taxable in Spesutia Upper Hundred, 1775.

HILL, Aron. Taxable in Gunpowder Lower Hundred, 1775.

HILL, Harman. Taxable in household of John Hill, Susquehanna Hundred, 1775.

HILL, Harmon. Taxable in household of John Hill, Susquehanna Hundred, 1776.

HILL, James. Taxable in Gunpowder Lower Hundred, 1775.

HILL, John. Taxable in Susquehanna Hundred, 1775, with taxable Harman Hill listed in his household.

HILL, John. Taxable in Susquehanna Hundred, 1776, with taxable Harman Hill listed in his household.

HILL, Stephen. Taxable in Spesutia Upper Hundred, 1775, with taxable George Mubury listed in his household.

HILL, Thomas. Taxable in Gunpowder Lower Hundred, 1775.

HILL, William. Taxable in Spesutia Lower Hundred, 1775.

HILL, William. Taxable in Bush River Upper Hundred, 1775.

HILL, William. Taxable in Deer Creek Lower Hundred, 1775.

HILL, William. Taxable in Spesutia Lower Hundred, 1776.

HINKS, Thomas. Taxable in Bush River Lower Hundred, 1775, with John Shinton as his security.

HITCHCOCK, Asell Jr. Taxable in Bush River Upper Hundred, 1775.

HITCHCOCK, Asell. Taxable in Bush River Upper Hundred, 1775, with taxables John Hitchcock and negroes Fill, Hannar, and Samma listed in his household.

HITCHCOCK, John. Taxable in household of Asell Hitchcock, Bush River Upper Hundred, 1775.

HITCHCOCK, Jos. Jr. Taxable in Bush River Upper Hundred, 1775.

HITCHCOCK, Joshua(?). Taxable in Bush River Upper Hundred, 1775. [The constable's scribbled handwriting makes this name appear to be "Johnus Hithcork," so it could be "Joshua Hitchcock"].

HITCHCOCK, Josiah. Taxable in Bush River Upper Hundred, 1775, with taxables Randel Hitchcock (son), John Molletsant, and negroes Marea and Hannah listed in his household.

HITCHCOCK, Randel (son of Josiah). Taxable in household of his father Josiah Hitchcock, Bush River Upper Hundred, 1775.

HITCHCOCK, William. Taxable in Bush River Upper Hundred, 1775, with tacxable John Pound (servant) listed in his household.

HOBS, James. Taxable in household of Thomas Ensor, Bush River Upper Hundred, 1775.

HODGES, Giles. Taxable in household of Joseph Hartley, Bush River Lower Hundred, 1775.

HODGES, John. Taxable in household of Benjamin Balis, Susquehanna Hundred, 1776.

EARLY HARFORD COUNTIANS: Supplement

HODGSKINS, James. Taxable in Bush River Upper Hundred, 1775.
HOLINGSWORTH, Samuel. Taxable in Susquehanna Hundred, 1775.
HOLLAND, Francis. Taxable in Spesutia Lower Hundred, 1776, with taxables Roger Obricon and negroes Tom, Bill, Toney, and Violet listed in his household.
HOLLIS, Amos. Taxable in Spesutia Lower Hundred, 1775, with taxable slaves Sambo and Luraney listed in his household.
HOLLIS, Clark. Taxable in the household of William Hollis, Sr., Spesutia Lower Hundred, 1775.
HOLLIS, William Jr. Taxable in the household of William Hollis, Sr., Spesutia Lower Hundred, 1775.
HOLLIS, William Sr. Taxable in Spesutia Lower Hundred, 1775, with taxables William Hollis, Jr., Clark, Hollis, and slaves Bendow, Jack, Toney, and Fann listed in his household.
HOLLIT, John. Taxable in household of Andrey [sic] Wilson, Susquehanna Hundred, 1776.
HOLLIWAY, Richard. Taxable in Gunpowder Lower Hundred, 1775. His name (among others) was listed on the back of the tax list.
HOLMES, James. Taxable in Bush River Lower Hundred, 1775, with taxable servant Thomas Sheredon and John Tilbrook listed in his household.
HOPE, Richard. Taxable in Bush River Upper Hundred, 1775.
HOPE, Thomas. Taxable in Bush River Upper Hundred, 1775.
HOPKINS, Jarret. Taxable in Deer Creek Lower Hundred, 1775, with taxable negroes Ben and Jenney listed in his household.
HOPKINS, John. Taxable in Deer Creek Lower Hundred, 1775.
HOPKINS, Joseph. Taxable in Deer Creek Lower Hundred, 1775, with taxable negroes Sharper, Hector, Duke, Poledor, Nan, and Hago listed in his household.
HOPKINS, Leven. Taxable in household of William Hopkins, Jr., Deer Creek Lower Hundred, 1775.
HOPKINS, Samuel. Taxable in Deer Creek Lower Hundred, 1775.
HOPKINS, William Jr. Taxable in Deer Creek Lower Hundred, 1775, with taxable Leven Hopkins listed in his household.
HOPKINS, William. Taxable in Deer Creek Lower Hundred, 1775, with taxable negroes Ned, Pompey, Neptune, Jack, James, Will, Tom, Isaac, Nanney, and Peg listed on his plantation.
HORNER, James. Taxable in Susquehanna Hundred, 1775, with taxable Patrick Nevin listed in his household.
HORNER, James. Taxable in Susquehanna Hundred, 1776.
HORNER, Nathan. Taxable in Gunpowder Lower Hundred, 1775, with taxable slave Hager listed in his household.
HORNER, Nathaniel. Taxable in household of John Wood, Spesutia Lower Hundred, 1776.
HORNER, William. Taxable in Susquehanna Hundred, 1775, with taxable negro Nan listed in his household.
HORNER, William. Taxable in Susquehanna Hundred, 1776, with taxable negro Nan listed in his household.
HORTEN, William. Taxable in Susquehanna Hundred, 1775, with taxabale negroes Tom and Dinah listed in his household.
HORTEN, William. Taxable in Susquehanna Hundred, 1776, with taxable negroes Tom and Dina listed in his household.
HOULEY, Thomas. Taxable in household of Andrew Meeks, Susquehanna Hundred, 1775.
HOW, William. Taxable (servant) in household of John Montgomery, Deer Creek Lower Hundred, 1775.
HOWARD, Benjamin. Taxable in Bush River Lower Hundred, 1775. Security for taxable negroes Harry, Nedd, Margaret, and Catron.
HOWARD, Benjamin's Quarters. Gunpowder Lower Hundred, 1775, with taxables William Bond and slaves Bumbrow, Dick, Wil, and Phillis listed at these quarters.
HOWARD, John (weaver). Taxable in Gunpowder Lower Hundred, 1775.
HOWARD, John Beal. Taxable in Gunpowder Lower Hundred, 1775.
HOWARD, John Gould. Taxable in Gunpowder Lower Hundred, 1775.
HOWARD, Lemuel. Taxable in Bush River Lower Hundred, 1775, with taxable negroes Guinea, Tom, Sam, and Marai listed in his household.
HOWARD, Nathaniel. Taxable in Gunpowder Lower Hundred, 1775, with taxable slave Nathan listed in hism household.
HOWARD, R. See "Negro Lydia," q.v.
HOWEL, Samuel. Taxable in household of William Vertchworth, Susquehanna Hundred, 1775.
HOWEL, Samuel. Taxable in Susquehanna Hundred, 1776, with taxable negroes Samson and Mererer listed in his household.
HOWELL, John. Taxable on the plantation of Amos Garrett, Spesutia Lower Hundred, 1775.
HOWLET, Andrew. Taxable in Deer Creek Lower Hundred, 1775, with taxable James Howlet (son) and man Philip Nevel (servant) listed in his household.
HOWLET, James (son of Andrew). Taxable in household of his father Andrew Howlet, Deer Creek Lower Hundred, 1775.
HUBBARD, George. Taxable in household of Edward

Ward, Deer Creek Lower Hundred, 1775.

HUCHINS, Richard. Taxable in Bush River Upper Hundred, 1775.

HUDSON, Thomas (son of William). Taxable in household of his father William Hudson, Deer Creek Upper Hundred, 1775.

HUDSON, William. Taxable in Deer Creek Upper Hundred, 1775, with taxable Thomas Hudson (son) listed in his household.

HUFF, Abram. Taxable in Bush River Upper Hundred, 1775.

HUFF, Garrett. Taxable in Bush River Upper Hundred, 1775.

HUFF, John. Taxable in Bush River Lower Hundred, 1775.

HUFF, John. Taxable in Bush River Upper Hundred, 1775.

HUFFIELD, Charles. Taxable at Jacob Giles' mill at Bush, Spesutia Lower Hundred, 1775.

HUGGINS, James. Taxable in Bush River Lower Hundred, 1775.

HUGGINS, Thomas. Taxable on the plantation of Amos Garrett, Spesutia Lower Hundred, 1775.

HUGHES, Aram. Taxable in Bush River Upper Hundred, 1775.

HUGHES, J--- [illegible]. Taxable in Susquehanna Hundred, 1775.

HUGHES, John Hall. Taxable at Thomas Frisby Henderson's Quarters, Spesutia Lower Hundred, 1775.

HUGHES, John Jr. Taxable in Susquehanna Hundred, 1775.

HUGHES, John Jr. Taxable in Susquehanna Hundred, 1776.

HUGHES, John Sr. Taxable in Susquehanna Hundred, 1776.

HUGHES, John. Taxable in Gunpowder Lower Hundred, 1775.

HUGHES, Nathanel. Taxable in Susquehanna Hundred, 1776

HUGHES, Nathaniel. Taxable in Susquehanna Hundred, 1775.

HUGHES, Neason. Taxable in Bush River Upper Hundred, 1775.

HUGHES, Nicholas. Taxable in Bush River Upper Hundred, 1775.

HUGHES, William (taylor). Taxable in Gunpowder Lower Hundred, 1775.

HUGHES, Zenas. Taxable in Bush River Upper Hundred, 1775, with a taxable servant man (no name given) listed in his household.

HUGHES, Zibidee. Taxable in Bush River Upper Hundred, 1775.

HUGHSTON, Alexander. Taxable in Bush River Lower Hundred, 1775.

HUGOM, William. Taxable in household of Clement Lewis, Bush River Lower Hundred, 1775.

HUMBLE, Isaac. Taxable in Susquehanna Hundred, 1776.

HUMES, James. Taxable in household of John Duzan, Spesutia Lower Hundred, 1775.

HUMPHRES, Richard. Taxable (servant) on plantation of Stephen Jay, Deer Creek Lower Hundred, 1775.

HUNT, Robert. Taxable in Spesutia Lower Hundred, 1775.

HUNT, Thomas. Taxable at William Buchanan's Quarters, Gunpowder Lower Hundred, 1775.

HUPES (HEEPES?), Robert Jr. Taxable in household of Robert Hupes (Heepes?), Bush River Upper Hundred, 1775.

HURLEY, James. Taxable in household of James Giles, Spesutia Lower Hundred, 1775.

HUSBAND, Joseph. Taxable in Susquehanna Hundred, 1775, with one taxable servant in his household (no name given).

HUSBANDS, Elizabeth (widow). Head of household in Deer Creek Lower Hundred, 1775, with taxable negroes Sam, James, George, and Mary listed in her household.

HUSBANDS, Joseph. Taxable in Susquehanna Hundred, 1776, with taxable Thomas Clark listed in his household.

HUSBANDS, William. See "Negro Sam," q.v.

HUSBANDS, William. Taxable in Deer Creek Lower Hundred, 1775.

HUSKINS, Thomas. Taxable in Bush River Upper Hundred, 1775.

HUSTON, Hugh. Taxable in Bush River Upper Hundred, 1775.

HUTCHENS, Thomas. Taxable in Bush River Lower Hundred, 1775, with taxable William Celly listed in his household.

HUTCHESON, James. Taxable in Deer Creek Upper Hundred, 1775, with taxable man J. Blanch (servant) listed in his household.

HUTCHINS, Richard. See "Richard Huchins," q.v.

HUTCHINSON, James. Taxable in Deer Creek Upper Hundred, 1775, with taxable John Reiley listed in his household.

INGRAM, Eleven. Taxable in Gunpowder Lower Hundred, 1775, with taxable John Clark listed in his household.

IRONS, John. Taxable in Bush River Lower Hundred, 1775.

IRONS, Peter. Taxable in household of William Boner, Jr., Susquehanna Hundred, 1775.

IRONS, Peter. Taxable in household of William Bonar, Jr., Susquehanna Hundred, 1776.

IRONS, William. Taxable in household of Moses Collins, Spesutia Lower Hundred, 1775.

JACKLIN, Andrew. Taxable (servant) in household of Benjamin Norris, Bush River Lower Hundred, 1775.

JACKSON, Isaiah. Taxable in Bush River Upper Hundred, 1775.

JACKSON, James. Taxable in Deer Creek Upper Hundred, 1775.

JACKSON, John. Taxable in household of Underwood Guiton, Bush River Lower Hundred, 1775.

JACKSON, John. Taxable in Deer Creek Upper Hundred, 1775.

JACKSON, Thomas. Taxable in Spesutia Lower Hundred, 1775.

JAKELIN(?), James. Taxable (servant) in household of William Beaty, Bush River Upper Hundred, 1775.

JAMES, John. Taxable in Deer Creek Upper Hundred, 1775.

JAMES, Richard. Taxable in Deer Creek Upper Hundred, 1775, with taxable Sedgwick James (son) listed in his household.

JAMES, Robert. Taxable in Deer Creek Lower Hundred, 1775.

JAMES, Sedgwick (son of Richard). Taxable in household of his father Richard James, Deer Creek Upper Hundred, 1775.

JAMES, Thomas Jr. Taxable in Bush River Upper Hundred, 1775.

JAMES, Thomas. Taxable in Bush River Lower Hundred, 1775.

JAMES, Thomas. Taxable in Bush River Upper Hundred, 1775, with taxable slaves Pam and Suck listed in his household.

JAMES, Tom (carpenter). See "Cumberland Forge," q.v.

JAMES, William. See "John Stuart," q.v.

JAMES, William. Taxable in Bush River Upper Hundred, 1775, with taxable servant ---- (no name given) listed in his household.

JAMESON (JAMSON), Edward. Taxable (servant) in household of Margret Akins, Bush River Upper Hundred, 1775.

JAMESON, John. Taxable in Spesutia Upper Hundred, 1775.

JAMISON, Alexander. Taxable in Susquehanna Hundred, 1775, with taxable John Jamison listed in his household.

JAMISON, John. Taxable in household of Alexander Jamison, Susquehanna Hundred, 1775.

JAMMESON, Ellexander. Taxable in household of John Jammeson, Susquehanna Hundred, 1776.

JAMMESON, John. Taxable in Susquehanna Hundred, 1776, with taxable Ellexander Jammeson listed in his household.

JANAER, James. Taxable in household of Jacob Giles, Susquehanna Hundred, 1775.

JARMAN, John. Taxable in household of Jacob Lemmon, Susquehanna Hundred, 1775.

JARRETT, Abraham. Taxable in Bush River Lower Hundred, 1775, with 4 taxables in his household, but only his name was given.

JARVES, William. Taxable in Susquehanna Hundred, 1775.

JARVIS, James. Taxable in Bush River Lower Hundred, 1775.

JARVIS, John. Taxable in Spesutia Upper Hundred, 1775.

JARVIS, Joshua. Taxable in Spesutia Upper Hundred, 1775.

JAY, Stephen. Taxable in Deer Creek Lower Hundred, 1775, with taxable men Richard Humphres (servant) and James Lamford (servant) and negores Prince, Frank, Sandey, Samp, Sip, Moll and Sall listed in his plantation.

JEFFERIES, William. Taxable in household of Jacob Forward, Spesutia Lower Hundred, 1775.

JEFFERY, William. Taxable in Spesutia Lower Hundred, 1776, with Thomas Browning as his security.

JEFFREY, Robert. Taxable in Spesutia Upper Hundred, 1775.

JEFFREYS, William. Taxable in Deer Creek Upper Hundred, 1775.

JEFFRY, Hugh. Taxable in Spesutia Upper Hundred, 1775.

JEFFRY, Thomas. Taxable in Spesutia Upper Hundred, 1775.

JENKENS, Jonathan. Taxable in household of William Jenkens, Bush River Lower Hundred, 1775.

JENKENS, William. Taxable in Bush River Lower Hundred, 1775, with taxables Nathaniel Price, John Thorn, and Jonathan Jenkens listed in his household.

JENKINS, Francis. Taxable in Spesutia Upper Hundred, 1775.

JENKINS, Samuel. Taxable in Spesutia Lower Hundred, 1775, with William Hall as his security. Taxable in Spesutia Lower Hundred, 1775.

JENKINS, Samuel. Taxable in Spesutia Lower Hundred, 1776, with taxable Roland Kimble listed in his household.

JENNINGS, Isaac. Taxable at Jacob Giles' Quarters at Romney, Spesutia Lower Hundred, 1775.

JEWELL, Robert. Taxable in Deer Creek Upper Hundred, 1775.

JEWL, Robert. Taxable in Spesutia Upper Hundred, 1775, with William Grafton as his security.

JINKINS, Samuel. Taxable in Deer Creek Upper Hundred, 1775.

JINNIS (GINNIS?), William. Taxable in household of Robert Glenn, Bush River Upper Hundred, 1775.

JOHNS, Nathan. Taxable in household of Richard Johns, Susquehanna Hundred, 1775.

JOHNS, Nathan. Taxable in Susquehanna Hundred, 1776.

JOHNS, Richard. Taxable in Susquehanna Hundred, 1775, with taxables Nathan Johns and negroes Tom, Wil, George, Mingo, Polydore, and Affey listed in his household.

JOHNS, Richard. Taxable in Susquehanna Hundred, 1776. See "Negro Thomas (a free negro)," q.v.

JOHNSN, John. Taxable in the household of Archibald Johnson, Sr., Spesutia Lower Hundred, 1775.

JOHNSON, An [Ann], widow of John. Head of household in Deer Creek Upper Hundred, 1775, with taxables Nathannile [sic] Dominick and negro Toney listed in her household.

JOHNSON, Archibald Jr. Taxable in Spesutia Lower Hundred, 1775.

JOHNSON, Archibald Jr. Taxable in Spesutia Lower Hundred, 1776.

JOHNSON, Archibald Sr. Taxable in Spesutia Lower Hundred, 1775, with taxable John Johnson listed in his household.

JOHNSON, Barnard (son of Hester). Taxable in household of his mother Hester Johnson, Spesutia Upper Hundred, 1775.

JOHNSON, Charles. Taxable in Deer Creek Upper Hundred, 1775.

JOHNSON, Hester. Head of household in Spesutia Upper Hundred, 1775, with taxables Barnard Johnson (son) and negroes Mingo and Moll listed in her household.

JOHNSON, Isaac. Taxable in Deer Creek Upper Hundred, 1775.

JOHNSON, John (free negro). Taxable in Deer Creek Lower Hundred, 1775, with William Fisher as his security.

JOHNSON, John. Taxable (servant) in household of William Bradford, Bush River Lower Hundred, 1775.

JOHNSON, John. Taxable in household of John Whiteford, Deer Creek Upper Hundred, 1775.

JOHNSON, John. Taxable in Deer Creek Upper Hundred, 1775.

JOHNSON, Joseph. See "Thomas Johnson," q.v.

JOHNSON, Joseph. Taxable in Spesutia Lower Hundred, 1775.

JOHNSON, Joseph. Taxable in Spesutia Lower Hundred, 1776.

JOHNSON, Mossus. Taxable in Bush River Upper Hundred, 1775, with taxables Richard Freen and William Charrett listed in his household.

JOHNSON, Rachel. Head of household in Spesutia Upper Hundred, 1775, with taxable negro Exedor listed in her household.

JOHNSON, Robert. Taxable in Spesutia Upper Hundred, 1775.

JOHNSON, Samuel. Taxable in household of Kent Mitchel, Susquehanna Hundred, 1775.

JOHNSON, Thomas (son of Joseph). Taxable in Deer Creek Lower Hundred, 1775.

JOHNSON, Thomas Sr. Taxable in Spesutia Upper Hundred, 1775, with taxable negroes Pugg, Nan, Comfort, and Doll listed in his household.

JOHNSON, Thomas. Taxable in Deer Creek Lower Hundred, 1775, with taxable man Francis Tipton (servant) listed in his household.

JOHNSON, William. Taxable in Spesutia Lower Hundred, 1775.

JOHNSON, William. Taxable in Spesutia Upper Hundred, 1775.

JOHNSON, William. Taxable in Spesutia Lower Hundred, 1776.

JOHSTON [sic], Samuel. Taxable in household of Kent Mitchel, Jr., Susquehanna Hundred, 1776.

JOICE, Elijah. Taxable in household of Jacob Bond, Sr., Bush River Lower Hundred, 1775.

JOLLEY, John. Taxable in Deer Creek Lower Hundred, 1775, with taxables Richard Chew and negroes Suck, Dampear, and Daniel listed in his household.

JONES, Benjamin. Taxable in Deer Creek Upper Hundred, 1775, with taxable man H. Reed (servant) listed in his household.

JONES, Gilbert. Taxable in Bush River Lower Hundred, 1775.

JONES, Griffith. Taxable in Spesutia Lower Hundred, 1775.

JONES, Griffith. Taxable in Spesutia Lower Hundred, 1776.

JONES, Howard. Taxable in household of William Jones, Bush River Upper Hundred, 1775.

JONES, Jacob. Taxable in Deer Creek Upper Hundred, 1775.

JONES, James. Taxable in household of Kent Mitchel, Susquehanna Hundred, 1775.

JONES, Jeremiah. Taxable in Bush River Lower Hundred, 1775.

JONES, John. Taxable in Gunpowder Lower Hundred, 1775.

JONES, John. Taxable in Gunpowder Lower Hundred, 1775. His name (among others) was listed on the back of the tax list.

JONES, John. Taxable in Gunpowder Lower Hundred, 1775. His name (among others) was listed on the back of the tax list.

JONES, John. Taxable at Dr. Henry Stephenson's Quarters, Spesutia Lower Hundred, 1775.

JONES, Joseph. Taxable in household of Shephard Armstrong, Bush River Lower Hundred, 1775.

JONES, Joseph. Taxable in Bush River Upper Hundred,

EARLY HARFORD COUNTIANS: Supplement

JONES, Joseph. Taxable in household of Baltus Fie, Spesutia Lower Hundred, 1776.
JONES, Joshua. Taxable in Bush River Upper Hundred, 1775.
JONES, Ruben. Taxable in Deer Creek Lower Hundred, 1775.
JONES, Thomas. Taxable in Deer Creek Upper Hundred, 1775, with taxable William Jones (son) listed in his household.
JONES, William (son of Thomas). Taxable in household of his father Thomas Jones, Deer Creek Upper Hundred, 1775.
JONES, William. Taxable in the household of Michael Kennard, Spesutia Lower Hundred, 1775.
JONES, William. Taxable in Bush River Upper Hundred, 1775, with taxable Howard Jones listed in his household.
JONES, William. Taxable in Deer Creek Upper Hundred, 1775, with taxable man Charles Martin (servant) listed in his household.
JOSHUA, Joash. Taxable in household of Jehu ---- (free negro), Susquehanna Hundred, 1775.
JOURDAN, Rinhard (Richard?). Taxable (servant) in the household of William Norris, Bush River Upper Hundred, 1775.
JUD, Daniel. Taxable in Susquehanna Hundred, 1776.
JUD, William. Taxable in Susquehanna Hundred, 1776.
JUDD, Daniel. Taxable in Susquehanna Hundred, 1775.
JUDD, Matthew. Taxable in household of Henry Waters, Spesutia Upper Hundred, 1775.
JUDD, William. Taxable in Susquehanna Hundred, 1775.
JUETT, Thaddeus. Taxable in Spesutia Upper Hundred, 1775, with taxable Thomas Winnet and negro Rachel listed in his household.
JURDON, Simon. Taxable in Deer Creek Upper Hundred, 1775.
JURY, Richard. Taxable in household of Caleb Beck, Spesutia Lower Hundred, 1775.
KAIN, John. Taxable in Bush River Upper Hundred, 1775.
KAINE, Edward. Taxable in household of James Giles, Spesutia Lower Hundred, 1775.
KANADAY, James. Taxable in Spesutia Upper Hundred, 1775, with taxable Micheal Gore listed in his household.
KANADAY, Thomas. Taxable in Spesutia Upper Hundred, 1775.
KEAN, James. Taxable in Spesutia Upper Hundred, 1775, with taxable John Kean listed in his household.
KEAN, John. Taxable in household of James Kean, Spesutia Upper Hundred, 1775.
KEEN, Timothy. See "Timmothon Ken," q.v.
KEEN, Timothy. Taxable in Susquehanna Hundred, 1775.
KELLEY, Allexander. Taxable in Susquehanna Hundred, 1776, with taxable Robert Kelley liste in his household.
KELLEY, Aurthur. Taxable in Deer Creek Upper Hundred, 1775.
KELLEY, James. Taxable in Spesutia Lower Hundred, 1776.
KELLEY, John. Taxable (servant) in household of James Parks, Deer Creek Lower Hundred, 1775.
KELLEY, Robert. Taxable in household of Allexander Kelley, Susquehanna Hundred, 1776,
KELLY, Alexander. Taxable in household of Alexander Kelly, Susquehanna Hundred, 1775.
KELLY, Alexander. Taxable in Susquehanna Hundred, 1775, with taxables Robert Kelly and Alexander Kelly listed in his household.
KELLY, Arthur. See "Aurthur Kelley," q.v.
KELLY, James. See "Michael Malarky," q.v.
KELLY, James. Taxable in Spesutia Lower Hundred, 1775.
KELLY, James. Taxable in Deer Creek Upper Hundred, 1775.
KELLY, M. Taxable (servant) in household of John McFadden, Deer Creek Upper Hundred, 1775.
KELLY, Robert. Taxable in household of Alexander Kelly, Susquehanna Hundred, 1775.
KEN, Timmothon. Taxable in Susquehanna Hundred, 1776. [The constable mistakenly entered the name as "Timmothon Ken" on this tax list, but it is actually "Timothy Keen" as shown on other lists].
KENNADY, John. Taxable in Bush River Lower Hundred, 1775.
KENNARD, Michael. Taxable in Spesutia Lower Hundred, 1775, with taxables Robert Forghtner and William Jones listed in his household [These names appeared at the end of the tax list].
KENT, Christopher. Taxable in Bush River Lower Hundred, 1775.
KENT, Jese [sic]. Taxable in Deer Creek Upper Hundred, 1775.
KERMAID, Michael. See "James Redman," q.v.
KERN, John. Taxable in household of William Gale, Gunpowder Lower Hundred, 1775.
KERR, Robert. Taxable in household of Charles Gilbert, Susquehanna Hundred, 1776.
KEY, Job. Taxable in Spesutia Upper Hundred, 1775, listed in same household with Peter Swaton.
KID, Henry. Taxable in Bush River Upper Hundred, 1775 [The constable's scribbled handwriting makes the name appear to be Heny Kid, but it is actually Henry Kid].
KID, James. Taxable in Bush River Upper Hundred, 1775. [The constable's scribbled handwriting makes

the name appear to be Jones Kid, but it is actually James Kid].

KID, Joshua. Taxable in Bush River Upper Hundred, 1775.

KID, William. Taxable in Bush River Upper Hundred, 1775.

KIGHT (RIGHT?), John. Taxable in household of John Carlile, Spesutia Lower Hundred, 1775.

KIMBLE, Giles. Taxable in Spesutia Lower Hundred, 1775.

KIMBLE, Giles. Taxable in Spesutia Lower Hundred, 1776.

KIMBLE, James. Taxable in Spesutia Lower Hundred, 1775, with taxables Rowland Kimble and slaves Will, Margaret, Judith, Jane, Hagur, and Fill listed in his household.

KIMBLE, James. Taxable in the household of Samuel Kimble, Spesutia Lower Hundred, 1775.

KIMBLE, James. Taxable in household of Samuel Kimble, Spesutia Lower Hundred, 1776.

KIMBLE, James. Taxable in Spesutia Lower Hundred, 1776, with taxable negroes William, Fill, Margaret, Judiah, Hager, and Jean listed in his household.

KIMBLE, John. Taxable in Spesutia Lower Hundred, 1775.

KIMBLE, John. Taxable in Spesutia Lower Hundred, 1776.

KIMBLE, Josias. Taxable in Spesutia Lower Hundred, 1775.

KIMBLE, Josias. Taxable in Spesutia Lower Hundred, 1776.

KIMBLE, Roland. Taxable in household of Samuel Jenkins, Spesutia Lower Hundred, 1776.

KIMBLE, Rowland. Taxable in the household of James Kimble, Spesutia Lower Hundred, 1775.

KIMBLE, Samuel. Taxable in Spesutia Lower Hundred, 1775, with taxables James Kimble, John Monroe, and slaves Sampson and Abigail listed in his household.

KIMBLE, Samuel. Taxable in Spesutia Lower Hundred, 1776, with taxables James Kimble, John Monroe, and negroes Abigail and Sampson listed in his household.

KIMBLE, Stephen. Taxable in Spesutia Lower Hundred, 1775.

KIMBLE, Stephen. Taxable in Spesutia Lower Hundred, 1776.

KING, William. Taxable in Bush River Lower Hundred, 1775.

KIRKPATRICK, Hugh. Taxable in Spesutia Upper Hundred, 1775, with taxable servant James ---- (no last name given).

KIRKPATRICK, James. Taxable in Spesutia Upper Hundred, 1775.

KIRKWOOD, Robert. Taxable in Bush River Upper Hundred, 1775.

KITELEY, Thomas. Taxable in Gunpowder Lower Hundred, 1775.

KITELY, William. Taxable in Bush River Lower Hundred, 1775, with taxables Abrm. Norris and 3 slaves (no names given) in his household.

KNIGHT, David. Taxable in Susquehanna Hundred, 1775.

KNIGHT, David. Taxable in household of David Knight, Susquehanna Hundred, 1776.

KNIGHT, David. Taxable in Susquehanna Hundred, 1776, with taxable David Knight listed in his household.

KNIGHT, George. Taxable in Susquehanna Hundred, 1776.

KNIGHT, John. Taxable (servant) in household of Barnard Riely, Bush River Lower Hundred, 1775.

KNIGHT, Jonothan. Taxable in Susquehanna Hundred, 1776.

KNIGHT, Light. Taxable in Susquehanna Hundred, 1776, with taxable William Knight listed in his household.

KNIGHT, Lite. Taxable in Susquehanna Hundred, 1775, with taxable William Knight listed in his household.

KNIGHT, Michael. Taxable in Susquehanna Hundred, 1775.

KNIGHT, Thomas Jr. Taxable in Susquehanna Hundred, 1775.

KNIGHT, Thomas. Taxable in Susquehanna Hundred, 1775.

KNIGHT, Thomas. Taxable in Spesutia Upper Hundred, 1775, with Jos. or Jas. Weatherall as his security.

KNIGHT, Thomas. Taxable in Susquehanna Hundred, 1776.

KNIGHT, William. Taxable in Susquehanna Hundred, 1775, with William Perkins as his security.

KNIGHT, William. Taxable in household of Lite Knight, Susquehanna Hundred, 1775.

KNIGHT, William. Taxable in household of Light Knight, Susquehanna Hundred, 1776.

KNIGHT, ---- [illegible; could be Thos. or Jno.?]. Taxable in Susquehanna Hundred, 1775.

KNOTT, William. Taxable in Deer Creek Lower Hundred, 1775.

KNOWLMAN, Anthony. Taxable in household of Martha Presbury, Gunpowder Lower Hundred, 1775.

KNOWLMAN, Richard. Taxable in Gunpowder Lower Hundred, 1775.

LAFFERTY, John. Taxable in Susquehanna Hundred, 1775.

LAFFERTY, William. Taxable in Susquehanna Hundred, 1775.

LAMFORD, James. Taxable (servant) on plantation of Stephen Jay, Deer Creek Lower Hundred, 1775.

LAMP, John. Taxable in household of Joseph Stiles,

Spesutia Upper Hundred, 1775.

LAMPRE, John. Taxable in Susquehanna Hundred, 1776.

LANAGAN, James. Taxable in Spesutia Lower Hundred, 1775.

LANCASTER, Benjamin. Taxable in Bush River Lower Hundred, 1775, with taxable Joseph Lancaster listed in his household.

LANCASTER, Jesse. Taxable in Bush River Lower Hundred, 1775.

LANCASTER, Joseph. Taxable in household of Benjamin Lancaster, Bush River Lower Hundred, 1775.

LANCASTER, Thomas. Taxable in Spesutia Lower Hundred, 1775.

LANCASTER, Thomas. Taxable in Spesutia Lower Hundred, 1776.

LARRANCE, John. Taxable in Susquehanna Hundred, 1776.

LARRIMORE, John. Taxable in Bush River Lower Hundred, 1775.

LARY, Laurence. Taxable in Spesutia Lower Hundred, 1776.

LASARUS, James. Taxable (servant) in household of Hugh Nivans, Bush River Upper Hundred, 1775.

LASEY, Amos. Taxable in household of Thomas Lasey, Sr., Bush River Lower Hundred, 1775.

LASEY, Samuel. Taxable in household of Thomas Lasey, Sr., Bush River Lower Hundred, 1775.

LASEY, Thomas Jr. Taxable in household of Thomas Lasey, Sr., Bush River Lower Hundred, 1775.

LASEY, Thomas Sr. Taxable in Bush River Lower Hundred, 1775, with taxables Thomas Lasey, Jr., William Lasey, Samuel Lasey, and Amos Lasey listed in his household.

LASEY, William. Taxable in household of Thomas Lasey, Sr., Bush River Lower Hundred, 1775.

LATTIMORE, William. Taxable in Bush River Upper Hundred, 1775, with Rev. George Worsley as his security.

LAUGHLAN, Peter. Taxable in Susquehanna Hundred, 1775, with taxable negro Sambo listed in his household.

LAWRENCE, John. Taxable in Susquehanna Hundred, 1775.

LEAGUE, Aquila. Taxable in Spesutia Lower Hundred, 1776.

LEAKIN, James. Taxable in Deer Creek Upper Hundred, 1775.

LEE, David. Taxable in Bush River Lower Hundred, 1775, with taxable servants John ---- and Samuel ---- (no last names given) listed in his household.

LEE, James Jr. Taxable in Spesutia Upper Hundred, 1775, with taxable negroes Sall and Sue listed in his household.

LEE, James. Taxable in Deer Creek Lower Hundred, 1775, with taxable negroes Dick, Forester, Nan, Hagar, Dutches, Tamer, Bob, Luke, Ceaser, and Sam listed on his plantation.

LEE, James. Taxable in Susquehanna Hundred, 1776.

LEE, John. Taxable in Spesutia Lower Hundred, 1776.

LEE, Josiah. Taxable in Deer Creek Upper Hundred, 1775, with taxable negroes Nell, Paraway, and Sucks listed in his household.

LEE, Samuel. Taxable in Bush River Lower Hundred, 1775.

LEE, Samuel. Taxable in Spesutia Upper Hundred, 1775, with taxable negroes Antony, Dick, Len, Clem, and Cato listed in his household.

LEGO, Spencer. Taxable in Gunpowder Lower Hundred, 1775. His name (among others) was listed on the back of the tax list.

LEGOE, Benedict. Taxable in Gunpowder Lower Hundred, 1775.

LEMMON, Jacob. See "Roger Dillon," q.v.

LEMMON, Jacob. Taxable in Susquehanna Hundred, 1775, with taxables John Jarman, Timothy Hallow, William Hewet, and William Deiey listed in his household.

LENHARD, Samuel. Taxable in Deer Creek Upper Hundred, 1775, with taxable men William Smith and James Barnard listed in his household.

LESTER, Norris. Taxable in Spesutia Lower Hundred, 1775.

LESTER, Norris. Taxable in Spesutia Lower Hundred, 1776, with taxable negro Sass listed in his household.

LEVEY, David. Taxable in household of John Wilson, Bush River Lower Hundred, 1775.

LEWIN, William. Taxable in Bush River Lower Hundred, 1775.

LEWIS, Clement. Taxable in Bush River Lower Hundred, 1775, with taxables William Hugom and John Asten listed in his household.

LEWIS, James. Taxable in Deer Creek Upper Hundred, 1775.

LEWIS, John. Taxable in Bush River Lower Hundred, 1775.

LEWIS, Thomas. Taxable in Bush River Upper Hundred, 1775.

LEWIS, Walter. Taxable in Deer Creek Upper Hundred, 1775.

LIGHTFOOT, Isaac. Taxable in Deer Creek Upper Hundred, 1775.

LIGOE, Judy. Head of household in Gunpowder Lower Hundred, 1775, with taxable slave Sate listed in her household.

LIGOE, Mary. Head of household in Gunpowder Lower Hundred, 1775, with taxable slave Fan listed in her household.

LINCH, John. Taxable in Spesutia Upper Hundred, 1775, with taxable negroes Sarah and Gin listed in his household.

LINCH, John. Taxable in household of James Fisher, Deer Creek Lower Hundred, 1775.

LINIAM, James. Taxable in Deer Creek Upper Hundred, 1775.

LINSEY, Andrew. Taxable in Deer Creek Upper Hundred, 1775.

LINTON, Isaiah. Taxable in Bush River Lower Hundred, 1775.

LISBE, Elisabeth. Head of household in Bush River Lower Hundred, 1775, with 2 taxables in her household (no names given).

LISBY, Joseph. Taxable in Gunpowder Lower Hundred, 1775, with taxable slave Sue listed in his household.

LITEL, James. Taxable in Bush River Upper Hundred, 1775.

LITHHILL, Tompain. Taxable in household of Jacob Giles, Susquehanna Hundred, 1775.

LITLE, Nathan. Taxable in household of John Patrick, Deer Creek Lower Hundred, 1775.

LITTEN, John. Taxable in Deer Creek Lower Hundred, 1775.

LITTEN, Samuel. Taxable in Susquehanna Hundred, 1775.

LITTLE, George. Taxable in Spesutia Lower Hundred, 1775, with taxable slaves Harry, Lottos, Prissa, and Fann listed in his household.

LITTLE, William. Taxable in Deer Creek Upper Hundred, 1775.

LITTON, Sammel. Taxable in Susquehanna Hundred, 1776.

LOCKWOOD, Stephen. Taxable (servant) in household of Sias Billingsly, Deer Creek Upper Hundred, 1775.

LOCKYEARE, John. Taxable in Spesutia Lower Hundred, 1775.

LOGAN, William. Taxable in Bush River Upper Hundred, 1775, with David Davis as his security.

LOGHLON, Peter. Taxable in Susquehanna Hundred, 1776, with taxable negro Samson listed in his household.

LOLAWAY, Henery. Taxable in Gunpowder Lower Hundred, 1775.

LONEY, John. Taxable in Spesutia Lower Hundred, 1775.

LONEY, Moses. See "Archibald McMurphey," q.v.

LONEY, Moses. Taxable in Spesutia Lower Hundred, 1775.

LONEY, Moses. Taxable in Spesutia Lower Hundred, 1776.

LONEY, William. Taxable in Spesutia Lower Hundred, 1775, with taxables Michael Coleman, Peter Font, and slave Cato listed in his household.

LONEY, William. Taxable in Spesutia Lower Hundred, 1776, with taxables Michael Coleman, Peter Font, John Wright, and negroe Kate listed in his household.

LONG, John Jr. Taxable in Bush River Upper Hundred, 1775.

LONG, John Sr. Taxable in Bush River Upper Hundred, 1775, with taxable Peter Long (son) listed in his household.

LONG, Peter. Taxable in household of his father John Long, Sr., Bush River Upper Hundred, 1775.

LOVE, James. Taxable in Deer Creek Lower Hundred, 1775.

LOVE, John. Taxable in Spesutia Upper Hundred, 1775, with taxable negroes Jack, Nan, and Prue listed in his household.

LOVEL, John. Taxable in household of Jacob Giles, Jr., Susquehanna Hundred, 1775.

LOVEL, John. Taxable on plantation of Jacob Giles, Jr., Susquehanna Hundred, 1776.

LOVEL, Peter. Taxable in Spesutia Lower Hundred, 1776.

LOVELL, Peter. Taxable in Spesutia Lower Hundred, 1775.

LOWERY, John. Taxable in Deer Creek Upper Hundred, 1775.

LOYAD, Thomas. Taxable in household of Ralph Piles, Spesutia Upper Hundred, 1775.

LUDWICK, Warner. Taxable in household of Jacob Forward, Spesutia Lower Hundred, 1775.

LUNAN, Osmond. Taxable at Jacob Forward's Quarters, Spesutia Lower Hundred, 1776.

LUSBY, Betty (widow). Head of household in Gunpowder Lower Hundred, 1775, with taxable slaves Hector and Jack listed in her household.

LUSBY, Milkey. Head of household in Gunpowder Lower Hundred, 1775, with taxable slave Rachael listed in her household.

LUTTERFEILD, Charles. Taxable on plantation of Jacob Giles, Susquehanna Hundred, 1776.

LYON, Jonathan. Taxable in Bush River Upper Hundred, 1775, with taxables Leonard Lyon (son) and slaves Tom and Fanny listed in his household.

LYON, Leonard. Taxable in household of Jonathan Lyon, Bush River Upper Hundred, 1775.

LYTLE, Elizabeth. Head of household in Gunpowder Lower Hundred, 1775, with taxable slaves Jim, Lawtur, Cupit, Toney, Hannah, and Gin listed in her household.

LYTLE, James. Taxable in Gunpowder Lower Hundred, 1775, with taxable slave Pol listed in his household.

MACKEY, George. Taxable in Susquehanna Hundred, 1775 [The tax list indicated 2 taxables in this household, but only named one].

MADDEN, James. Taxable in Bush River Upper

Hundred, 1775.

MADDEN, Philip. Taxable in Bush River Upper Hundred, 1775.

MAFITT, Andrew. Taxable in Gunpowder Lower Hundred, 1775, with taxable Pat Mullan listed in his household.

MAGILL, William. Taxable in Susquehanna Hundred, 1775, with a taxable servant man, no name given, listed in his household.

MAHAN, William. Taxable in Susquehanna Hundred, 1775.

MAHHAN, John. See "Thomas Coen," q.v.

MAHHON, James. Taxable in Susquehanna Hundred, 1776.

MAHHON, William. Taxable in Susquehanna Hundred, 1776.

MAHON, John. See "Thomas Cowan," q.v.

MAHON, John. Taxable in Susquehanna Hundred, 1775.

MAJOR, John. Taxable in household of Samuel Griffith, Spesutia Lower Hundred, 1775.

MAJOR, John. Taxable in Deer Creek Upper Hundred, 1775.

MAJOR, John. Taxable on plantation of Samuel Griffith, Spesutia Lower Hundred, 1776.

MAJOR, Thomas. Taxable in Bush River Upper Hundred, 1775.

MAJORS, Thomas. Taxable in Bush River Lower Hundred, 1775.

MAKENSON, Andrew Jr. Taxable in Bush River Upper Hundred, 1775.

MAKENSON, Andrew Sr. Taxable in Bush River Upper Hundred, 1775.

MAKENSON, John. Taxable in Bush River Upper Hundred, 1775.

MALARKY, Michael. Taxable in Spesutia Lower Hundred, 1775, with James Kelly as his security.

MALEN, Patrick. Taxable in household of David Benfield, Bush River Lower Hundred, 1775.

MALFELD, Daniel. Taxable in Susquehanna Hundred, 1776.

MANLEY, Jesse. Taxable in Spesutia Lower Hundred, 1775.

MARCHEL, John. Taxable in Susquehanna Hundred, 1776.

MARNHAM, John. Taxable on the plantation of Amos Garrett, Spesutia Lower Hundred, 1775.

MARRICK, William. Taxable in Bush River Lower Hundred, 1775, with 2 taxables in his household, but only his name was given.

MARROTT, William. Taxable in Bush River Lower Hundred, 1775.

MARSH, Lloyd. Taxable in Spesutia Lower Hundred, 1775.

MARSH, Lloyd. Taxable in Spesutia Lower Hundred, 1776.

MARSHAL, John. Taxable in Susquehanna Hundred, 1775.

MARTHEW, Patrick. Taxable in household of Samson Eagon, Bush River Upper Hundred, 1775.

MARTIN, Able. Taxable in household of Thomas Ruchman, Deer Creek Upper Hundred, 1775.

MARTIN, Alexander. Taxable in Susquehanna Hundred, 1775.

MARTIN, Charles. Taxable (servant) in household of William Jones, Deer Creek Upper Hundred, 1775.

MARTIN, Edward. Taxable in Susquehanna Hundred, 1775. [Following his name on the list is William ---- (blank), so it is possible his name was William Martin. He is listed in a separate household from Edward Martin because each name has the number "1" after it rather than a total of "2"].

MARTIN, Isaac. Taxable (servant) in household of Thomas Waltham, Gunpowder Lower Hundred, 1775.

MARTIN, Walter. Taxable in Bush River Lower Hundred, 1775.

MARTIN, William. See "Edwad Martin," q.v.

MARTIN, William. Taxable in Susquehanna Hundred, 1775.

MARTIN, William. Taxable (servant) in household of Benjamin Biddel, Bush River Upper Hundred, 1775.

MARTON, Allexander. Taxable in Susquehanna Hundred, 1776.

MARTON, Edward. Taxable in Susquehanna Hundred, 1776.

MARTON, James. Taxable in household of Mathew Marton, Susquehanna Hundred, 1776.

MARTON, Mathew. Taxable in Susquehanna Hundred, 1776, with taxable James Marton listed in his household.

MARTON, William. Taxable in Susquehanna Hundred, 1776.

MATHERS, James. Taxable in Bush River Lower Hundred, 1775, with taxables Michael Mathers, Thomas Mathers, and servant Darby Duyr [sic] listed in his household.

MATHERS, Michael. Taxable in household of James Mathers, Bush River Lower Hundred, 1775.

MATHERS, Thomas. Taxable in household of James Mathers, Bush River Lower Hundred, 1775.

MATHEW, Michael. Taxable (servant) in household of Alexander Rigdon, Deer Creek Upper Hundred, 1775.

MATHEWS, John (captain). Taxable in Spesutia Lower Hundred, 1776, with taxables Roger Mathews, John Mathews, and negroes Nobb, George, George Jr., Joe, Thomasine, Rachael, and June listed on his plantation.

MATHEWS, John. Taxable in household of Capt. John Mathews, Spesutia Lower Hundred, 1776.

MATHEWS, Leven. Taxable in Spesutia Lower

Hundred, 1776, with taxable negroes Sip, Jacob, Phillis, and Bett listed in his household.

MATHEWS, Roger. Taxable in household of Capt. John Mathews, Spesutia Lower Hundred, 1776.

MATTHEWS, Bennett. Taxable in Spesutia Upper Hundred, 1775, with taxables William Williams and negroes Sharper, Dick, Fillis, and Grace listed in his household.

MATTHEWS, Ignatius. Taxable in Spesutia Upper Hundred, 1775, with taxable negroes David, Jacob, Charles, and Dino listed in his household.

MATTHEWS, James. Security for Daniel Dugless (molato), 1775.

MATTHEWS, James. Taxable in Bush River Lower Hundred, 1775. [The entry is worded as "James Mathews, Negroes & Servants - 5" followed by the words "Burnt Sqr. hands" and then followed by a straight line "----" and then with a large "X" through the entire entry].

MATTHEWS, John Jr. Taxable in household of John Matthews, Spesutia Lower Hundred, 1775.

MATTHEWS, John. Taxable in Spesutia Lower Hundred, 1775, with taxables Roger Matthews, John Matthews, Jr., and slaves Will, Nob, Sharper, Old George, George 2nd, Joe, Tomson, Rachael, Barb, and another slave (name illegible) listed on his plantation.

MATTHEWS, Leven. Taxable in Spesutia Lower Hundred, 1775, with taxables John Whitekar and slaves Phillis, Sip, Jack, and Bett listed in his household.

MATTHEWS, Patrick. See "Samson Eagon," q.v.

MATTHEWS, Roger. Taxable in household of John Matthews, Spesutia Lower Hundred, 1775.

MAULSBY, David. Taxable in Bush River Lower Hundred, 1775, with taxables John Maulsby and Wheeler Maulsby listed in his household.

MAULSBY, John. Taxable in household of David Maulsby, Bush River Lower Hundred, 1775.

MAULSBY, Wheeler. Taxable in household of David Maulsby, Bush River Lower Hundred, 1775.

MAXWELL, James (captain). Taxable in Gunpowder Lower Hundred, 1775, with taxables James Maxwell (son) and slaves Prince, Cornelius, Zedor, Soldier, Charles, Dick, Sam, Gin, Sal, Hanna, Beck, and Phy listed in his household.

MAXWELL, James (son of James). Taxable in household of his father Capt. James Maxwell, Gunpowder Lower Hundred, 1775.

MAY, James. Taxable in Spesutia Upper Hundred, 1775.

MAY, William. Taxable in Spesutia Upper Hundred, 1775.

McADOW, John. Taxable in Spesutia Upper Hundred, 1775.

McANTOS, Hugh. Taxable in household of Robert Culver, Susquehanna Hundred, 1776.

McBRIDE, John. Taxable in Spesutia Lower Hundred, 1775.

McCALHANEY, Marthew. Taxable in Bush River Upper Hundred, 1775.

McCALL, John Sr. Taxable in Deer Creek Upper Hundred, 1775.

McCALL, John. Taxable in household of John Whiteford, Deer Creek Upper Hundred, 1775.

McCAN, Patrick. See "Patrick Mecan," q.v.

McCANDLES, William. Taxable in Susquehanna Hundred, 1776.

McCANDLESS, William. Taxable in Susquehanna Hundred, 1775.

McCANNA, George. Taxable in Bush River Upper Hundred, 1775.

McCARDEL, Patrick. Taxable in Susquehanna Hundred, 1775.

McCARTIE, Daniel. Taxable in Spesutia Lower Hundred, 1775.

McCARTIE, Samuel. Taxable in Spesutia Lower Hundred, 1775.

McCARTY, Jacob. Taxable in Susquehanna Hundred, 1775.

McCARTY, Owen. Taxable in household of Josias Hall, Susquehanna Hundred, 1776.

McCARTY, Sarah. Head of household in Susquehanna Hundred, 1775, with taxable Joss Bendal listed in her household.

McCARY, Robert. Taxable in Deer Creek Upper Hundred, 1775.

McCASKEY, John. Taxable in Deer Creek Upper Hundred, 1775.

McCENSY, Edward. Taxable in Spesutia Upper Hundred, 1775.

McCLAIN, Patrick. Taxable in Spesutia Lower Hundred, 1776.

McCLAN, John. Taxable in Bush River Upper Hundred, 1775, with taxable John Orr (servant) listed in his household.

McCLANE, Alexander. Taxable in Spesutia Upper Hundred, 1775.

McCLENTICK, Mathew (son of Mathew). Taxable in household of his father Mathew McClentick, Spesutia Upper Hundred, 1775.

McCLENTICK, Mathew. Taxable in Spesutia Upper Hundred, 1775, with taxable Mathew McClentick (son) listed in his household.

McCLOSKY, Joseph. Taxable in Bush River Upper Hundred, 1775.

McCLUER, Robert. Taxable in Spesutia Upper Hundred, 1775.

McCLUER, William. Taxable in Spesutia Upper

Hundred, 1775.

McCLUGHLEN, John. Taxable in Deer Creek Upper Hundred, 1775.

McCLUNG, Adam. Taxable in Bush River Upper Hundred, 1775, with a taxable servant (no name given) listed in his household.

McCLURA (McCLUNA?), Nathan. Taxable in Bush River Upper Hundred, 1775, with taxable William Night listed in his household.

McCLURE, John. Taxable in Bush River Upper Hundred, 1775.

McCOMAS, Aaron. Taxable in Bush River Lower Hundred, 1775.

McCOMAS, Alexander. Taxable in Bush River Lower Hundred, 1775, with taxable slaves Pegg and Sall listed in his household.

McCOMAS, Alexander. Taxable in Spesutia Lower Hundred, 1775.

McCOMAS, Benjamin (son of Alexander). Taxable in Spesutia Lower Hundred, 1775.

McCOMAS, Daniel. See "Donnill McCommos," q.v.

McCOMAS, Daniel. Taxable in Bush River Lower Hundred, 1775, with taxable negroes Triall and John listed in his household.

McCOMAS, Edward. Taxable in Bush River Lower Hundred, 1775.

McCOMAS, James. Taxable in Bush River Lower Hundred, 1775, with taxable negroes Buck, Toney, Dider, and Luta listed in his household.

McCOMAS, John (son of Alexander). Taxable in Spesutia Lower Hundred, 1775.

McCOMAS, John. Taxable in Bush River Lower Hundred, 1775, with taxable Thomas Bove listed in his household.

McCOMAS, John. Taxable in Bush River Lower Hundred, 1775, with taxable negroes Samson and Grace listed in his household.

McCOMAS, John. Taxable in Bush River Upper Hundred, 1775.

McCOMAS, Martha. Head of household in Bush River Lower Hundred, 1775, with taxable negroes Samson and Phebe listed in her household.

McCOMAS, Moses. Taxable in Bush River Lower Hundred, 1775, with taxable servant Patrick Ford listed in his household.

McCOMAS, Sarah (widow). See "Sarrah McCommos (widdow)," q.v.

McCOMAS, Solomon. Taxable in Bush River Lower Hundred, 1775, with taxables William McComas and negro Ceesar listed in his household.

McCOMAS, William. See "William McCommos," q.v.

McCOMAS, William. Taxable in household of Solomon McComas, Bush River Lower Hundred, 1775.

McCOMMOS, Donnill. Taxable in Bush River Upper Hundred, 1775, with taxable negro Dina listed in his household.

McCOMMOS, Sarrah (widdow). Head of household in Bush River Upper Hundred, 1775, with taxable negroes Pomp and Tamar listed in her household.

McCOMMOS, William Sr. Taxable in Bush River Upper Hundred, 1775, with taxable negro wench Dina listed in his household.

McCOMMOS, William. Taxable in Bush River Upper Hundred, 1775, with taxable negroes Dina and Filus listed in his household.

McCORMICK, John. Taxable in Gunpowder Lower Hundred, 1775.

McCOY, Andrew. See "Robert McCoy" and "William McCoy," q.v.

McCOY, Robert. Taxable in Deer Creek Upper Hundred, 1775, with Andrew McCoy as his security.

McCOY, William. Taxable in Deer Creek Upper Hundred, 1775, with Andrew McCoy as his security.

McCRACKIN, James. Taxable in Spesutia Lower Hundred, 1775, with taxables Thomas Nowlen and Garrett Fitsjarrold listed in his household.

McCRACKIN, James. Taxable in Spesutia Lower Hundred, 1776, with taxable Thomas Noulon listed in his household.

McCULGAN, Chirnelius. Taxable in Bush River Lower Hundred, 1775.

McCULICK, David. Taxable in Bush River Upper Hundred, 1775.

McCULLACK, Alexander. Taxable in Bush River Upper Hundred, 1775, with taxables James McCullack (son) and William McCullack (son) listed in his household.

McCULLACK, James (son of Alexander). Taxable in household of his father Alexander McCullack, Bush River Upper Hundred, 1775.

McCULLACK, William (son of Alexander). Taxable in household of his father Alexander McCullack, Bush River Upper Hundred, 1775.

McCULLOUGH, John. Taxable in Deer Creek Lower Hundred, 1775.

McCULLOUGH, Thomas. See "Jonathan Starrat," q.v.

McCURDEY, Archable. Taxable in Susquehanna Hundred, 1776.

McCURDY, Archabald. Taxable in Susquehanna Hundred, 1775.

McDANIEL, Neale. Taxable in Bush River Upper Hundred, 1775.

McDANIEL, Thomas. Taxable in the household of William Young, Spesutia Lower Hundred, 1775.

McDONNEL, Curnelus. Taxable in Bush River Upper Hundred, 1775, with taxables John McDonnel (son) and a servant man (no name given) listed in his household.

McDONNEL, John. Taxable in household of Curnelus

McDonnel, Bush River Upper Hundred, 1775.

McDORNEL, Thomas. Taxable in the household of William Young, Spesutia Lower Hundred, 1775.

McDOWELL, John. Taxable on the plantation of Amos Garrett, Spesutia Lower Hundred, 1775.

McFADDEN, John. Taxable in Deer Creek Upper Hundred, 1775, with taxable man M. Kelly (servant) listed in his household.

McFADDON, Joseph. Taxable in Susquehanna Hundred, 1776.

McFADEN, Joseph. Taxable in Susquehanna Hundred, 1775.

McFADON, Samuel. Taxable in Susquehanna Hundred, 1775.

McFAUL, Daniel. Taxable in Susquehanna Hundred, 1775.

McGILL, William. See "William Megill," q.v.

McGILLIGAN, Thomas. Taxable in Bush River Upper Hundred, 1775.

McGILTON, ---- (no first name given). Taxable (servant) in household of Robert Hawkins, Deer Creek Upper Hundred, 1775.

McGOMERY, Thomas. Taxable in Deer Creek Upper Hundred, 1775.

McGOUGH, Hugh. Taxable in Deer Creek Upper Hundred, 1775.

McGUIER, Phillip. Taxable in Spesutia Upper Hundred, 1775.

McHALLAN, Patrick. Taxable in household of William Ashmore, Deer Creek Upper Hundred, 1775.

McILHANEY, Matthew. See "Marthew McIlhaney," q.v.

McINTOSH, Hugh. See "Hugh McAntos," q.v.

McINTOSH, Hugh. Taxable in household of Robert Culver, Susquehanna Hundred, 1775.

McKINDLEY, Roger. Taxable in Bush River Upper Hundred, 1775.

McKISSON, John. Taxable in Deer Creek Lower Hundred, 1775.

McLAUGHLIN, ----. See "George McLaughlin," q.v.

McLAUGHLIN, George. Taxable in Spesutia Upper Hundred, 1775, with taxable son (name not given) listed in his household. [The actual entry looks like "& son" were added later and the number of taxables was changed from 1 to 2].

McMASTERS, Alexander. Taxable in Bush River Upper Hundred, 1775.

McMATH, Samuel. Taxable in Spesutia Upper Hundred, 1775. [It is interesting to note that although his name is the only one listed as a taxable in this household, the constable made the "S" on Samuel very large and inserted the number "2" in the bottom loop of the "S"].

McMATH, William. Taxable in Bush River Lower Hundred, 1775.

McMOLE(?), William. Taxable in Deer Creek Upper Hundred, 1775.

McMULLEN, Samuel. Taxable in Bush River Lower Hundred, 1775, with Edward Norris (son of Joseph) as his security.

McMULLEN, William. Taxable in Bush River Lower Hundred, 1775, with Edward Norris (son of Joseph) as his security.

McMURPHEY, Archibald. Taxable in Spesutia Lower Hundred, 1775.

McMURPHEY, Archibald. Taxable in Spesutia Lower Hundred, 1776, with Moses Loney as his security.

McNABB, James. Taxable in Deer Creek Lower Hundred, 1775.

McNAIR, Robert. Taxable in Deer Creek Upper Hundred, 1775, with taxable man John Gladden (servant) listed in his household.

McNEMARER, Joseph. Taxable in household of William Ashmore, Deer Creek Upper Hundred, 1775.

MEADS, James Jr. Taxable in Bush River Upper Hundred, 1775, with a taxable servant man (no name given) listed in his household.

MEADS, James. Taxable in Bush River Upper Hundred, 1775.

MEAK, Andra. Taxable in Susquehanna Hundred, 1776, with taxable John Crage listed in his household.

MECAN, Auther. Taxable in Susquehanna Hundred, 1776.

MECAN, Patrick. Taxable in Susquehanna Hundred, 1776.

MEED, Benjamin. Taxable in Gunpowder Lower Hundred, 1775, with taxable slave Daphney listed in his household. See "James Or," q.v.

MEEKS, Andrew. Taxable in Susquehanna Hundred, 1775, with taxable Thomas Houley listed inmhis household.

MEGAY, George. Taxable in the household of Robert Megay, Spesutia Lower Hundred, 1775.

MEGAY, Robert. Taxable in Spesutia Lower Hundred, 1775, with taxables George Megay and John Richards listed in his household.

MEGILL, William. Taxable in Susquehanna Hundred, 1776, with taxable John Owen listed in his household.

MELONE, Hugh. Taxable (servant) in household of Samuel Calwell, Bush River Lower Hundred, 1775.

MICHAEL, Balcher. Taxable in Susquehanna Hundred, 1775, with taxables John Hardin and Negro Sall listed in his household.

MICHEL, John. Taxable in household of William Coal (carpenter), Deer Creek Lower Hundred, 1775.

MIDLETON, Joseph. Taxable in Gunpowder Lower Hundred, 1775.

MIERS, John. Taxable in Spesutia Lower Hundred, 1775.

MILES, Aquila. See "Joshua Miles," q.v.

EARLY HARFORD COUNTIANS: Supplement

MILES, John. Taxable in Deer Creek Upper Hundred, 1775.
MILES, Joshua. Taxable in Bush River Upper Hundred, 1775, with taxable servant(?) Aquil Mills [sic] and negro Moll listed in his household. [In spite of what it appears, this "Aquil Mills" could actually be "Aquila Miles" who was the brother of Joshua Miles, as shown on another tax list].
MILES, McGough. Taxable in Deer Creek Upper Hundred, 1775.
MILES, Peter. Taxable in Bush River Upper Hundred, 1775, with Thomas Bond as his security.
MILL, Thomas. See "William Diven," q.v.
MILLAR, Margaret (widow). Head of household in Susquehanna Hundred, 1776, with taxable Samuel Millar listed in her household.
MILLAR, Samuel. Taxable in household of Margaret Millar (widow), Susquehanna Hundred, 1776.
MILLER, John. Taxable on plantation of William Webb, Deer Creek Upper Hundred, 1775.
MILLER, Joseph. Taxable in Deer Creek Upper Hundred, 1775, with William Ashmore as his security.
MILLS, Aquil. See "Joshua Miles," q.v.
MILLS, John. Taxable in household of Robert Miles, Susquehanna Hundred, 1775.
MILLS, Richard. Taxable in Gunpowder Lower Hundred, 1775.
MILLS, Robert. Taxable in Susquehanna Hundred, 1775, with taxable John Miles listed in his household. See "Robert Smith," q.v.
MILLS, Thomas. Taxable in Gunpowder Lower Hundred, 1775, with taxable slave Fan listed in his household.
MILS, John. Taxable in household of Robert Mils [sic], Susquehanna Hundred, 1776.
MILS [sic], Robert. Taxable in Susquehanna Hundred, 1776, with taxables John Dockket, James Grant, and John Mils listed in his household.
MITCHEL, Edward. Taxable in Susquehanna Hundred, 1775, with taxable negro Tom listed in his household.
MITCHEL, Edward. Taxable in Susquehanna Hundred, 1776, with taxable negroes Tom and Mary listed in his household.
MITCHEL, Gabril. Taxable in household of John Mitchel, Susquehanna Hundred, 1776.
MITCHEL, James (farmer). Taxable in Susquehanna Hundred, 1775.
MITCHEL, James (weaver). Taxable in Susquehanna Hundred, 1776, with taxables Mical Belshur, John Harton, and negro Sal listed in his household.
MITCHEL, James. Taxable in Susquehanna Hundred, 1775.
MITCHEL, James. Taxable in Susquehanna Hundred, 1776, with taxable William Price listed in his household.
MITCHEL, John. Taxable in Susquehanna Hundred, 1775, with taxable John Mitchel listed in his household. [The entry actually had "John Mitchel" written on one line, with "Ditto" written beneath it, and the number of taxables as 2, thus indicating that both taxables were named John Mitchel].
MITCHEL, John. Taxable in Susquehanna Hundred, 1776, with taxables Gabril Mitchel and Richard Perkins listed in his household.
MITCHEL, Kent Jr. Taxable in Susquehanna Hundred, 1776, with taxable Samuel Johston [sic] listed in his household.
MITCHEL, Kent. Taxable in Susquehanna Hundred, 1775, with taxables Samuel Johnson and James Jones listed in his household.
MITCHEL, Kent. Taxable in Susquehanna Hundred, 1775, with taxable negro Pug listed in his household.
MITCHEL, Kent. Taxable in Susquehanna Hundred, 1776, with taxable negro Smug listed in his household.
MITCHEL, Micaja. Taxable in Susquehanna Hundred, 1775, with taxable negro Tomey listed in his household. [The name looked like "Meiaja Mitchel" on the tax list, but it is undoubtedly "Micajah Mitchell" who was a private in the Harford County militia in 1775].
MITCHEL, Micajh [Micajah]. Taxable in Susquehanna Hundred, 1776, with taxable negro Toney listed in his household.
MITCHEL, Thomas Jr. Taxable in Susquehanna Hundred, 1776, with taxable negro Hagro listed in his household.
MITCHEL, Thomas. Taxable in Susquehanna Hundred, 1775, with taxable negro Bob listed in his household.
MITCHEL, Thomas. Taxable in Susquehanna Hundred, 1775, with taxable negro Hagar listed in his household.
MITCHEL Thomas. Taxable in Susquehanna Hundred, 1776, with taxable negro Bob listed in his household.
MITCHEL, William. Taxable in Susquehanna Hundred, 1775.
MITCHEL, William. Taxable in Susquehanna Hundred, 1776.
MITCHELL, Robert. Taxable in Bush River Lower Hundred, 1775.
MOLLETSANT, John. Taxable in household of Josiah Hitchcock, Bush River Upper Hundred, 1775.
MONK, Richard. Taxable in Gunpowder Lower Hundred, 1775, with taxable William Monk listed in his household.
MONK, William. Taxable in household of Richard Monk, Gunpowder Lower Hundred, 1775.

MONROE, John. Taxable in the household of Samuel Kimble, Spesutia Lower Hundred, 1775.

MONROE, John. Taxable in household of Samuel Kimble, Spesutia Lower Hundred, 1776.

MONTGOMERY, John. Taxable in Deer Creek Lower Hundred, 1775, with taxable man Willam How (servant) listed in his household.

MONTGOMERY, William. Taxable in Deer Creek Lower Hundred, 1775.

MOOBERRY, William Jr. Taxable in Spesutia Lower Hundred, 1775, with John Diemer as his security.

MOOBERRY, William. Taxable in Spesutia Lower Hundred, 1775, with "a James Phillips." [Note: Both appear to have been taxable, but the constable wrote "1" instead of "2" for the total number taxed].

MOOBERRY, William. Taxable in Spesutia Lower Hundred, 1776.

MOORE, Daniel. Taxable in Deer Creek Upper Hundred, 1775.

MOORE, James (doctor). Taxable in Bush River Upper Hundred, 1775.

MOORE, James. Taxable in Bush River Lower Hundred, 1775.

MOORE, Willliam. Taxable in Deer Creek Upper Hundred, 1775.

MORATTA, Dannael. Taxable in Spesutia Upper Hundred, 1775.

MORES, James (son of John). Taxable in household of James Mores, Spesutia Upper Hundred, 1775.

MORES, James. See "Robert Hart," q.v.

MORES, James. Taxable in Spesutia Upper Hundred, 1775, with taxables Henry Ruff, Jr., James Mores (son of John), and negroes Toney, Jack, Rose, and Easter listed in his household.

MORGAN, Elizabeth. Head of household in Deer Creek Lower Hundred, 1775, with taxable negros James and Priss listed in her household. [This information was added at the end of the tax list].

MORGAN, John. Taxable in Deer Creek Lower Hundred, 1775. See "Thomas Stephenson" and "William Ellis," q.v.

MORGAN, Robert. Taxable in Deer Creek Lower Hundred, 1775, with taxable negroes J----, P----, and Mike listed in his household. [part of tax list dark and illegible].

MORGAN, Samuel. Taxable in Deer Creek Upper Hundred, 1775, with taxable negroes Ned, Kate, and Sall listed in his household. See "William Connelly" and "James Cooper," q.v.

MORGAN, William. Taxable in Deer Creek Upper Hundred, 1775, with taxable negroes Phil, Tom, Nan, and Vilet listed in his household.

MORISON, Dugal. Taxable in Deer Creek Lower Hundred, 1775.

MORRIS, Edward. Taxable in Spesutia Lower Hundred, 1775.

MORRIS, John. Taxable (servant) in household of Charles Baker, Bush River Upper Hundred, 1775.

MORRIS, John. Taxable in household of Timothy Murphey, Spesutia Lower Hundred, 1776.

MORRIS, Michael. Taxable in Spesutia Lower Hundred, 1775.

MOULDER (MOULDEN?), Richard. Taxable (servant) in household of Edward Robeson, Bush River Upper Hundred, 1775.

MUBURY, George. Taxable in household of Stephen Hill, Spesutia Upper Hundred, 1775.

MULATTO Daniel. See "Daniel Dugless" and "Sarah Dugless," q.v.

MULLAN, Pat. Taxable in household of Andrew Mafitt, Gunpowder Lower Hundred, 1775.

MUNDAY, James. Taxable in Bush River Lower Hundred, 1775.

MURDOCH, William. Taxable in Deer Creek Upper Hundred, 1775.

MURFEY, James. Taxable in Susquehanna Hundred, 1776.

MURFEY, Partrick. Taxable in household of Rev. John Clark, Bush River Upper Hundred, 1775.

MURFORD, Stephen. Taxable in Deer Creek Upper Hundred, 1775, with John Scharbrough as his security.

MURPHEY, Edward. Taxable in Spesutia Lower Hundred, 1775.

MURPHEY, Timothy. Taxable in Spesutia Lower Hundred, 1776, with taxable John Morris listed in his household.

MURPHEY, William (cooper). Taxable in Spesutia Lower Hundred, 1776.

MURPHEY, William. Taxable in Spesutia Lower Hundred, 1776, with taxable William Hailey listed in his household.

MURPHY, Hugh (son of Patrick). Taxable in household of his father Patrick Murphy, Spesutia Upper Hundred, 1775.

MURPHY, Patrick. See "Partrick Murfey," q.v.

MURPHY, Patrick. Taxable in Spesutia Upper Hundred, 1775, with taxable Hugh Murphy (son) listed in his household.

MURPHY, Peter. Taxable in household of Garret Garretson, Spesutia Lower Hundred, 1775.

MURPHY, Timothy. Taxable in Spesutia Lower Hundred, 1775, with Amos Cord as his security.

MURPHY, William (cooper). Taxable in Spesutia Lower Hundred, 1775.

MURPHY, William. See "William Hailey," q.v.

MURPHY, William. Taxable in household of Samuel Forwood, Spesutia Upper Hundred, 1775.

MURRAY, Edward. Taxable in Susquehanna Hundred, 1775. [tax list smudged; difficult to read].

MURRAY, James. Taxable in household of Richard Ruff, Spesutia Upper Hundred, 1775.

MURRY, ---- (son of Alexander). Taxable in household of his father Alexander Murry, Deer Creek Lower Hundred, 1775.

MURRY, Alexander. Taxable in Deer Creek Lower Hundred, 1775, with taxable son (no name given) listed in his household.

MUSGROVE, Francis. Taxable in household of William Hawkins, Susquehanna Hundred, 1775.

MUSKGROVE, Francis. Taxable in household of William Hawkins, Susquehanna Hundred, 1776.

NEALE, Charles. Taxable in household of William Bradford, Spesutia Upper Hundred, 1775.

NEEGLE, James. Taxable in the household of Samuel Sutton, Spesutia Lower Hundred, 1775.

NEGRO ---- (illegible). Taxable on plantation of John Matthews, Spesutia Lower Hundred, 1775.

NEGRO ---- (no name given). Taxable in Bush River Lower Hundred, 1775, owned by William Downs.

NEGRO ---- (no name given). See "Daniel Anderson, Sr.," q.v.

NEGRO ---- (no name given). See "Walter Tolley," q.v.

NEGRO ---- (no name given). Taxable in household of Edward Bessie (Bessic?), Bush River Upper Hundred, 1775.

NEGRO ---- (no name given). Taxable at Zacheus Onion's Quarters, Bush River Upper Hundred, 1775.

NEGRO Aaron. Taxable in household of Casandra Sheridine (widow), Deer Creek Lower Hundred, 1775.

NEGRO Abey. Taxable on plantation of William Hall, Spesutia Lower Hundred, 1776.

NEGRO Abigail. Taxable on plantation of Capt. John Hall, Spesutia Lower Hundred, 1775.

NEGRO Abigail. Taxable in household of Samuel Griffith, Spesutia Lower Hundred, 1775.

NEGRO Abigail. Taxable in the household of Samuel Kimble, Spesutia Lower Hundred, 1775.

NEGRO Abigail. Taxable in household of Samuel Kimble, Spesutia Lower Hundred, 1776.

NEGRO Abigail. Taxable on plantation of Samuel Griffith, Spesutia Lower Hundred, 1776.

NEGRO Abner. Taxable in household of Thomas Wheler, Spesutia Upper Hundred, 1775.

NEGRO Abraham. Taxable in household of William Hall, Spesutia Lower Hundred, 1775.

NEGRO Abraham. Taxable in household of Larrance Clark, Spesutia Upper Hundred, 1775.

NEGRO Abraham. Taxable in household of Moses Ruth, Jr., Spesutia Upper Hundred, 1775.

NEGRO Abraham. Taxable in household of Francis Downing, Deer Creek Lower Hundred, 1775.

NEGRO Abraham. Taxable on plantation of William Hall, Spesutia Lower Hundred, 1776.

NEGRO Abraham. Taxable in household of Henry Spencer, Susquehanna Hundred, 1776.

NEGRO Abram. Taxable in household of Thomas Whelar, Bush River Upper Hundred, 1775.

NEGRO Aby. Taxable in household of William Hall, Spesutia Lower Hundred, 1775.

NEGRO Ada. Taxable in Susquehanna Hundred, 1775 William Wilson, Susquehanna Hundred, 1775.

NEGRO Adam. Taxable in household of Peter Bond, Bush River Lower Hundred, 1775.

NEGRO Adam. Taxable in household of John Peca, Bush River Lower Hundred, 1775.

NEGRO Adam. Taxable at William Smith's Quarters, Susquehanna Hundred, 1775.

NEGRO Adam. Taxable in household of Godfrey Waters, Susquehanna Hundred, 1775.

NEGRO Adam. Taxable in household of Josias William Dallam, Spesutia Lower Hundred, 1775.

NEGRO Adam. Taxable on plantation of Josias William Dallam, Spesutia Lower Hundred, 1776.

NEGRO Adam. Taxable in household of Henry Vansickleton, Spesutia Lower Hundred, 1776.

NEGRO Adam. Taxable in household of William Wilson, Susquehanna Hundred, 1776.

NEGRO Adam. Taxable in household of Godfery Watters, Susquehanna Hundred, 1776.

NEGRO Addam. Taxable in household of Henry Green, Spesutia Upper Hundred, 1775.

NEGRO Addam. Taxable in household of Martin Preston, Spesutia Upper Hundred, 1775.

NEGRO Affey. Taxable in Bush River Lower Hundred, 1775, with Henry Wilson, Sr. as her security.

NEGRO Affey. Taxable in household of Richard Johns, Susquehanna Hundred, 1775.

NEGRO Affey. Taxable in household of Negro Thomas (a free negro), Susquehanna Hundred, 1776.

NEGRO Agnus. Taxable at William Paca's Quarters, Spesutia Lower Hundred, 1775.

NEGRO Agnus. Taxable on plantation of Thomas Gash, Spesutia Lower Hundred, 1776.

NEGRO Akhilles. Taxable in household of Robbert Bishop, Gunpowder Lower Hundred, 1775.

NEGRO Aleck. Taxable in household of Richard Hargrove, Spesutia Upper Hundred, 1775.

NEGRO Alexander. Taxable in household of John Diemer, Spesutia Lower Hundred, 1775.

NEGRO Alice. Taxable in the household of James Taylor, Sr., Spesutia Lower Hundred, 1775.

NEGRO Alice. Taxable in household of James Taylor, Sr., Spesutia Lower Hundred, 1776.

NEGRO Ambo. Taxable at Thomas Harrison's Quarters,

Susquehanna Hundred, 1775.
NEGRO Amey. Taxable in household of Benjaman Wilson, Deer Creek Lower Hundred, 1775.
NEGRO Amey. Taxable on plantation of Hannah Hall, Spesutia Lower Hundred, 1776.
NEGRO Amey. Taxable at Dr. Henry Stephenson's Quarters, Spesutia Lower Hundred, 1776.
NEGRO Ammey. Taxable in household of Phillip Henderson, Spesutia Upper Hundred, 1775.
NEGRO Anderson. Taxable in household of John Archer, Spesutia Upper Hundred, 1775.
NEGRO Andrew. Taxable in household of Thomas Peregrin Frisby, Spesutia Lower Hundred, 1775.
NEGRO Andrew. Taxable at Cumberland Forge, Deer Creek Lower Hundred, 1775.
NEGRO Andrew. Taxable on plantation of George Ford, Spesutia Lower Hundred, 1776.
NEGRO Andrew. Taxable in household of Thomas Peregrine Frisby, Spesutia Lower Hundred, 1776.
NEGRO Ann. Taxable in household of Freeborn Garretson, Spesutia Lower Hundred, 1775.
NEGRO Ann. Taxable in household of Thomas Peregrine Frisby, Spesutia Lower Hundred, 1776.
NEGRO Ann. Taxable in household of Daniel Anderson, Susquehanna Hundred, 1776.
NEGRO Anna. Taxable in household of Jacob Giles, Susquehanna Hundred, 1775.
NEGRO Annabaal. Taxable at Cumberland Forge, Deer Creek Lower Hundred, 1775.
NEGRO Annaboe. Taxable at Thomas Harrison's Quarters, Susquehanna Hundred, 1776.
NEGRO Anneble. Taxables on plantation of Col. Thomas White, Susquehanna Hundred, 1776.
NEGRO Antinoy. Taxable in household of Daniel Nutawell, Susquehanna Hundred, 1776.
NEGRO Antony. Taxable in household of Jacob Bond, Sr., Bush River Lower Hundred, 1775.
NEGRO Antony. Taxable in household of Samuel Lee, Spesutia Upper Hundred, 1775.
NEGRO Araco. Taxable in household of John Hays, Sr., Spesutia Upper Hundred, 1775.
NEGRO Augustus. Taxable on plantation of Hannah Hall, Spesutia Lower Hundred, 1775.
NEGRO Augustus. Taxable on plantation of Hannah Hall, Spesutia Lower Hundred, 1776.
NEGRO Austin. Taxable "at ye glebe" of Rev. William West, Spesutia Lower Hundred, 1775.
NEGRO Bacchus. Taxable on plantation of Capt. John Hall, Spesutia Lower Hundred, 1775.
NEGRO Bacheus. Taxable in household of Isaac Webster, Spesutia Upper Hundred, 1775.
NEGRO Bachus. Taxable in household of Nathaniel Rigbie, Deer Creek Lower Hundred, 1775.
NEGRO Bachus. Taxable in household of William Wells, Deer Creek Upper Hundred, 1775.
NEGRO Bale. Taxable in household of Archibald Beaty, Spesutia Lower Hundred, 1775.
NEGRO Barb. Taxable on plantation of John Matthews, Spesutia Lower Hundred, 1775.
NEGRO Barbara. Taxable in household of Freeborn Brown, Spesutia Lower Hundred, 1775.
NEGRO Basiel. Taxable in household of Joseph Everest, Spesutia Lower Hundred, 1775.
NEGRO Basiel. Taxable in household of Joseph Everest, Spesutia Lower Hundred, 1776.
NEGRO Batrice. Taxable in household of John Rumsey, Susquehanna Hundred, 1776.
NEGRO Beatrice. Taxable in household of John Rumsey, Susquehanna Hundred, 1775.
NEGRO Beck. Taxable in household of Capt. James Maxwell, Gunpowder Lower Hundred, 1775.
NEGRO Beck. Taxable in household of Josias William Dallam, Spesutia Lower Hundred, 1775.
NEGRO Beck. Taxable on plantation of Capt. John Hall, Spesutia Lower Hundred, 1775.
NEGRO Beck. Taxable in household of Richard Willmot, Spesutia Upper Hundred, 1775.
NEGRO Beck. Taxable in household of William Fisher, Deer Creek Lower Hundred, 1775.
NEGRO Beck. Taxable on plantation of Josias William Dallam, Spesutia Lower Hundred, 1776.
NEGRO Bell. Taxable in household of Samuel Forwood, Spesutia Upper Hundred, 1775.
NEGRO Bell. Taxable in household of Edmond Bull, Spesutia Upper Hundred, 1775.
NEGRO Ben. Taxable in household of Thomas Bond, Sr., Bush River Lower Hundred, 1775.
NEGRO Ben. Taxable in household of Benjamin Norris, Bush River Lower Hundred, 1775.
NEGRO Ben. Taxable in household of William Debrular, Gunpowder Lower Hundred, 1775.
NEGRO Ben. Taxable in household of Jacob Giles, Susquehanna Hundred, 1775.
NEGRO Ben. Taxable on plantation of John Lee Webster, Spesutia Lower Hundred, 1775.
NEGRO Ben. Taxable at William Paca's Quarters, Spesutia Lower Hundred, 1775.
NEGRO Ben. Taxable in household of George Bradford, Spesutia Upper Hundred, 1775.
NEGRO Ben. Taxable in household of Isaac Webster, Spesutia Upper Hundred, 1775.
NEGRO Ben. Taxable in household of Thomas Streett, Bush River Upper Hundred, 1775.
NEGRO Ben. Taxable in household of Winston Smith, Bush River Upper Hundred, 1775.
NEGRO Ben. Taxable in household of Richard Dalam, Deer Creek Lower Hundred, 1775.
NEGRO Ben. Taxable in household of Phillip Coal, Deer

EARLY HARFORD COUNTIANS: Supplement

Creek Lower Hundred, 1775.
NEGRO Ben. Taxable in household of Grace Wallace, Deer Creek Lower Hundred, 1775.
NEGRO Ben. Taxable on plantation of Thomas Gash, Spesutia Lower Hundred, 1776.
NEGRO Ben. Taxable on plantation of John Lee Webster, Spesutia Lower Hundred, 1776.
NEGRO Ben. Taxable on plantation of Jacob Giles, Susquehanna Hundred, 1776.
NEGRO Bendow. Taxable in the household of William Hollis, Sr., Spesutia Lower Hundred, 1775.
NEGRO Bes. Taxable in household of John Bedle Hall, Susquehanna Hundred, 1776.
NEGRO Bes. Taxable on plantation of Jacob Giles, Susquehanna Hundred, 1776.
NEGRO Bess. Taxable in household of Jacob Giles, Susquehanna Hundred, 1775.
NEGRO Bess. Taxable in household of John Bots, Susquehanna Hundred, 1776.
NEGRO Bess. Taxable in household of Aquila Paca, Jr., Spesutia Lower Hundred, 1776.
NEGRO Bet. Taxable in household of Aaburella Smith, Gunpowder Lower Hundred, 1775.
NEGRO Bet. Taxable in household of Samuel Ricketts, Gunpowder Lower Hundred, 1775.
NEGRO Bet. Taxable in household of John Botts, Susquehanna Hundred, 1775.
NEGRO Bet. Taxable in household of Elizabeth Gallion, Spesutia Lower Hundred, 1775.
NEGRO Bet. Taxable in Spesutia Upper Hundred, 1775 [page torn; name of owner not known, but last name started with letter "B"].
NEGRO Bett. Taxable in the household of Leven Matthews, Spesutia Lower Hundred, 1775.
NEGRO Bett. Taxable in the household of Edward Carvel Tolley, Spesutia Lower Hundred, 1775.
NEGRO Bett. Taxable in the household of Aquila Paca, Jr., Spesutia Lower Hundred, 1775.
NEGRO Bett. Taxable in household of Micheal Hannor, Spesutia Upper Hundred, 1775.
NEGRO Bett. Taxable in Spesutia Upper Hundred, 1775.
NEGRO Bett. Taxable in household of Thomas Wheler, Spesutia Upper Hundred, 1775.
NEGRO Bett. Taxable in household of William Coal, Deer Creek Lower Hundred, 1775.
NEGRO Bett. Taxable on plantation of William Webb, Deer Creek Upper Hundred, 1775.
NEGRO Bett. Taxable in household of Elizabeth Gallion, Spesutia Lower Hundred, 1776.
NEGRO Bett. Taxable in household of Leven Mathews, Spesutia Lower Hundred, 1776.
NEGRO Bett. Taxable on plantation of William Smith, Jr., Spesutia Lower Hundred, 1776.
NEGRO Bett. Taxable on plantation of Edward Carvel Tolley, Spesutia Lower Hundred, 1776.
NEGRO Betty. Taxable in household of Benjamin Rumsey, Gunpowder Lower Hundred, 1775.
NEGRO Betty. Taxable in Susquehanna Hundred, 1775 William Wilson, Susquehanna Hundred, 1775.
NEGRO Betty. Taxable in household of Samuel Wilson, Susquehanna Hundred, 1776.
NEGRO Bill. Taxable in household of William Hall, Spesutia Lower Hundred, 1775.
NEGRO Bill. Taxable in household of Ignatius Wheeler, Jr., Deer Creek Upper Hundred, 1775.
NEGRO Bill. Taxable in household of Francis Holland, Spesutia Lower Hundred, 1776.
NEGRO Bill. Taxable on plantation of William Hall, Spesutia Lower Hundred, 1776.
NEGRO Bill. Taxable on plantation of Samuel Griffith, Spesutia Lower Hundred, 1776.
NEGRO Bimah. Taxable in household of Charles Gilbert, Susquehanna Hundred, 1775.
NEGRO Binar. Taxable in household of Charles Gilbert, Susquehanna Hundred, 1776.
NEGRO Bine. Taxable in household of Rev. John Davis, Bush River Upper Hundred, 1775.
NEGRO Black John. Taxable at Cumberland Forge, Deer Creek Lower Hundred, 1775.
NEGRO Boatswain. Taxable in household of John Worthington, Deer Creek Lower Hundred, 1775.
NEGRO Bob. Taxable in household of Jacob Bull, Sr. Bush River Lower Hundred, 1775.
NEGRO Bob. Taxable in household of William Richardson, Bush River Lower Hundred, 1775.
NEGRO Bob. Taxable in household of John Peca, Bush River Lower Hundred, 1775.
NEGRO Bob. Taxable in household of William Smith, Gunpowder Lower Hundred, 1775.
NEGRO Bob. Taxable in household of Thomas Mitchel, Susquehanna Hundred, 1775.
NEGRO Bob. Taxable in household of Phebe Gallion, Spesutia Lower Hundred, 1775.
NEGRO Bob. Taxable in household of Josias William Dallam, Spesutia Lower Hundred, 1775.
NEGRO Bob. Taxable in the household of Aquila Paca, Jr., Spesutia Lower Hundred, 1775.
NEGRO Bob. Taxable on plantation of James Lee, Deer Creek Lower Hundred, 1775.
NEGRO Bob. Taxable in household of Thomas Mitchel, Susquehanna Hundred, 1776.
NEGRO Bobb. Taxable in household of Isaac Webster, Spesutia Upper Hundred, 1775.
NEGRO Bobb. Taxable in household of Clemonsy Preston, Spesutia Upper Hundred, 1775.
NEGRO Bobb. Taxable on plantation of Josias William Dallam, Spesutia Lower Hundred, 1776.
NEGRO Bolt. Taxable in household of Robbert Bishop,

Gunpowder Lower Hundred, 1775.

NEGRO Boner. Taxable in household of Samuel Gott, Gunpowder Lower Hundred, 1775.

NEGRO Bridget. Taxable in household of Benjamin Rumsey, Gunpowder Lower Hundred, 1775.

NEGRO Brista. Taxable at Jacob Bond's Quarters, Gunpowder Lower Hundred, 1775.

NEGRO Buck. Taxable in household of James McComas, Bush River Lower Hundred, 1775.

NEGRO Bumbrow. Taxable at Benjamin Howard's Quarters, Gunpowder Lower Hundred, 1775.

NEGRO Caesar. Taxable in household of John Rumsey, Susquehanna Hundred, 1775.

NEGRO Caesar. Taxable in household of Greenberry Dorsey, Spesutia Lower Hundred, 1776.

NEGRO Caesar. Taxable on plantation of Samuel Griffith, Spesutia Lower Hundred, 1776.

NEGRO Caesar. Taxable in household of James Taylor, Sr., Spesutia Lower Hundred, 1776.

NEGRO Caeser. Taxable on plantation of George Ford, Spesutia Lower Hundred, 1776.

NEGRO Caeser. Taxable on plantation of Josias William Dallam, Spesutia Lower Hundred, 1776.

NEGRO Caff. Taxable in household of John Brown, Spesutia Lower Hundred, 1775.

NEGRO Carpenter Tom. Taxable at Cumberland Forge, Deer Creek Lower Hundred, 1775.

NEGRO Cash. Taxable in household of Alexander Cowen, Gunpowder Lower Hundred, 1775.

NEGRO Cate. Taxable in household of Jacob Bond, Sr., Bush River Lower Hundred, 1775.

NEGRO Cate. Taxable in household of Ephriam Andrews, Susquehanna Hundred, 1775.

NEGRO Cate. Taxable at William Paca's Quarters, Spesutia Lower Hundred, 1775.

NEGRO Cate. Taxable in household of Sarah Grafton, Spesutia Upper Hundred, 1775.

NEGRO Cate. Taxable in household of Elizabeth Wheler, Spesutia Upper Hundred, 1775.

NEGRO Cate. Taxable in household of Thomas Bond, Jr., Bush River Upper Hundred, 1775.

NEGRO Cate. Taxable on plantation of Thomas Gash, Spesutia Lower Hundred, 1776.

NEGRO Cate. Taxable on plantation of Ephrem Andres, Susquehanna Hundred, 1776.

NEGRO Cato. Taxable in household of John Taylor, Bush River Lower Hundred, 1775.

NEGRO Cato. Taxable in household of Jacob Giles, Jr., Susquehanna Hundred, 1775.

NEGRO Cato. Taxable in household of Jacob Giles, Susquehanna Hundred, 1775.

NEGRO Cato. Taxable at Richard Dallam's Quarters at Romney, Spesutia Lower Hundred, 1775.

NEGRO Cato. Taxable on plantation of James Phillips, Spesutia Lower Hundred, 1775.

NEGRO Cato. Taxable in the household of Edward Carvel Tolley, Spesutia Lower Hundred, 1775.

NEGRO Cato. Taxable in the household of William Loney, Spesutia Lower Hundred, 1775.

NEGRO Cato. Taxable in household of George Bradford, Spesutia Upper Hundred, 1775.

NEGRO Cato. Taxable at Thomas Gash's Quarters, Spesutia Upper Hundred, 1775.

NEGRO Cato. Taxable in household of Samuel Lee, Spesutia Upper Hundred, 1775.

NEGRO Cato. Taxable in household of Thomas Giles, Spesutia Lower Hundred, 1776.

NEGRO Cato. Taxable at Jacob Giles, Jr.'s Quarters, Spesutia Lower Hundred, 1776.

NEGRO Cato. Taxable on plantation of Jacob Giles, Jr., Susquehanna Hundred, 1776.

NEGRO Cato. Taxable on plantation of Edward Carvel Tolley, Spesutia Lower Hundred, 1776.

NEGRO Catron. Taxable in Bush River Lower Hundred, 1775, with Benjamin Howard as security.

NEGRO Catto. Taxable at Giles & Smith's Rock Run Plantation, Susquehanna Hundred, 1776.

NEGRO Ceaser. Taxable in household of Greenberry Dorsey, Spesutia Lower Hundred, 1775.

NEGRO Ceaser. Taxable in household of Josias William Dallam, Spesutia Lower Hundred, 1775.

NEGRO Ceaser. Taxable in household of George Ford, Spesutia Lower Hundred, 1775.

NEGRO Ceaser. Taxable in the household of John Hanson, Sr., Spesutia Lower Hundred, 1775.

NEGRO Ceaser. Taxable in household of Micheal Hannor, Spesutia Upper Hundred, 1775.

NEGRO Ceaser. Taxable in household of William Coal, Deer Creek Lower Hundred, 1775.

NEGRO Ceaser. Taxable on plantation of James Lee, Deer Creek Lower Hundred, 1775.

NEGRO Ceaser. Taxable in household of Martha Smith, Deer Creek Lower Hundred, 1775.

NEGRO Ceaser. Taxable in household of Samuel Worthington, Deer Creek Lower Hundred, 1775.

NEGRO Ceaser. Taxable in household of John Rumsey, Susquehanna Hundred, 1776.

NEGRO Ceazer. Taxable in household of Danniel Preston, Spesutia Upper Hundred, 1775.

NEGRO Ceesar. Taxable in household of Solomon McComas, Bush River Lower Hundred, 1775.

NEGRO Cesar. Taxable in household of William Amos, Sr., Bush River Lower Hundred, 1775.

NEGRO, Cesar. Taxable in household of Jacob Bull, Sr. Bush River Lower Hundred, 1775.

NEGRO Cesar. Taxable in household of Jacob Bond, Sr., Bush River Lower Hundred, 1775.

NEGRO Cesar. Taxable in household of Benjamin

Rumsey, Gunpowder Lower Hundred, 1775.

NEGRO Cesar. Taxable at Asel Gittings' Quarters, Gunpowder Lower Hundred, 1775.

NEGRO Cesaro. Taxable at Giles & Smith's Rock Run Plantation, Susquehanna Hundred, 1776.

NEGRO Ceser. Taxable at Giles & Smith's Rock Run Plantation, Susquehanna Hundred, 1776.

NEGRO Cesor. Taxable in household of Joshua Amoss, Bush River Upper Hundred, 1775.

NEGRO Chan. Taxable in household of John Day (son of Edward), Gunpowder Lower Hundred, 1775.

NEGRO Charity. Taxable in household of Josias Carvel Hall, Spesutia Lower Hundred, 1775.

NEGRO Charity. Taxable at Dr. Henry Stephenson's Quarters, Spesutia Lower Hundred, 1775.

NEGRO Charity. Taxable on plantation of Dr. Josias Carvell Hall, Spesutia Lower Hundred, 1776.

NEGRO Charles. Taxable in household of Jacob Bond, Sr., Bush River Lower Hundred, 1775.

NEGRO Charles. Taxable in household of Thomas Waltham, Gunpowder Lower Hundred, 1775.

NEGRO Charles. Taxable at William Buchanan's Quarters, Gunpowder Lower Hundred, 1775.

NEGRO Charles. Taxable in household of Capt. James Maxwell, Gunpowder Lower Hundred, 1775.

NEGRO Charles. Taxable on plantation of James Phillips, Spesutia Lower Hundred, 1775.

NEGRO Charles. Taxable in household of Ignatius Matthews, Spesutia Upper Hundred, 1775.

NEGRO Charles. Taxable in household of Henry Waters, Spesutia Upper Hundred, 1775.

NEGRO Charles. Taxable in household of Benjamin Amoss, Bush River Upper Hundred, 1775.

NEGRO Charles. Taxable in household of Joshua Amoss, Bush River Upper Hundred, 1775.

NEGRO Charles. Taxable on plantation of William Smith, Sr, Bush River Upper Hundred, 1775.

NEGRO Charles. Taxable in household of Jobe Barnes, Deer Creek Lower Hundred, 1775.

NEGRO Chloe. Taxable in household of Gregory Barnes, Susquehanna Hundred, 1775.

NEGRO Chloe. Taxable in household of Robert Hawkins, Susquehanna Hundred, 1775.

NEGRO Chloe. Taxable in household of Jacob Giles, Jr., Susquehanna Hundred, 1775.

NEGRO Chloe. Taxable in Susquehanna Hundred, 1775 William Wilson, Susquehanna Hundred, 1775.

NEGRO Chloe. Taxable on plantation of Hannah Hall, Spesutia Lower Hundred, 1776.

NEGRO Ciser. Taxable in household of J. Beale Boadley, Gunpowder Lower Hundred, 1775.

NEGRO Cleetus. Taxable on plantation of James Phillips, Spesutia Lower Hundred, 1775.

NEGRO Clem. Taxable in household of Samuel Lee, Spesutia Upper Hundred, 1775.

NEGRO Clem. Taxable in household of Robert Hawkins, Susquehanna Hundred, 1776.

NEGRO Clem. Taxable in household of Samuel Wilson, Susquehanna Hundred, 1776.

NEGRO Clo. Taxable in household of Robbert Bishop, Gunpowder Lower Hundred, 1775.

NEGRO Cloe. Taxable in household of Lambert Wilmer, Gunpowder Lower Hundred, 1775.

NEGRO Cloe. Taxable on plantation of Hannah Hall, Spesutia Lower Hundred, 1775.

NEGRO Cloe. Taxable in household of Micheal Hannor, Spesutia Upper Hundred, 1775.

NEGRO Cloe. Taxable in the household of John Copeland, Spesutia Lower Hundred, 1775.

NEGRO Cloe. Taxable in household of Nathaniel Rigbie, Deer Creek Lower Hundred, 1775.

NEGRO Cloe. Taxable in household of Thomas Baker Rigdon, Deer Creek Upper Hundred, 1775.

NEGRO Cloe. Taxable in household of William Wilson, Susquehanna Hundred, 1776.

NEGRO Cloe. Taxable in household of Samuel Wilson, Susquehanna Hundred, 1776.

NEGRO Clove. Taxable in household of Ignatius Wheeler, Jr., Deer Creek Upper Hundred, 1775.

NEGRO Coff. Taxable in household of Christon Baker, Spesutia Upper Hundred, 1775.

NEGRO Coffy. Taxable in household of David Clark, Spesutia Upper Hundred, 1775.

NEGRO Coleme. Taxable in Susquehanna Hundred, 1775 William Wilson, Susquehanna Hundred, 1775.

NEGRO Combo. Taxable in household of John Brown, Spesutia Lower Hundred, 1776.

NEGRO Combo. Taxable in household of Richard Garrettson, Spesutia Lower Hundred, 1776.

NEGRO Combow. Taxable in household of Richard Garretson, Spesutia Lower Hundred, 1775.

NEGRO Comfort. Taxable in household of Thomas Johnson, Sr., Spesutia Upper Hundred, 1775.

NEGRO Cook. Taxable in household of Mary Carlile, Bush River Lower Hundred, 1775.

NEGRO Cook. Taxable in household of Benjamin Rumsey, Gunpowder Lower Hundred, 1775.

NEGRO Cook. Taxable in household of Thomas Wheler, Spesutia Upper Hundred, 1775.

NEGRO Cornelius. Taxable in household of Capt. James Maxwell, Gunpowder Lower Hundred, 1775.

NEGRO Crafet. Taxable in household of Josias Hall, Susquehanna Hundred, 1776.

NEGRO Crommell. Taxable on plantation of Josias William Dallam, Spesutia Lower Hundred, 1776.

NEGRO Cromwell. Taxable in household of Josias William Dallam, Spesutia Lower Hundred, 1775.

NEGRO Cudgo. Taxable on plantation of Aquila Hall,

Spesutia Lower Hundred, 1775.
NEGRO Cuff. Taxable in household of Garret Garretson, Spesutia Lower Hundred, 1775.
NEGRO Cuff. Taxable on plantation of Capt. John Hall, Spesutia Lower Hundred, 1775.
NEGRO Cuff. Taxable on the plantation of Amos Garrett, Spesutia Lower Hundred, 1775.
NEGRO Cuff. Taxable in household of John Hawkins, Deer Creek Lower Hundred, 1775.
NEGRO Cuff. Taxable in household of John Brown, Spesutia Lower Hundred, 1776.
NEGRO Cuff. Taxable in household of Garrett Garrettson (son of James), Spesutia Lower Hundred, 1776.
NEGRO Cuff. Taxable in household of John Bedle Hall, Susquehanna Hundred, 1776.
NEGRO Cumbo. Taxable in household of John Brown, Spesutia Lower Hundred, 1775.
NEGRO Cupit. Taxable in household of Elizabeth Lytle, Gunpowder Lower Hundred, 1775.
NEGRO Cupit. Taxable at Cumberland Forge, Deer Creek Lower Hundred, 1775.
NEGRO Cynthia. Taxable on plantation of Hannah Hall, Spesutia Lower Hundred, 1776.
NEGRO Da--- [page torn]. Taxable in household of Burgess Chaney, Bush River Lower Hundred, 1775.
NEGRO Daff. Taxable in household of Thomas Bussey, Bush River Lower Hundred, 1775.
NEGRO Dal. Taxable in household of Richard Dalam, Deer Creek Lower Hundred, 1775.
NEGRO Dampear. Taxable in household of John Jolley, Deer Creek Lower Hundred, 1775.
NEGRO Damphies. Taxable on plantation of Samuel Griffith, Spesutia Lower Hundred, 1776.
NEGRO Dan. Taxable at Richard Dallam's Quarters at Romney, Spesutia Lower Hundred, 1775.
NEGRO Dana. Taxable in household of James Amoss, Bush River Upper Hundred, 1775.
NEGRO Danby. Taxable on plantation of John Lee Webster, Spesutia Lower Hundred, 1776.
NEGRO Dandee. Taxable at Cumberland Forge, Deer Creek Lower Hundred, 1775.
NEGRO Daniel. Taxable in household of Philip Gover, Susquehanna Hundred, 1775.
NEGRO Daniel. Taxable in household of Jacob Giles, Jr., Susquehanna Hundred, 1775.
NEGRO Daniel. Taxable in household of John Jolley, Deer Creek Lower Hundred, 1775.
NEGRO Daniel. Taxable at Jacob Giles, Jr.'s Quarters, Spesutia Lower Hundred, 1776.
NEGRO Daniel. Taxable on plantation of Jacob Giles, Jr., Susquehanna Hundred, 1776.
NEGRO Daniel. Taxable on plantation of Philip Gover, Susquehanna Hundred, 1776.
NEGRO Daphney. Taxable in household of Benjamin Meed, Gunpowder Lower Hundred, 1775.
NEGRO Darbe. Taxable in household of Philip Gover, Susquehanna Hundred, 1775.
NEGRO Darbey. Taxable on plantation of Philip Gover, Susquehanna Hundred, 1776.
NEGRO Darby. Taxable in household of Joseph Presbury, Gunpowder Lower Hundred, 1775.
NEGRO Darby. Taxable at Joseph Presbury's Quarters, Spesutia Upper Hundred, 1775.
NEGRO Darby. Taxable in household of Joshua Amoss, Bush River Upper Hundred, 1775.
NEGRO Darcus. Taxable on plantation of Hannah Hall, Spesutia Lower Hundred, 1775.
NEGRO Darcus. Taxable on plantation of Hannah Hall, Spesutia Lower Hundred, 1776.
NEGRO Darkish. Taxable in household of Thomas Wheler, Spesutia Upper Hundred, 1775.
NEGRO Davey. Taxable in household of Samuel Worthington, Deer Creek Lower Hundred, 1775.
NEGRO David. Taxable at William Paca's Quarters, Spesutia Lower Hundred, 1775.
NEGRO David. Taxable on plantation of John Lee Webster, Spesutia Lower Hundred, 1775.
NEGRO David. Taxable at Clark Young's Quarters, Spesutia Lower Hundred, 1775.
NEGRO David. Taxable in household of Ignatius Matthews, Spesutia Upper Hundred, 1775.
NEGRO David. Taxable on plantation of Samuel Griffith, Spesutia Lower Hundred, 1776.
NEGRO David. Taxable in household of Thomas Giles, Spesutia Lower Hundred, 1776.
NEGRO David. Taxable on plantation of Thomas Gash, Spesutia Lower Hundred, 1776.
NEGRO David. Taxable in household of Robert Stokes, Spesutia Lower Hundred, 1776.
NEGRO David. Taxable on plantation of John Lee Webster, Spesutia Lower Hundred, 1776.
NEGRO Davy. Taxable in household of Jacob Giles, Susquehanna Hundred, 1775.
NEGRO Davy. Taxable in household of Goldsmith Garretson, Spesutia Lower Hundred, 1775.
NEGRO Davy. Taxable "at ye glebe" of Rev. William West, Spesutia Lower Hundred, 1775.
NEGRO Debb. Taxable in household of Richard Willmot, Spesutia Upper Hundred, 1775.
NEGRO Defany. Taxable in household of Ephraim Andrews, Susquehanna Hundred, 1775.
NEGRO Defany. Taxable in household of Bathia Barnes, Susquehanna Hundred, 1775.
NEGRO Dell. Taxable in the household of James Osborn, Jr., Spesutia Lower Hundred, 1775.
NEGRO Demitres. Taxable at Cumberland Forge, Deer Creek Lower Hundred, 1775.
NEGRO Denal. Taxable in household of Burgess

EARLY HARFORD COUNTIANS: Supplement

Chaney, Bush River Lower Hundred, 1775.
NEGRO Derry. Taxable in household of William Norris, Bush River Upper Hundred, 1775.
NEGRO Dic. Taxable on plantation of Aquila Hall, Spesutia Lower Hundred, 1775.
NEGRO Dick. Taxable in household of Ann Bond, Bush River Lower Hundred, 1775.
NEGRO Dick. Taxable in household of John Peca, Bush River Lower Hundred, 1775.
NEGRO Dick. Taxable in household of Samuel Ricketts, Gunpowder Lower Hundred, 1775.
NEGRO Dick. Taxable in household of Capt. James Maxwell, Gunpowder Lower Hundred, 1775.
NEGRO Dick. Taxable in household of Groumbrit Bailey, Gunpowder Lower Hundred, 1775.
NEGRO Dick. Taxable in household of Stephen Waters, Gunpowder Lower Hundred, 1775.
NEGRO Dick. Taxable at Benjamin Howard's Quarters, Gunpowder Lower Hundred, 1775.
NEGRO Dick. Taxable in household of Thomas Waltham, Gunpowder Lower Hundred, 1775.
NEGRO Dick. Taxable in household of Greenberry Dorsey, Spesutia Lower Hundred, 1775.
NEGRO Dick. Taxable at Richard Dallam's Quarters at Swan Creek, Spesutia Lower Hundred, 1775.
NEGRO Dick. Taxable in household of William Hall, Spesutia Lower Hundred, 1775.
NEGRO Dick. Taxable on plantation of John Lee Webster, Spesutia Lower Hundred, 1775.
NEGRO Dick. Taxable at William Paca's Quarters, Spesutia Lower Hundred, 1775.
NEGRO Dick. Taxable in household of Samel Daugherty, Spesutia Upper Hundred, 1775.
NEGRO Dick. Taxable in household of Samuel Lee, Spesutia Upper Hundred, 1775.
NEGRO Dick. Taxable in household of Bennett Matthews, Spesutia Upper Hundred, 1775.
NEGRO Dick. Taxable in household of John Barclay, Deer Creek Lower Hundred, 1775.
NEGRO Dick. Taxable in household of John Peacock, Deer Creek Lower Hundred, 1775.
NEGRO Dick. Taxable on plantation of James Lee, Deer Creek Lower Hundred, 1775.
NEGRO Dick. Taxable in household of William Fisher, Deer Creek Lower Hundred, 1775.
NEGRO Dick. Taxable on plantation of Thomas Gash, Spesutia Lower Hundred, 1776.
NEGRO Dick. Taxable on plantation of Amos Garrett, Spesutia Lower Hundred, 1776.
NEGRO Dick. Taxable in household of Greenberry Dorsey, Spesutia Lower Hundred, 1776.
NEGRO Dick. Taxable on plantation of William Hall, Spesutia Lower Hundred, 1776.
NEGRO Dick. Taxable on plantation of John Lee Webster, Spesutia Lower Hundred, 1776.
NEGRO Dider. Taxable in household of James McComas, Bush River Lower Hundred, 1775.
NEGRO Dido. Taxable in household of John Garretson, Spesutia Lower Hundred, 1775.
NEGRO Dido. Taxable on plantation of John Lee Webster, Spesutia Lower Hundred, 1775.
NEGRO Dido. Taxable in the household of James Stewart, Spesutia Lower Hundred, 1775.
NEGRO Dido. Taxable in household of James Rigbie, Deer Creek Lower Hundred, 1775.
NEGRO Dido. Taxable in household of James Stewart, Spesutia Lower Hundred, 1776.
NEGRO Dido. Taxable on plantation of John Lee Webster, Spesutia Lower Hundred, 1776.
NEGRO Dido. Taxable at Thomas Harrison's Quarters, Susquehanna Hundred, 1776.
NEGRO Diels. Taxable in household of Ellender Durham, Bush River Lower Hundred, 1775.
NEGRO Dill. Taxable in household of Hugh Dorran, Bush River Upper Hundred, 1775.
NEGRO Dimcort. Taxable in household of Josias Hall, Susquehanna Hundred, 1776.
NEGRO Dina. Taxable in household of Nicholas Alender, Gunpowder Lower Hundred, 1775.
NEGRO Dina. Taxable in household of Lambert Wilmer, Gunpowder Lower Hundred, 1775.
NEGRO Dina. Taxable in household of Mary Scott, Gunpowder Lower Hundred, 1775.
NEGRO Dina. Taxable in household of William Amoss (son of James), Bush River Upper Hundred, 1775.
NEGRO Dina. Taxable in household of William Norris, Bush River Upper Hundred, 1775.
NEGRO Dina. Taxable in household of John Daul, Bush River Upper Hundred, 1775.
NEGRO Dina. Taxable in household of William McCommos," q.v.
NEGRO Dina. Taxable in household of William McCommos, Sr., Bush River Upper Hundred, 1775.
NEGRO Dina. Taxable in household of Dannill Bond, Bush River Upper Hundred, 1775.
NEGRO Dina. Taxable in household of Donnill McCommos, Bush River Upper Hundred, 1775.
NEGRO Dina. Taxable in household of George Vogan, Bush River Upper Hundred, 1775.
NEGRO Dina. Taxable in household of Abram Whitekar, Bush River Upper Hundred, 1775.
NEGRO Dina. Taxable in household of William Horten, Susquehanna Hundred, 1776.
NEGRO Dinah. Taxable in household of Jacob Bond, Sr., Bush River Lower Hundred, 1775.
NEGRO Dinah. Taxable in household of William Ady, Bush River Lower Hundred, 1775.
NEGRO Dinah. Taxable in household of Jacob Bond, Sr.,

Bush River Lower Hundred, 1775.
NEGRO Dinah. Taxable in household of Peter Potee, Bush River Lower Hundred, 1775.
NEGRO Dinah. Taxable at Asel Gittings' Quarters, Gunpowder Lower Hundred, 1775.
NEGRO Dinah. Taxable in household of Martha Presbury, Gunpowder Lower Hundred, 1775.
NEGRO Dinah. Taxable in household of William Horten, Susquehanna Hundred, 1775.
NEGRO Dinah. Taxable in household of Philip Gover, Susquehanna Hundred, 1775.
NEGRO Dinah. Taxable in household of William Hall, Spesutia Lower Hundred, 1775.
NEGRO Dinah. Taxable in household of George Chancey, Jr., Spesutia Lower Hundred, 1775.
NEGRO Dinah. Taxable in household of Phebe Gallion, Spesutia Lower Hundred, 1775.
NEGRO Dinah. Taxable in household of George Garretson, Spesutia Lower Hundred, 1775.
NEGRO Dinah. Taxable on the plantation of Amos Garrett, Spesutia Lower Hundred, 1775.
NEGRO Dinah. Taxable on plantation of Hannah Hall, Spesutia Lower Hundred, 1775.
NEGRO Dinah. Taxable in the household of Benjamin Hanson, Spesutia Lower Hundred, 1775.
NEGRO Dinah. Taxable at William Paca's Quarters, Spesutia Lower Hundred, 1775.
NEGRO Dinah. Taxable on plantation of James Phillips, Spesutia Lower Hundred, 1775.
NEGRO Dinah. Taxable in the household of William Osborn, Sr., Spesutia Lower Hundred, 1775.
NEGRO Dinah. Taxable on plantation of John Lee Webster, Spesutia Lower Hundred, 1775.
NEGRO Dinah. Taxable in household of Joseph Brownley, Spesutia Upper Hundred, 1775.
NEGRO Dinah. Taxable in household of Jobe Barnes, Deer Creek Lower Hundred, 1775.
NEGRO Dinah. Taxable in household of Grace Wallace, Deer Creek Lower Hundred, 1775.
NEGRO Dinah. Taxable in household of Elizabeth Gover, Deer Creek Lower Hundred, 1775.
NEGRO Dinah. Taxable in household of Robert Clerk, Sr., Deer Creek Upper Hundred, 1775.
NEGRO Dinah. Taxable in household of Martha Garrettson, Spesutia Lower Hundred, 1776.
NEGRO Dinah. Taxable on plantation of Thomas Gash, Spesutia Lower Hundred, 1776.
NEGRO Dinah. Taxable on plantation of Hannah Hall, Spesutia Lower Hundred, 1776.
NEGRO Dinah. Taxable in household of John Garrettson, Spesutia Lower Hundred, 1776.
NEGRO Dinah. Taxable in household of Freeborn Brown, Susquehanna Hundred, 1776.
NEGRO Dinar. Taxable on plantation of Philip Gover, Susquehanna Hundred, 1776.
NEGRO Diniah. Taxable in household of Mary Renshaw, Deer Creek Upper Hundred, 1775.
NEGRO Dinnah. Taxable in household of Christon Baker, Spesutia Upper Hundred, 1775.
NEGRO Dinnah. Taxable in household of John Archer, Spesutia Upper Hundred, 1775.
NEGRO Dinnah. Taxable in household of Edward Hanson, Spesutia Upper Hundred, 1775.
NEGRO Dinnah. Taxable in household of Joseph Stiles, Spesutia Upper Hundred, 1775.
NEGRO Dinnah. Taxable in household of Ann Stevenson, Spesutia Upper Hundred, 1775.
NEGRO Dino. Taxable in household of Ignatius Matthews, Spesutia Upper Hundred, 1775.
NEGRO Dofney. Taxable in household of Bethiah Barns, Susquehanna Hundred, 1776.
NEGRO Doll. Taxable in household of John Bond, Sr., Bush River Lower Hundred, 1775.
NEGRO Doll. Taxable in household of Ann Bond, Bush River Lower Hundred, 1775.
NEGRO Doll. Taxable in household of Joseph Renshaw, Sr., Bush River Lower Hundred, 1775.
NEGRO Doll. Taxable in household of Thomas Johnson, Sr., Spesutia Upper Hundred, 1775.
NEGRO Dongo. Taxable in household of George Chancey, Sr., Spesutia Lower Hundred, 1775.
NEGRO Dorinder. Taxable on plantation of Hannah Hall, Spesutia Lower Hundred, 1775.
NEGRO Dublin. Taxable in household of Robbert Bishop, Gunpowder Lower Hundred, 1775.
NEGRO Duke. Taxable in household of Ann Bond, Bush River Lower Hundred, 1775.
NEGRO Duke. Taxable in household of Jacob Giles, Susquehanna Hundred, 1775.
NEGRO Duke. Taxable at Amos Garrett's Quarters, Spesutia Lower Hundred, 1775.
NEGRO Duke. Taxable in household of George Garretson, Spesutia Lower Hundred, 1775.
NEGRO Duke. Taxable in household of John Barton, Bush River Upper Hundred, 1775.
NEGRO Duke. Taxable in household of Joseph Hopkins, Deer Creek Lower Hundred, 1775.
NEGRO Duke. Taxable on plantation of Amos Garrett, Spesutia Lower Hundred, 1776.
NEGRO Duke. Taxable in household of Martha Garrettson, Spesutia Lower Hundred, 1776.
NEGRO Duke. Taxable on plantation of Jacob Giles, Susquehanna Hundred, 1776.
NEGRO Dull. Taxable in household of William Fisher, Jr., Deer Creek Upper Hundred, 1775.
NEGRO Dundee. Taxable on plantation of William Smith, Sr, Bush River Upper Hundred, 1775.
NEGRO Dupea. Taxable in household of Martha

EARLY HARFORD COUNTIANS: Supplement

Garrettson, Spesutia Lower Hundred, 1776.
NEGRO Dutches. Taxable in household of George Bradford, Spesutia Upper Hundred, 1775.
NEGRO Dutches. Taxable on plantation of James Lee, Deer Creek Lower Hundred, 1775.
NEGRO Dutchess. Taxable in household of Freeborn Brown, Spesutia Lower Hundred, 1775.
NEGRO Dutchess. Taxable on the plantation of Amos Garrett, Spesutia Lower Hundred, 1775.
NEGRO Dutchess. Taxable on plantation of Amos Garrett, Spesutia Lower Hundred, 1776.
NEGRO Dutchess. Taxable on plantation of William Smith, Jr., Spesutia Lower Hundred, 1776.
NEGRO Dydo. Taxable at Thomas Harrison's Quarters, Susquehanna Hundred, 1775.
NEGRO Dyner. Taxable in household of Henry Wilson, Jr., Bush River Lower Hundred, 1775.
NEGRO Eag. Taxable in household of Robert Briarly, Bush River Upper Hundred, 1775.
NEGRO Easter. Taxable at William Paca's Quarters, Spesutia Upper Hundred, 1775.
NEGRO Easter. Taxable in household of James Mores, Spesutia Upper Hundred, 1775.
NEGRO Easther. Taxable on plantation of John Lee Webster, Spesutia Lower Hundred, 1775.
NEGRO Eff. Taxable in household of James Norris, Bush River Lower Hundred, 1775.
NEGRO Emanuel. Taxable at Thomas Hall's plantation, Spesutia Upper Hundred, 1775.
NEGRO Emmy. Taxable on plantation of Hannah Hall, Spesutia Lower Hundred, 1775.
NEGRO Emy. Taxable in household of Mary Scott, Gunpowder Lower Hundred, 1775.
NEGRO Esther. Taxable in household of William Chapel, Susquehanna Hundred, 1775.
NEGRO Esther. Taxable in household of Col. Thomas White, Susquehanna Hundred, 1775.
NEGRO Esther. Taxable in household of Samuel Griffith, Spesutia Lower Hundred, 1775.
NEGRO Esther. Taxable on the plantation of Amos Garrett, Spesutia Lower Hundred, 1775.
NEGRO Esther. Taxable on plantation of James Phillips, Spesutia Lower Hundred, 1775.
NEGRO Esther. Taxable in the household of Cyrus Osborn, Spesutia Lower Hundred, 1775.
NEGRO Esther. Taxable on plantation of Amos Garrett, Spesutia Lower Hundred, 1776.
NEGRO Esther. Taxable in household of Benedict Edward Hall, Spesutia Lower Hundred, 1776.
NEGRO Esther. Taxable on plantation of Samuel Griffith, Spesutia Lower Hundred, 1776.
NEGRO Esther. Taxable on plantation of John Lee Webster, Spesutia Lower Hundred, 1776.
NEGRO Eve. Taxable in household of Martha Presbury, Gunpowder Lower Hundred, 1775.
NEGRO Eve. Taxable at Amos Garrett's Quarters, Spesutia Lower Hundred, 1775.
NEGRO Exedor. Taxable in household of Rachel Johnson, Spesutia Upper Hundred, 1775.
NEGRO Eyester. Taxables on plantation of Col. Thomas White, Susquehanna Hundred, 1776.
NEGRO Fan. Taxable in household of Lambert Wilmer, Gunpowder Lower Hundred, 1775.
NEGRO Fan. Taxable in household of Mary Ligoe, Gunpowder Lower Hundred, 1775.
NEGRO Fan. Taxable in household of Micheal Hannor, Spesutia Upper Hundred, 1775.
NEGRO Fan. Taxable in household of John Barton, Bush River Upper Hundred, 1775.
NEGRO Fan. Taxable in household of Richard Dalam, Deer Creek Lower Hundred, 1775.
NEGRO Faney. Taxables on plantation of Samuel Harris, Deer Creek Lower Hundred, 1775.
NEGRO Fann. Taxable in household of John Brown, Spesutia Lower Hundred, 1775.
NEGRO Fann. Taxable in household of Thomas Everest, Spesutia Lower Hundred, 1775.
NEGRO Fann. Taxable in the household of George Little, Spesutia Lower Hundred, 1775.
NEGRO Fann. Taxable in the household of William Hollis, Sr., Spesutia Lower Hundred, 1775.
NEGRO Fann. Taxable on plantation of Aquila Hall, Spesutia Lower Hundred, 1775.
NEGRO Fann. Taxable in the household of Rev. William West, Spesutia Lower Hundred, 1775.
NEGRO Fann. Taxable in household of John Brown, Spesutia Lower Hundred, 1776.
NEGRO Fann. Taxable in household of Thomas Everest, Spesutia Lower Hundred, 1776.
NEGRO Fanney. Taxable in household of John Peca, Bush River Lower Hundred, 1775.
NEGRO Fanney. Taxable in household of John Worthington, Deer Creek Lower Hundred, 1775.
NEGRO Fanny. Taxable in household of Ellender Durham, Bush River Lower Hundred, 1775.
NEGRO Fanny. Taxable in household of Mary Carlile, Bush River Lower Hundred, 1775.
NEGRO Fanny. Taxable in household of William Hall, Spesutia Lower Hundred, 1775.
NEGRO Fanny. Taxable in household of Jonathan Lyon, Bush River Upper Hundred, 1775.
NEGRO Fany. Taxable in household of Nicklaus Amoss, Bush River Upper Hundred, 1775.
NEGRO Feby. Taxable in household of Walter Billingsley, Spesutia Upper Hundred, 1775.
NEGRO Feby. Taxable in household of James Scott, Bush River Upper Hundred, 1775.
NEGRO Feby. Taxable in household of Henry Stump,

Susquehanna Hundred, 1776.
NEGRO Feeb. Taxable in household of J. Beale Boadley, Gunpowder Lower Hundred, 1775.
NEGRO Felis. Taxable in household of James Scott, Bush River Upper Hundred, 1775.
NEGRO Fellis. Taxable in household of John Griffeth, Susquehanna Hundred, 1776.
NEGRO Femy. Taxable on plantation of Amos Garrett, Spesutia Lower Hundred, 1776.
NEGRO Fender. Taxable in household of J. Beale Boadley, Gunpowder Lower Hundred, 1775.
NEGRO Fiby. Taxable in household of John Rutlage, Bush River Upper Hundred, 1775.
NEGRO Fie. Taxable in household of John Day (son of Edward), Gunpowder Lower Hundred, 1775.
NEGRO Filis. Taxable in household of Thomas Streett, Bush River Upper Hundred, 1775.
NEGRO Fill. Taxable on plantation of Capt. John Hall, Spesutia Lower Hundred, 1775.
NEGRO Fill. Taxable in the household of James Kimble, Spesutia Lower Hundred, 1775.
NEGRO Fill. Taxable in household of Asell Hitchcock, Bush River Upper Hundred, 1775.
NEGRO Fill. Taxable in household of James Kimble, Spesutia Lower Hundred, 1776.
NEGRO Fillis. Taxable in household of Bennett Matthews, Spesutia Upper Hundred, 1775.
NEGRO Fillis. Taxable in household of Moses Ruth, Jr., Spesutia Upper Hundred, 1775.
NEGRO FIllis. Taxable on plantation of Jacob Giles, Susquehanna Hundred, 1776.
NEGRO Filulbes. Taxable in household of Jacob Giles, Susquehanna Hundred, 1775.
NEGRO Filus. Taxable in household of William McCommos," q.v.
NEGRO Flora. Taxable in household of Ann Bond, Bush River Lower Hundred, 1775.
NEGRO Flora. Taxable in household of Thomas Smithson, Sr., Bush River Lower Hundred, 1775.
NEGRO Flora. Taxable in Susquehanna Hundred, 1775 William Wilson, Susquehanna Hundred, 1775.
NEGRO Flora. Taxable in household of James Armstrong, Spesutia Upper Hundred, 1775.
NEGRO Floro. Taxable in household of Rachel Wilson, Susquehanna Hundred, 1776.
NEGRO Forester. Taxable on plantation of James Lee, Deer Creek Lower Hundred, 1775.
NEGRO Frank. Taxable on plantation of John Lee Webster, Spesutia Lower Hundred, 1775.
NEGRO Frank. Taxable on plantation of Stephen Jay, Deer Creek Lower Hundred, 1775.
NEGRO Frank. Taxable on plantation of Ephrem Andres, Susquehanna Hundred, 1776.
NEGRO Frank. Taxable on plantation of John Lee Webster, Spesutia Lower Hundred, 1776.
NEGRO Gambowel. Taxable in the household of John Ruff, Spesutia Lower Hundred, 1775.
NEGRO Gee. Taxable in household of Dannill Bond, Bush River Upper Hundred, 1775.
NEGRO George 2nd. Taxable on plantation of John Matthews, Spesutia Lower Hundred, 1775.
NEGRO George Jr. Taxable on plantation of Capt. John Mathews, Spesutia Lower Hundred, 1776.
NEGRO George. Taxable in household of Elijah Blackstone, Gunpowder Lower Hundred, 1775.
NEGRO George. Taxable in household of Richard Johns, Susquehanna Hundred, 1775.
NEGRO George. Taxable at Thomas Harrison's Quarters, Susquehanna Hundred, 1775.
NEGRO George. Taxable in household of George Ford, Spesutia Lower Hundred, 1775.
NEGRO George. Taxable on the plantation of Amos Garrett, Spesutia Lower Hundred, 1775.
NEGRO George. Taxable on plantation of John Lee Webster, Spesutia Lower Hundred, 1775.
NEGRO George. Taxable on plantation of Hannah Hall, Spesutia Lower Hundred, 1775.
NEGRO George. Taxable on plantation of Aquila Hall, Spesutia Lower Hundred, 1775.
NEGRO George. Taxable in household of William Prigg, Sr., Spesutia Upper Hundred, 1775.
NEGRO George. Taxable in household of Skipwith Coal, Deer Creek Lower Hundred, 1775.
NEGRO George. Taxable in household of Elizabeth Husbands (widow), Deer Creek Lower Hundred, 1775.
NEGRO George. Taxable in household of Grace Wallace, Deer Creek Lower Hundred, 1775.
NEGRO George. Taxable in household of Mary Renshaw, Deer Creek Upper Hundred, 1775.
NEGRO George. Taxable at Aquila Hall's Quarters, Spesutia Lower Hundred, 1776.
NEGRO George. Taxable on plantation of George Ford, Spesutia Lower Hundred, 1776.
NEGRO George. Taxable on plantation of Hannah Hall, Spesutia Lower Hundred, 1776.
NEGRO George. Taxable on plantation of Amos Garrett, Spesutia Lower Hundred, 1776.
NEGRO George. Taxable on plantation of Capt. John Mathews, Spesutia Lower Hundred, 1776.
NEGRO George. Taxable on plantation of John Lee Webster, Spesutia Lower Hundred, 1776.
NEGRO George. Taxable in household of Negro Thomas (a free negro), Susquehanna Hundred, 1776.
NEGRO George. Taxable at Thomas Harrison's Quarters, Susquehanna Hundred, 1776.
NEGRO Gin. Taxable in household of Rachel Thorp, Bush River Lower Hundred, 1775.

NEGRO Gin. Taxable in household of Capt. James Maxwell, Gunpowder Lower Hundred, 1775.
NEGRO Gin. Taxable in household of Nicholas Alender, Gunpowder Lower Hundred, 1775.
NEGRO Gin. Taxable in household of Thomas Waltham, Gunpowder Lower Hundred, 1775.
NEGRO Gin. Taxable in household of Elizabeth Lytle, Gunpowder Lower Hundred, 1775.
NEGRO Gin. Taxable in household of Micheal Hannor, Spesutia Upper Hundred, 1775.
NEGRO Gin. Taxable in household of John Hays, Sr., Spesutia Upper Hundred, 1775.
NEGRO Gin. Taxable in household of Walter Billingsley, Spesutia Upper Hundred, 1775.
NEGRO Gin. Taxable in household of Joseph Butler, Spesutia Upper Hundred, 1775.
NEGRO Gin. Taxable in household of John Linch, Spesutia Upper Hundred, 1775.
NEGRO Grace. Taxable in household of William Amos, Sr., Bush River Lower Hundred, 1775.
NEGRO Grace. Taxable in household of Burgess Chaney, Bush River Lower Hundred, 1775.
NEGRO Grace. Taxable in household of John McComas, Bush River Lower Hundred, 1775.
NEGRO Grace. Taxable in household of William Robinson, Sr., Bush River Lower Hundred, 1775.
NEGRO Grace. Taxable in household of Michael Gilbert, Susquehanna Hundred, 1775.
NEGRO Grace. Taxable in the household of Aquila Paca, Jr., Spesutia Lower Hundred, 1775.
NEGRO Grace. Taxable at Dr. Henry Stephenson's Quarters, Spesutia Lower Hundred, 1775.
NEGRO Grace. Taxable in the household of John Copeland, Spesutia Lower Hundred, 1775.
NEGRO Grace. Taxable in household of Bennett Matthews, Spesutia Upper Hundred, 1775.
NEGRO Grace. Taxable in household of William Allender, Deer Creek Upper Hundred, 1775.
NEGRO Grace. Taxable in household of Hugh Whiteford, Jr., Deer Creek Upper Hundred, 1775.
NEGRO Grace. Taxable in household of Aquila Paca, Jr., Spesutia Lower Hundred, 1776.
NEGRO Grace. Taxable at Dr. Henry Stephenson's Quarters, Spesutia Lower Hundred, 1776.
NEGRO Grace. Taxable in household of Michal Gilbert, Susquehanna Hundred, 1776.
NEGRO Grace. Taxable on plantation of Jacob Giles, Susquehanna Hundred, 1776.
NEGRO Gras. Taxable in household of Robert Amoss, Bush River Upper Hundred, 1775.
NEGRO Gras. Taxable in household of Joshua Chalk, Bush River Upper Hundred, 1775.
NEGRO Grove. Taxable in household of Thomas Bond, Jr., Bush River Upper Hundred, 1775.
NEGRO Guinea. Taxable in household of Lemuel Howard, Bush River Lower Hundred, 1775.
NEGRO Guy. Taxable in household of Mordicai Amos, Bush River Lower Hundred, 1775.
NEGRO Hagar. Taxable in household of Jacob Bull, Sr. Bush River Lower Hundred, 1775.
NEGRO Hagar. Taxable in household of Jacob Giles, Susquehanna Hundred, 1775.
NEGRO Hagar. Taxable in household of Thomas Mitchel, Susquehanna Hundred, 1775.
NEGRO Hagar. Taxable in the household of James Osborn, Jr., Spesutia Lower Hundred, 1775.
NEGRO Hagar. Taxable on plantation of Aquila Hall, Spesutia Lower Hundred, 1775.
NEGRO Hagar. Taxable on plantation of James Lee, Deer Creek Lower Hundred, 1775.
NEGRO Hager. Taxable in household of Nathan Horner, Gunpowder Lower Hundred, 1775.
NEGRO Hager. Taxable in household of Richard Willmot, Spesutia Upper Hundred, 1775.
NEGRO Hager. Taxable in household of James Amoss, Bush River Upper Hundred, 1775.
NEGRO Hager. Taxable in household of John Wilson, Deer Creek Lower Hundred, 1775.
NEGRO Hager. Taxable in household of James Kimble, Spesutia Lower Hundred, 1776.
NEGRO Hager. Taxable in household of Godfery Watters, Susquehanna Hundred, 1776.
NEGRO Hago. Taxable in household of Joseph Presbury, Gunpowder Lower Hundred, 1775.
NEGRO Hago. Taxable in household of Aquilla Paca, Gunpowder Lower Hundred, 1775.
NEGRO Hago. Taxable in household of Joseph Hopkins, Deer Creek Lower Hundred, 1775.
NEGRO Hagro. Taxable in household of Thomas Mitchel, Jr., Susquehanna Hundred, 1776.
NEGRO Hagur. Taxable in the household of James Kimble, Spesutia Lower Hundred, 1775.
NEGRO Hagur. Taxable in the household of Benjamin Hanson, Spesutia Lower Hundred, 1775.
NEGRO Ham. Taxable in the household of John Ruff, Spesutia Lower Hundred, 1775.
NEGRO Hamdon. Taxable in household of J. Beale Boadley, Gunpowder Lower Hundred, 1775.
NEGRO Hamond. Taxable in household of Ellender Durham, Bush River Lower Hundred, 1775.
NEGRO Hanary. Taxable on plantation of Ignatious Wheler, Spesutia Upper Hundred, 1775.
NEGRO Hanibal. Taxable in household of Col. Thomas White, Susquehanna Hundred, 1775.
NEGRO Hanibol. Taxable in household of Dr. Moses Haslet, Gunpowder Lower Hundred, 1775.
NEGRO Hanna. Taxable in household of Martha Presbury, Gunpowder Lower Hundred, 1775.

NEGRO Hanna. Taxable in household of Capt. James Maxwell, Gunpowder Lower Hundred, 1775.

NEGRO Hannah (a free negro). Head of household in Susquehanna Hundred, 1776.

NEGRO Hannah Jr. Taxable at Dr. Henry Stephenson's Quarters, Spesutia Lower Hundred, 1776.

NEGRO Hannah. Taxable in household of Ann Bond, Bush River Lower Hundred, 1775.

NEGRO Hannah. Taxable in household of John Hays, Jr., Bush River Lower Hundred, 1775.

NEGRO Hannah. Taxable in household of John Peca, Bush River Lower Hundred, 1775.

NEGRO Hannah. Taxable in household of Thomas Smithson, Sr., Bush River Lower Hundred, 1775.

NEGRO Hannah. Taxable in household of Edward Talbott, Bush River Lower Hundred, 1775.

NEGRO Hannah. Taxable at Jacob Bond's Quarters, Gunpowder Lower Hundred, 1775.

NEGRO Hannah. Taxable in household of Elizabeth Lytle, Gunpowder Lower Hundred, 1775.

NEGRO Hannah. Taxable in household of Greenberry Dorsey, Spesutia Lower Hundred, 1775.

NEGRO Hannah. Taxable at Richard Dallam's Quarters at Romney, Spesutia Lower Hundred, 1775.

NEGRO Hannah. Taxable in household of George Chancey, Sr., Spesutia Lower Hundred, 1775.

NEGRO Hannah. Taxable in household of Samuel Griffith, Spesutia Lower Hundred, 1775.

NEGRO Hannah. Taxable in household of Benjamin Ford, Spesutia Lower Hundred, 1775.

NEGRO Hannah. Taxable on plantation of James Phillips, Spesutia Lower Hundred, 1775.

NEGRO Hannah. Taxable on plantation of Hannah Hall, Spesutia Lower Hundred, 1775.

NEGRO Hannah. Taxable in the household of John Hanson, Sr., Spesutia Lower Hundred, 1775.

NEGRO Hannah. Taxable on plantation of Aquila Hall, Spesutia Lower Hundred, 1775.

NEGRO Hannah. Taxable in household of William Bradford, Spesutia Upper Hundred, 1775.

NEGRO Hannah. Taxable in household of Aquila Hall, Jr., Spesutia Upper Hundred, 1775.

NEGRO Hannah. Taxable in household of William Prigg, Sr., Spesutia Upper Hundred, 1775.

NEGRO Hannah. Taxable in household of Josiah Hitchcock, Bush River Upper Hundred, 1775.

NEGRO Hannah. Taxable in household of Hugh Dorran, Bush River Upper Hundred, 1775.

NEGRO Hannah. Taxable in household of Henry Guspey, Deer Creek Lower Hundred, 1775.

NEGRO Hannah. Taxable in household of Francis Downing, Deer Creek Lower Hundred, 1775.

NEGRO Hannah. Taxable on plantation of Hannah Hall, Spesutia Lower Hundred, 1776.

NEGRO Hannah. Taxable on plantation of George Ford, Spesutia Lower Hundred, 1776.

NEGRO Hannah. Taxable in household of Greenberry Dorsey, Spesutia Lower Hundred, 1776.

NEGRO Hannah. Taxable on plantation of Samuel Griffith, Spesutia Lower Hundred, 1776.

NEGRO Hannah. Taxable at Dr. Henry Stephenson's Quarters, Spesutia Lower Hundred, 1776.

NEGRO Hannah. Taxable in household of Isaac Tulock, Spesutia Lower Hundred, 1776.

NEGRO Hannah. Taxable in household of Josias Hall, Susquehanna Hundred, 1776.

NEGRO Hannar. Taxable in household of Asell Hitchcock, Bush River Upper Hundred, 1775.

NEGRO Hannibal. Taxable at Dr. Henry Stephenson's Quarters, Spesutia Lower Hundred, 1775.

NEGRO Harkellees. Taxable on plantation of Jacob Giles, Susquehanna Hundred, 1776.

NEGRO Harrey. Taxable in household of Charles Worthington, Deer Creek Lower Hundred, 1775.

NEGRO Harry. Taxable in Bush River Lower Hundred, 1775, with Benjamin Howard as security.

NEGRO Harry. Taxable in household of John Peca, Bush River Lower Hundred, 1775.

NEGRO Harry. Taxable in household of George Copland, Spesutia Lower Hundred, 1775.

NEGRO Harry. Taxable in Susquehanna Hundred, 1775 William Wilson, Susquehanna Hundred, 1775.

NEGRO Harry. Taxable in household of Benjamin Ford, Spesutia Lower Hundred, 1775.

NEGRO Harry. Taxable in the household of George Little, Spesutia Lower Hundred, 1775.

NEGRO Harry. Taxable on plantation of James Phillips, Spesutia Lower Hundred, 1775.

NEGRO Harry. Taxable in the household of William Smith, Spesutia Lower Hundred, 1775.

NEGRO Harry. Taxable in the household of William Osborn, Jr., Spesutia Lower Hundred, 1775.

NEGRO Harry. Taxable "at ye glebe" of Rev. William West, Spesutia Lower Hundred, 1775.

NEGRO Harry. Taxable in household of Danniel Richardson, Spesutia Upper Hundred, 1775.

NEGRO Harry. Taxable in household of Winston Smith, Bush River Upper Hundred, 1775.

NEGRO Harry. Taxable on plantation of William Smith, Jr., Spesutia Lower Hundred, 1776.

NEGRO Harry. Taxable in household of William Wilson, Susquehanna Hundred, 1776.

NEGRO Hary. Taxable at Isaac Whiteker's Quarters, Spesutia Upper Hundred, 1775.

NEGRO Hazard. Taxable in the household of Edward Ward, Spesutia Lower Hundred, 1775.

NEGRO Hazard. Taxable in household of Benjaman Wilson, Deer Creek Lower Hundred, 1775.

NEGRO Hazard. Taxable in household of Edward Ward, Spesutia Lower Hundred, 1776.
NEGRO Hector. Taxable in household of Betty Lusby, Gunpowder Lower Hundred, 1775.
NEGRO Hector. Taxable on plantation of Hannah Hall, Spesutia Lower Hundred, 1775.
NEGRO Hector. Taxable in household of Joseph Hopkins, Deer Creek Lower Hundred, 1775.
NEGRO Hector. Taxable in household of Joseph Hopkins, Deer Creek Lower Hundred, 1775.
NEGRO Hector. Taxable on plantation of Hannah Hall, Spesutia Lower Hundred, 1776.
NEGRO Henny. Taxable in household of Benjaman Wheler, Spesutia Upper Hundred, 1775.
NEGRO Henny. Taxable on plantation of Ignatious Wheler, Spesutia Upper Hundred, 1775.
NEGRO Henry. Taxable in household of Ann Bond, Bush River Lower Hundred, 1775.
NEGRO Henry. Taxable on plantation of John Lee Webster, Spesutia Lower Hundred, 1776.
NEGRO Herculees. Taxable in household of Jonathan Woodland, Gunpowder Lower Hundred, 1775.
NEGRO Herculees. Taxable in household of Jacob Giles, Susquehanna Hundred, 1775.
NEGRO Herculees. Taxable in household of Benjamin Ford, Spesutia Lower Hundred, 1775.
NEGRO Herculees. Taxable on plantation of George Ford, Spesutia Lower Hundred, 1776.
NEGRO Hercules. Taxable on plantation of Aquila Hall, Spesutia Lower Hundred, 1775.
NEGRO Hester. Taxable in the household of Benedict Edward Hall, Spesutia Lower Hundred, 1775.
NEGRO Hester. Taxable on plantation of Ignatious Wheler, Spesutia Upper Hundred, 1775.
NEGRO Hettey. Taxable on plantation of William Smith, Jr., Spesutia Lower Hundred, 1776.
NEGRO Holaday. Taxable in household of Thomas Chew, Deer Creek Lower Hundred, 1775.
NEGRO Holliday. Taxable in household of Thomas Richardson, Sr., Bush River Lower Hundred, 1775.
NEGRO Honour. Taxable in household of Jacob Bond, Sr., Bush River Lower Hundred, 1775.
NEGRO Isaac. Taxable in the household of James Osborn, Jr., Spesutia Lower Hundred, 1775.
NEGRO Isaac. Taxable in household of Richard Wells, Deer Creek Lower Hundred, 1775.
NEGRO Isaac. Taxable on plantation of George Ford, Spesutia Lower Hundred, 1776.
NEGRO Isaac. Taxables on plantation of William Hopkins, Deer Creek Lower Hundred, 1775.
NEGRO Isac. Taxable in household of Ignatius Wheeler, Jr., Deer Creek Upper Hundred, 1775.
NEGRO Isibiler. Taxable in household of Ann Norris, Bush River Lower Hundred, 1775.

NEGRO J----. Taxable in household of Robert Morgan, Deer Creek Lower Hundred, 1775.
NEGRO Ja--- [page torn]. Taxable in household of Mary Carlile, Bush River Lower Hundred, 1775.
NEGRO Jack 2nd. Taxable in household of Freeborn Brown, Spesutia Lower Hundred, 1775.
NEGRO Jack Jr. Taxable in household of Sarah Brown, Spesutia Lower Hundred, 1776.
NEGRO Jack or Jacob [sic]. Taxable on plantation of Samuel Griffith, Spesutia Lower Hundred, 1776.
NEGRO Jack. Taxable in household of William Smithson, Bush River Lower Hundred, 1775.
NEGRO Jack. Taxable in household of Thomas Richardson, Sr., Bush River Lower Hundred, 1775.
NEGRO Jack. Taxable in household of Ann Scott, Bush River Lower Hundred, 1775.
NEGRO Jack. Taxable in household of Daniel Scott, Bush River Lower Hundred, 1775.
NEGRO Jack. Taxable at Asel Gittings' Quarters, Gunpowder Lower Hundred, 1775.
NEGRO Jack. Taxable in Gunpowder Lower Hundred, 1775.
NEGRO Jack. Taxable in household of Martha Presbury, Gunpowder Lower Hundred, 1775.
NEGRO Jack. Taxable in household of Thomas Waltham, Gunpowder Lower Hundred, 1775.
NEGRO Jack. Taxable in household of Betty Lusby, Gunpowder Lower Hundred, 1775.
NEGRO Jack. Taxable in household of William Creswell, Susquehanna Hundred, 1775.
NEGRO Jack. Taxable in household of Ephraim Andrews, Susquehanna Hundred, 1775.
NEGRO Jack. Taxable in household of Henery Stump, Susquehanna Hundred, 1775.
NEGRO Jack. Taxable in household of Freeborn Brown, Spesutia Lower Hundred, 1775.
NEGRO Jack. Taxable in household of Samuel Griffith, Spesutia Lower Hundred, 1775.
NEGRO Jack. Taxable in the household of William Hollis, Sr., Spesutia Lower Hundred, 1775.
NEGRO Jack. Taxable on the plantation of Amos Garrett, Spesutia Lower Hundred, 1775.
NEGRO Jack. Taxable on plantation of James Phillips, Spesutia Lower Hundred, 1775.
NEGRO Jack. Taxable in the household of Leven Matthews, Spesutia Lower Hundred, 1775.
NEGRO Jack. Taxable in the household of Aquila Paca, Jr., Spesutia Lower Hundred, 1775.
NEGRO Jack. Taxable in the household of Benjamin Hanson, Spesutia Lower Hundred, 1775.
NEGRO Jack. Taxable in household of Sillina Clark, Spesutia Upper Hundred, 1775.
NEGRO Jack. Taxable at Clark Young's Quarters, Spesutia Lower Hundred, 1775.

NEGRO Jack. Taxable at Dr. Henry Stephenson's Quarters, Spesutia Lower Hundred, 1775.
NEGRO Jack. Taxable in household of John Love, Spesutia Upper Hundred, 1775.
NEGRO Jack. Taxable in household of Thomas Wheler, Spesutia Upper Hundred, 1775.
NEGRO Jack. Taxable in household of Elizabeth Wheler, Spesutia Upper Hundred, 1775.
NEGRO Jack. Taxable in household of Barnard Preston, Spesutia Upper Hundred, 1775.
NEGRO Jack. Taxable in household of James Mores, Spesutia Upper Hundred, 1775.
NEGRO Jack. Taxable in household of Benjaman Wheler, Spesutia Upper Hundred, 1775.
NEGRO Jack. Taxable at Cumberland Forge, Deer Creek Lower Hundred, 1775.
NEGRO Jack. Taxable on plantation of William Smith, Sr, Bush River Upper Hundred, 1775.
NEGRO Jack. Taxable in household of Skipwith Coal, Deer Creek Lower Hundred, 1775.
NEGRO Jack. Taxable in household of William Fisher, Deer Creek Lower Hundred, 1775.
NEGRO Jack. Taxable in household of Sarah Brown, Spesutia Lower Hundred, 1776.
NEGRO Jack. Taxable on plantation of Amos Garrett, Spesutia Lower Hundred, 1776.
NEGRO Jack. Taxable at Dr. Henry Stephenson's Quarters, Spesutia Lower Hundred, 1776.
NEGRO Jack. Taxable on plantation of Ephrem Andres, Susquehanna Hundred, 1776.
NEGRO Jack. Taxable in household of William Creswell, Susquehanna Hundred, 1776.
NEGRO Jack. Taxable in household of Aquila Paca, Jr., Spesutia Lower Hundred, 1776.
NEGRO Jack. Taxable in household of John Bedle Hall, Susquehanna Hundred, 1776.
NEGRO Jack. Taxable at Thomas Harrison's Quarters, Susquehanna Hundred, 1776.
NEGRO Jack. Taxable in household of Henry Stump, Susquehanna Hundred, 1776.
NEGRO Jack. Taxables on plantation of William Hopkins, Deer Creek Lower Hundred, 1775.
NEGRO Jacob. Taxable in household of Aquila Scott, Bush River Lower Hundred, 1775.
NEGRO Jacob. Taxable in household of J. Beale Boadley, Gunpowder Lower Hundred, 1775.
NEGRO Jacob. Taxable at Thomas Harrison's Quarters, Susquehanna Hundred, 1775.
NEGRO Jacob. Taxable in household of George Ford, Spesutia Lower Hundred, 1775.
NEGRO Jacob. Taxable in household of Josias Carvel Hall, Spesutia Lower Hundred, 1775.
NEGRO Jacob. Taxable on plantation of Capt. John Hall, Spesutia Lower Hundred, 1775.
NEGRO Jacob. Taxable on the plantation of Amos Garrett, Spesutia Lower Hundred, 1775.
NEGRO Jacob. Taxable on plantation of James Phillips, Spesutia Lower Hundred, 1775.
NEGRO Jacob. Taxable on plantation of Aquila Hall, Spesutia Lower Hundred, 1775.
NEGRO Jacob. Taxable in the household of Cyrus Osborn, Spesutia Lower Hundred, 1775.
NEGRO Jacob. Taxable in household of Henry Cooper, Spesutia Upper Hundred, 1775.
NEGRO Jacob. Taxable in household of Ignatius Matthews, Spesutia Upper Hundred, 1775.
NEGRO Jacob. Taxable in household of George Chalk, Bush River Upper Hundred, 1775.
NEGRO Jacob. Taxable in household of James Rigbie, Deer Creek Lower Hundred, 1775.
NEGRO Jacob. Taxable in household of Casandra Sheridine (widow), Deer Creek Lower Hundred, 1775.
NEGRO Jacob. Taxable in household of Leven Mathews, Spesutia Lower Hundred, 1776.
NEGRO Jacob. Taxable at Aquila Hall's Quarters, Spesutia Lower Hundred, 1776.
NEGRO Jacob. Taxable on plantation of Dr. Josias Carvell Hall, Spesutia Lower Hundred, 1776.
NEGRO Jacob. Taxable on plantation of George Ford, Spesutia Lower Hundred, 1776.
NEGRO Jacob. Taxable on plantation of Amos Garrett, Spesutia Lower Hundred, 1776.
NEGRO Jacob. Taxable at Thomas Harrison's Quarters, Susquehanna Hundred, 1776.
NEGRO Jain. Taxable in household of Danniel Richardson, Spesutia Upper Hundred, 1775.
NEGRO Jam. Taxable in household of Thomas Peregrine Frisby, Spesutia Lower Hundred, 1776.
NEGRO James. Taxable in household of John Green, Bush River Lower Hundred, 1775.
NEGRO James. Taxable in household of Rachel Thorp, Bush River Lower Hundred, 1775.
NEGRO James. Taxable at Jacob Giles' Quarters at Romney, Spesutia Lower Hundred, 1775.
NEGRO James. Taxable at William Smith's Quarters, Spesutia Lower Hundred, 1775.
NEGRO James. Taxable on plantation of Hannah Hall, Spesutia Lower Hundred, 1775.
NEGRO James. Taxable in the household of Joseph Puntney, Spesutia Lower Hundred, 1775.
NEGRO James. Taxable in household of John Archer, Spesutia Upper Hundred, 1775.
NEGRO James. Taxable in household of Micheal Hannor, Spesutia Upper Hundred, 1775.
NEGRO James. Taxable in household of James Amoss, Bush River Upper Hundred, 1775.
NEGRO James. Taxable on plantation of William Smith,

Sr, Bush River Upper Hundred, 1775.

NEGRO James. Taxable at Cumberland Forge, Deer Creek Lower Hundred, 1775.

NEGRO James. Taxable in household of William Coal, Deer Creek Lower Hundred, 1775.

NEGRO James. Taxable in household of John Hawkins, Deer Creek Lower Hundred, 1775.

NEGRO James. Taxable in household of Elizabeth Morgan, Deer Creek Lower Hundred, 1775.

NEGRO James. Taxable in household of Elizabeth Husbands (widow), Deer Creek Lower Hundred, 1775.

NEGRO James. Taxable in household of Elizabeth Gover, Deer Creek Lower Hundred, 1775.

NEGRO James. Taxable on plantation of William Webb, Deer Creek Upper Hundred, 1775.

NEGRO James. Taxable in household of Thomas Giles, Spesutia Lower Hundred, 1776.

NEGRO James. Taxable on plantation of William Smith, Jr., Spesutia Lower Hundred, 1776.

NEGRO James. Taxables on plantation of William Hopkins, Deer Creek Lower Hundred, 1775.

NEGRO Jane. Taxable in household of Jacob Giles, Jr., Susquehanna Hundred, 1775.

NEGRO Jane. Taxable in Susquehanna Hundred, 1775 William Wilson, Susquehanna Hundred, 1775.

NEGRO Jane. Taxable in household of Freeborn Brown, Spesutia Lower Hundred, 1775.

NEGRO Jane. Taxable on plantation of James Phillips, Spesutia Lower Hundred, 1775.

NEGRO Jane. Taxable on plantation of Hannah Hall, Spesutia Lower Hundred, 1775.

NEGRO Jane. Taxable in the household of James Kimble, Spesutia Lower Hundred, 1775.

NEGRO Jane. Taxable in household of Mary Chalk (widow), Bush River Upper Hundred, 1775.

NEGRO Jane. Taxable on plantation of Hannah Hall, Spesutia Lower Hundred, 1776.

NEGRO Jane. Taxable on plantation of Samuel Griffith, Spesutia Lower Hundred, 1776.

NEGRO Jane. Taxable on plantation of John Lee Webster, Spesutia Lower Hundred, 1776.

NEGRO Jane. Taxable in household of Rachel Wilson, Susquehanna Hundred, 1776.

NEGRO Jason. Taxable in household of James Armstrong, Spesutia Upper Hundred, 1775.

NEGRO Jean. Taxable in household of William Amos, Sr., Bush River Lower Hundred, 1775.

NEGRO Jean. Taxable in household of Samuel Durham, Bush River Lower Hundred, 1775.

NEGRO Jean. Taxable in household of John Wain, Bush River Lower Hundred, 1775.

NEGRO Jean. Taxable in household of Sarah Brown, Spesutia Lower Hundred, 1776.

NEGRO Jean. Taxable in household of James Kimble, Spesutia Lower Hundred, 1776.

NEGRO Jeany. Taxable in household of Josias Carvel Hall, Spesutia Lower Hundred, 1775.

NEGRO Jeaoh. Taxable in household of Negro Jehue (a free negro), Susquehanna Hundred, 1776.

NEGRO Jeffery. Taxable in household of Ashberry Cord, Spesutia Lower Hundred, 1776.

NEGRO Jeffery. Taxable in household of Thomas Smith, Susquehanna Hundred, 1776.

NEGRO Jeffery. Taxable on plantation of Philip Gover, Susquehanna Hundred, 1776.

NEGRO Jeffrey. Taxable in household of David Sweeny, Jr., Deer Creek Lower Hundred, 1775.

NEGRO Jeffry. Taxable in household of Philip Gover, Susquehanna Hundred, 1775.

NEGRO Jefro. Taxable in the household of John Copeland, Spesutia Lower Hundred, 1775.

NEGRO Jehu. Taxable in Susquehanna Hundred, 1775, a free negro, with a taxable named "Joash Joshua" listed in his household.

NEGRO Jehue (a free negro). Head of household in Susquehanna Hundred, 1776, with taxable Jeaoh and Joshua listed in his household.

NEGRO Jemey. Taxable on plantation of Amos Garrett, Spesutia Lower Hundred, 1776.

NEGRO Jemima. Taxable on plantation of Thomas Gash, Spesutia Lower Hundred, 1776.

NEGRO Jemima. Taxable in household of William Wilson (overseer), Susquehanna Hundred, 1776.

NEGRO Jemimah. Taxable at William Wilson's Quarter, Susquehanna Hundred, 1775.

NEGRO Jemina. Taxable in household of Martha Garrettson, Spesutia Lower Hundred, 1776.

NEGRO Jemmy. Taxable in household of James Giles, Spesutia Lower Hundred, 1776.

NEGRO Jenney. Taxable in household of William Coal, Deer Creek Lower Hundred, 1775.

NEGRO Jenney. Taxable in household of Mordica Craford, Deer Creek Lower Hundred, 1775.

NEGRO Jenney. Taxable in household of John Worthington, Deer Creek Lower Hundred, 1775.

NEGRO Jenney. Taxable on plantation of Edward Carvel Tolley, Spesutia Lower Hundred, 1776.

NEGRO Jenney. Taxable at Samuel Thomas' Quarters, Susquehanna Hundred, 1776.

NEGRO Jenny. Taxable in household of Thomas Bond, Sr., Bush River Lower Hundred, 1775.

NEGRO Jenny. Taxable in household of John Taylor, Bush River Lower Hundred, 1775.

NEGRO Jenny. Taxable in household of William Gale, Gunpowder Lower Hundred, 1775.

NEGRO Jenny. Taxable at Samuel Thomas' Quarters, Susquehanna Hundred, 1775.

NEGRO Jenny. Taxable in household of William Clark, Spesutia Upper Hundred, 1775.

NEGRO Jenny. Taxable in household of Nicholous Waters, Spesutia Upper Hundred, 1775.

NEGRO Jenny. Taxable on plantation of George Ford, Spesutia Lower Hundred, 1776.

NEGRO Jenny. Taxable in household of Daniel Anderson, Susquehanna Hundred, 1776.

NEGRO Jere. Taxable at Thomas Harrison's Quarters, Susquehanna Hundred, 1776.

NEGRO Jeremiah. Taxable in household of Isaac Daws, Bush River Lower Hundred, 1775.

NEGRO Jeremiah. Taxable in household of George Garretson, Spesutia Lower Hundred, 1775.

NEGRO Jeremiah. Taxable at William Paca's Quarters, Spesutia Lower Hundred, 1775.

NEGRO Jerry. Taxable in household of James Giles, Spesutia Lower Hundred, 1775.

NEGRO Jerry. Taxable on the plantation of Amos Garrett, Spesutia Lower Hundred, 1775.

NEGRO Jerry. Taxable at Clark Young's Quarters, Spesutia Lower Hundred, 1775.

NEGRO Jerry. Taxable on plantation of Amos Garrett, Spesutia Lower Hundred, 1776.

NEGRO Jerry. Taxable on plantation of George Ford, Spesutia Lower Hundred, 1776.

NEGRO Jerry. Taxable in household of Robert Stokes, Spesutia Lower Hundred, 1776.

NEGRO Jess. Taxable in household of Ignatius Wheeler, Jr., Deer Creek Upper Hundred, 1775.

NEGRO Jessee. Taxable in household of Col. Thomas White, Susquehanna Hundred, 1775.

NEGRO Jessey. Taxables on plantation of Col. Thomas White, Susquehanna Hundred, 1776.

NEGRO Jim. Taxable in household of Elizabeth Lytle, Gunpowder Lower Hundred, 1775.

NEGRO Jim. Taxable in household of Henery Wetherell, Gunpowder Lower Hundred, 1775.

NEGRO Jim. Taxable in household of Basil Smith, Gunpowder Lower Hundred, 1775.

NEGRO Jim. Taxable in household of John Day (son of Edward), Gunpowder Lower Hundred, 1775.

NEGRO Jim. Taxable in household of Greenberry Dorsey, Spesutia Lower Hundred, 1775.

NEGRO Jim. Taxable in household of Benjamin Ford, Spesutia Lower Hundred, 1775.

NEGRO Jim. Taxable in household of Thomas Peregrin Frisby, Spesutia Lower Hundred, 1775.

NEGRO Jim. Taxable in household of Henry Cooper, Spesutia Upper Hundred, 1775.

NEGRO Jim. Taxable in household of John Craton, Spesutia Upper Hundred, 1775.

NEGRO Jim. Taxable in household of Isaac Webster, Spesutia Upper Hundred, 1775.

NEGRO Jim. Taxable in household of Joseph Wheler, Spesutia Upper Hundred, 1775.

NEGRO Jim. Taxable in household of Henry Ruff, Spesutia Upper Hundred, 1775.

NEGRO Jim. Taxable in household of George Vogan, Bush River Upper Hundred, 1775.

NEGRO Jim. Taxable on plantation of George Ford, Spesutia Lower Hundred, 1776.

NEGRO Jim. Taxable in household of Greenberry Dorsey, Spesutia Lower Hundred, 1776.

NEGRO Jimguin. Taxable in household of William Hall, Spesutia Lower Hundred, 1775.

NEGRO Jimmey. Taxable on plantation of William Hall, Spesutia Lower Hundred, 1776.

NEGRO Jo. Taxable in household of Danile Brown, Jr., Gunpowder Lower Hundred, 1775.

NEGRO Jo. Taxable in household of Isaac Webster, Spesutia Upper Hundred, 1775.

NEGRO Jocka. Taxable in household of Edward Talbott, Bush River Lower Hundred, 1775.

NEGRO Joe. Taxable in household of Elizabeth Davis, Bush River Lower Hundred, 1775.

NEGRO Joe. Taxable in household of Buckler Bond, Bush River Lower Hundred, 1775.

NEGRO Joe. Taxable in household of Aquilla Paca, Gunpowder Lower Hundred, 1775.

NEGRO Joe. Taxable in household of Charles Gilbert, Susquehanna Hundred, 1775.

NEGRO Joe. Taxable in household of Henery Stump, Susquehanna Hundred, 1775.

NEGRO Joe. Taxable on plantation of John Matthews, Spesutia Lower Hundred, 1775.

NEGRO Joe. Taxable in the household of Henry Vansickleton, Spesutia Lower Hundred, 1775.

NEGRO Joe. Taxable on plantation of John Lee Webster, Spesutia Lower Hundred, 1775.

NEGRO Joe. Taxable on plantation of James Phillips, Spesutia Lower Hundred, 1775.

NEGRO Joe. Taxable at Dr. Henry Stephenson's Quarters, Spesutia Lower Hundred, 1775.

NEGRO Joe. Taxable in household of Andrew Norris, Bush River Upper Hundred, 1775.

NEGRO Joe. Taxable at Jacob Giles, Jr.'s Quarters, Spesutia Lower Hundred, 1776.

NEGRO Joe. Taxable on plantation of Capt. John Mathews, Spesutia Lower Hundred, 1776.

NEGRO Joe. Taxable in household of Henry Vansickleton, Spesutia Lower Hundred, 1776.

NEGRO Joe. Taxable on plantation of John Lee Webster, Spesutia Lower Hundred, 1776.

NEGRO Joe. Taxable at Dr. Henry Stephenson's Quarters, Spesutia Lower Hundred, 1776.

NEGRO Joe. Taxable on plantation of Jacob Giles, Jr., Susquehanna Hundred, 1776.

NEGRO Joe. Taxable in household of Michel Gilbert (son of Charles), Susquehanna Hundred, 1776.
NEGRO Joe. Taxable in household of Henry Stump, Susquehanna Hundred, 1776.
NEGRO John Johnson. See "John Johnson (free negro)," q.v.
NEGRO John. Taxable in household of Daniel McComas, Bush River Lower Hundred, 1775.
NEGRO John. Taxable in household of Dannill Bond, Bush River Upper Hundred, 1775.
NEGRO John. Taxable in household of Thomas Baker Rigdon, Deer Creek Upper Hundred, 1775.
NEGRO John. Taxable in household of Thomas Foster, Deer Creek Upper Hundred, 1775.
NEGRO Jone. Taxable in household of Sarah Norris, Bush River Lower Hundred, 1775.
NEGRO Jone. Taxable in household of Henry Green, Spesutia Upper Hundred, 1775.
NEGRO Jone. Taxable on plantation of Ignatious Wheler, Spesutia Upper Hundred, 1775.
NEGRO Joshua. Taxable in household of Walter Billingsley, Spesutia Upper Hundred, 1775.
NEGRO Joshua. Taxable in household of William Clark, Spesutia Upper Hundred, 1775.
NEGRO Joshua. Taxable in household of Negro Jehue (a free negro), Susquehanna Hundred, 1776.
NEGRO Juba. Taxable in household of Josias Carvel Hall, Spesutia Lower Hundred, 1775.
NEGRO Juda. Taxable in Bush River Lower Hundred, 1775, with Henry Wilson, Sr. as her security.
NEGRO Jude. Taxable in household of Thomas Richardson, Sr., Bush River Lower Hundred, 1775.
NEGRO Judiah. Taxable on plantation of Hannah Hall, Spesutia Lower Hundred, 1776.
NEGRO Judiah. Taxable in household of James Kimble, Spesutia Lower Hundred, 1776.
NEGRO Judie. Taxable in household of Philip Gover, Susquehanna Hundred, 1775.
NEGRO Judie. Taxable in household of Charles Gilbert, Susquehanna Hundred, 1775.
NEGRO Judith. Taxable on plantation of Capt. John Hall, Spesutia Lower Hundred, 1775.
NEGRO Judith. Taxable in the household of James Kimble, Spesutia Lower Hundred, 1775.
NEGRO Judy. Taxable on plantation of Hannah Hall, Spesutia Lower Hundred, 1775.
NEGRO Judy. Taxable in the household of Edward Carvel Tolley, Spesutia Lower Hundred, 1775.
NEGRO Judy. Taxable in household of David Clark, Spesutia Upper Hundred, 1775.
NEGRO Judy. Taxable in the household of Edward Ward, Spesutia Lower Hundred, 1775.
NEGRO Judy. Taxable in household of William Prigg, Sr., Spesutia Upper Hundred, 1775.
NEGRO Judy. Taxable in household of Thomas Chew, Deer Creek Lower Hundred, 1775.
NEGRO Judy. Taxable on plantation of Philip Gover, Susquehanna Hundred, 1776.
NEGRO Juelia. Taxable on plantation of Edward Carvel Tolley, Spesutia Lower Hundred, 1776.
NEGRO Jula. Taxable in household of Benjamin Rumsey, Gunpowder Lower Hundred, 1775.
NEGRO Juley. Taxable on plantation of Dr. Josias Carvell Hall, Spesutia Lower Hundred, 1776.
NEGRO June. Taxable on plantation of Capt. John Mathews, Spesutia Lower Hundred, 1776.
NEGRO Jupiter. Taxable in household of Benjamin Ford, Spesutia Lower Hundred, 1775.
NEGRO Jupiter. Taxable in household of Phebe Gallion, Spesutia Lower Hundred, 1775.
NEGRO Jupiter. Taxable on plantation of John Lee Webster, Spesutia Lower Hundred, 1775.
NEGRO Jupiter. Taxable in household of Casandra Sheridine (widow), Deer Creek Lower Hundred, 1775.
NEGRO Jupiter. Taxable on plantation of George Ford, Spesutia Lower Hundred, 1776.
NEGRO Kate. Taxable in household of George Garretson, Bush River Lower Hundred, 1775.
NEGRO Kate. Taxable in the household of Edward Hall, Spesutia Lower Hundred, 1775.
NEGRO Kate. Taxable in household of John Archer, Spesutia Upper Hundred, 1775.
NEGRO Kate. Taxable in household of Samuel Morgan, Deer Creek Upper Hundred, 1775.
NEGRO Kate. Taxable in household of William Loney, Spesutia Lower Hundred, 1776.
NEGRO Kate. Taxable on plantation of John Lee Webster, Spesutia Lower Hundred, 1776.
NEGRO Kimish. Taxable in household of Thomas Baker Rigdon, Deer Creek Upper Hundred, 1775.
NEGRO Laury. Taxable at Richard Dallam's Quarters at Swan Creek, Spesutia Lower Hundred, 1775.
NEGRO Lawtur. Taxable in household of Elizabeth Lytle, Gunpowder Lower Hundred, 1775.
NEGRO Leah. Taxable on plantation of Aquila Hall, Spesutia Lower Hundred, 1775.
NEGRO Leah. Taxable in household of Nathaniel Rigbie, Deer Creek Lower Hundred, 1775.
NEGRO Leander. Taxable in household of Ruth Barnes, Susquehanna Hundred, 1775.
NEGRO Leander. Taxable on plantation of Aquila Hall, Spesutia Lower Hundred, 1775.
NEGRO Leander. Taxable on plantation of Hannah Hall, Spesutia Lower Hundred, 1775.
NEGRO Leander. Taxable on plantation of Hannah Hall, Spesutia Lower Hundred, 1776.
NEGRO Lear. Taxable at Aquila Hall's Quarters, Spesutia

Lower Hundred, 1776.

NEGRO Learles. Taxable in household of John Rumsey, Susquehanna Hundred, 1776.

NEGRO Len. Taxable in household of Samuel Lee, Spesutia Upper Hundred, 1775.

NEGRO Levi. Taxable in household of Robert Nelson, Bush River Upper Hundred, 1775.

NEGRO Lew. Taxable in household of Josias William Dallam, Spesutia Lower Hundred, 1775.

NEGRO Lew. Taxable on plantation of Hannah Hall, Spesutia Lower Hundred, 1776.

NEGRO Lew. Taxable on plantation of Josias William Dallam, Spesutia Lower Hundred, 1776.

NEGRO Lewshore. Taxable in household of John Peca, Bush River Lower Hundred, 1775.

NEGRO Lida. Taxable in household of Edward Ward, Deer Creek Lower Hundred, 1775.

NEGRO Liddy. Taxable in household of Mary Waters, Gunpowder Lower Hundred, 1775.

NEGRO Limbrick. Taxable on the plantation of Amos Garrett, Spesutia Lower Hundred, 1775.

NEGRO Limbrick. Taxable on plantation of Amos Garrett, Spesutia Lower Hundred, 1776.

NEGRO Limpal. Taxable in household of Col. Thomas White, Susquehanna Hundred, 1775.

NEGRO Lin. Taxables on plantation of Col. Thomas White, Susquehanna Hundred, 1776.

NEGRO Lingas. Taxable in household of Elizabeth Gover, Deer Creek Lower Hundred, 1775.

NEGRO Little Dinah. Taxable on plantation of Aquila Hall, Spesutia Lower Hundred, 1775.

NEGRO London. Taxable in household of Benjamin Rumsey, Gunpowder Lower Hundred, 1775.

NEGRO London. Taxable in household of James Giles, Spesutia Lower Hundred, 1775.

NEGRO London. Taxable in household of Aquila Hall, Jr., Spesutia Upper Hundred, 1775.

NEGRO London. Taxable in household of Skipwith Coal, Deer Creek Lower Hundred, 1775.

NEGRO London. Taxable in household of Richard Wells, Deer Creek Lower Hundred, 1775.

NEGRO Long Fanney. Taxable in household of John Peca, Bush River Lower Hundred, 1775.

NEGRO Lonnon. Taxable in household of Edmond Bull, Spesutia Upper Hundred, 1775.

NEGRO Lot. Taxable at Jacob Giles' Quarters at Romney, Spesutia Lower Hundred, 1775.

NEGRO Lotto. Taxable in household of Henry Green, Spesutia Upper Hundred, 1775.

NEGRO Lottos. Taxable in the household of George Little, Spesutia Lower Hundred, 1775.

NEGRO Lowrey. Taxable in household of Daniel Durbin, Spesutia Lower Hundred, 1776.

NEGRO Luce. Taxable in household of Henry Green, Spesutia Upper Hundred, 1775.

NEGRO Luce. Taxable in household of Benjamin Green, Spesutia Upper Hundred, 1775.

NEGRO Lucey. Taxable in household of Benedict Edward Hall, Spesutia Lower Hundred, 1776.

NEGRO Lucy. Taxable in household of Alexander Cowen, Gunpowder Lower Hundred, 1775.

NEGRO Lue. Taxable on plantation of Jacob Giles, Jr., Susquehanna Hundred, 1776.

NEGRO Luke. Taxable on plantation of James Lee, Deer Creek Lower Hundred, 1775.

NEGRO Lundon. Taxable on plantation of Philip Gover, Susquehanna Hundred, 1776.

NEGRO Luraner. Taxable on plantation of Hannah Hall, Spesutia Lower Hundred, 1775.

NEGRO Luraney. Taxable in household of Amos Hollis, Spesutia Lower Hundred, 1775.

NEGRO Luta. Taxable in household of James McComas, Bush River Lower Hundred, 1775.

NEGRO Lyda. Taxable in Bush River Lower Hundred, 1775, with Henry Wilson, Sr. as her security.

NEGRO Lydia. Taxable in Bush River Lower Hundred, 1775, owned by R. Howard.

NEGRO Lynita. Taxable on plantation of Hannah Hall, Spesutia Lower Hundred, 1776.

NEGRO Mana. Taxable in household of Benedict Edward Hall, Spesutia Lower Hundred, 1776.

NEGRO Manner. Taxable in household of James Giles, Spesutia Lower Hundred, 1775.

NEGRO Manuel. Taxable on plantation of Aquila Hall, Spesutia Lower Hundred, 1775.

NEGRO Many. Taxable in household of Thomas Bond, Sr., Bush River Lower Hundred, 1775.

NEGRO Marai. Taxable in household of Lemuel Howard, Bush River Lower Hundred, 1775.

NEGRO Marai. Taxable in household of Ellender Durham, Bush River Lower Hundred, 1775.

NEGRO Marcus. Taxable at Cumberland Forge, Deer Creek Lower Hundred, 1775.

NEGRO Marea. Taxable in household of Josiah Hitchcock, Bush River Upper Hundred, 1775.

NEGRO Margaret. Taxable in Bush River Lower Hundred, 1775, with Benjamin Howard as security.

NEGRO Margaret. Taxable at Luke Griffin's Quarters, Spesutia Lower Hundred, 1775.

NEGRO Margaret. Taxable in the household of James Kimble, Spesutia Lower Hundred, 1775.

NEGRO Margaret. Taxable on plantation of George Ford, Spesutia Lower Hundred, 1776.

NEGRO Margaret. Taxable at Luke Griffith's Quarters, Spesutia Lower Hundred, 1776.

NEGRO Margaret. Taxable in household of James Kimble, Spesutia Lower Hundred, 1776.

NEGRO Maria. Taxable in household of Freeborn

Brown, Spesutia Lower Hundred, 1775.

NEGRO Maria. Taxable in household of William Hall, Spesutia Lower Hundred, 1775.

NEGRO Maria. Taxable in household of George Garretson, Spesutia Lower Hundred, 1775.

NEGRO Maria. Taxable in the household of Benedict Edward Hall, Spesutia Lower Hundred, 1775.

NEGRO Maria. Taxable in the household of Joseph Puntney, Spesutia Lower Hundred, 1775.

NEGRO Maria. Taxable at William Paca's Quarters, Spesutia Lower Hundred, 1775.

NEGRO Mariah. Taxable in household of Robert Culver, Susquehanna Hundred, 1775.

NEGRO Mariah. Taxable in household of William Creswell, Susquehanna Hundred, 1775.

NEGRO Marier. Taxable in household of Ignatius Wheeler, Jr., Deer Creek Upper Hundred, 1775.

NEGRO Marmur. Taxable in household of Mary Carlile, Bush River Lower Hundred, 1775.

NEGRO Mary. Taxable in household of Ephraim Andrews, Susquehanna Hundred, 1775.

NEGRO Mary. Taxable in household of John Brown, Spesutia Lower Hundred, 1775.

NEGRO Mary. Taxable at William Paca's Quarters, Spesutia Lower Hundred, 1775.

NEGRO Mary. Taxable "at ye glebe" of Rev. William West, Spesutia Lower Hundred, 1775.

NEGRO Mary. Taxable in household of Richard Willmot, Spesutia Upper Hundred, 1775.

NEGRO Mary. Taxable in household of Abram Whitekar, Bush River Upper Hundred, 1775.

NEGRO Mary. Taxable in household of Elizabeth Husbands (widow), Deer Creek Lower Hundred, 1775.

NEGRO Mary. Taxable in household of Casandra Sheridine (widow), Deer Creek Lower Hundred, 1775.

NEGRO Mary. Taxable on plantation of Thomas Gash, Spesutia Lower Hundred, 1776.

NEGRO Mary. Taxable on plantation of Ephrem Andres, Susquehanna Hundred, 1776.

NEGRO Mary. Taxable in household of Edward Mitchel, Susquehanna Hundred, 1776.

NEGRO Maud. Taxable in the household of Benedict Edward Hall, Spesutia Lower Hundred, 1775.

NEGRO Maud. Taxable in household of Benedict Edward Hall, Spesutia Lower Hundred, 1776.

NEGRO Medars. Taxable in household of Col. Thomas White, Susquehanna Hundred, 1775.

NEGRO Medary. Taxables on plantation of Col. Thomas White, Susquehanna Hundred, 1776.

NEGRO Melford. Taxable in household of John Rumsey, Susquehanna Hundred, 1775.

NEGRO Melkey. Taxable in household of Michal Gilbert, Susquehanna Hundred, 1776.

NEGRO Merer. Taxable in household of William Creswell, Susquehanna Hundred, 1776.

NEGRO Merer. Taxable in household of Robert Culver, Susquehanna Hundred, 1776.

NEGRO Mererer. Taxable in household of Samuel Howel, Susquehanna Hundred, 1776.

NEGRO Meriah. Taxable in household of William Vertchworth, Susquehanna Hundred, 1775.

NEGRO Meriah. Taxable in household of John Worthington, Deer Creek Lower Hundred, 1775.

NEGRO Michael. Taxable on plantation of Aquila Hall, Spesutia Lower Hundred, 1775.

NEGRO Mick. Taxable in household of William Hall, Spesutia Lower Hundred, 1775.

NEGRO Mike. Taxable in household of Thomas Waltham, Gunpowder Lower Hundred, 1775.

NEGRO Mike. Taxable in household of Robert Morgan, Deer Creek Lower Hundred, 1775.

NEGRO Mike. Taxable on plantation of William Hall, Spesutia Lower Hundred, 1776.

NEGRO Mike. Taxable at Aquila Hall's Quarters, Spesutia Lower Hundred, 1776.

NEGRO Milbourn. Taxable on plantation of John Lee Webster, Spesutia Lower Hundred, 1776.

NEGRO Milcah. Taxable on plantation of Capt. John Hall, Spesutia Lower Hundred, 1775.

NEGRO Milford. Taxable in household of John Rumsey, Susquehanna Hundred, 1776.

NEGRO Mingo. Taxable in household of Ann Norris, Bush River Lower Hundred, 1775.

NEGRO Mingo. Taxable in household of Richard Johns, Susquehanna Hundred, 1775.

NEGRO Mingo. Taxable in household of James Giles, Spesutia Lower Hundred, 1775.

NEGRO Mingo. Taxable in the household of James Stewart, Spesutia Lower Hundred, 1775.

NEGRO Mingo. Taxable in the household of Edward Ward, Spesutia Lower Hundred, 1775.

NEGRO Mingo. Taxable in household of Hester Johnson, Spesutia Upper Hundred, 1775.

NEGRO Mingo. Taxable in household of Aquila Amoss, Bush River Upper Hundred, 1775.

NEGRO Mingo. Taxable on plantation of John Lee Webster, Spesutia Lower Hundred, 1776.

NEGRO Mingo. Taxable in household of James Stewart, Spesutia Lower Hundred, 1776.

NEGRO Mingo. Taxable in household of Negro Thomas (a free negro), Susquehanna Hundred, 1776.

NEGRO Mingoe. Taxable in household of Thomas Baker Rigdon, Deer Creek Upper Hundred, 1775.

NEGRO Mint. Taxable in household of Robbert Bishop, Gunpowder Lower Hundred, 1775.

NEGRO Mint. Taxable at Thomas Frisby Henderson's

Quarters, Spesutia Lower Hundred, 1775.
NEGRO Mint. Taxable in household of William Ditto, Bush River Upper Hundred, 1775.
NEGRO Mobber. Taxable on plantation of Josias William Dallam, Spesutia Lower Hundred, 1776.
NEGRO Modey. Taxable at William Buchanan's Quarters, Gunpowder Lower Hundred, 1775.
NEGRO Mol. Taxable at William Buchanan's Quarters, Gunpowder Lower Hundred, 1775.
NEGRO Mol. Taxable in household of Thomas Waltham, Gunpowder Lower Hundred, 1775.
NEGRO Mol. Taxable at Samuel Thomas' Quarters, Susquehanna Hundred, 1776.
NEGRO Moll 2nd. Taxable on plantation of James Phillips, Spesutia Lower Hundred, 1775.
NEGRO Moll 2nd. Taxable at William Paca's Quarters. Spesutia Lower Hundred, 1775.
NEGRO Moll. Taxable in household of Joseph Renshaw, Sr., Bush River Lower Hundred, 1775.
NEGRO Moll. Taxable in household of Patrick Creighton, Susquehanna Hundred, 1775.
NEGRO Moll. Taxable in household of Peter Bennett, Spesutia Lower Hundred, 1775.
NEGRO Moll. Taxable at Samuel Thomas' Quarters, Susquehanna Hundred, 1775.
NEGRO Moll. Taxable in household of Richard Garretson, Spesutia Lower Hundred, 1775.
NEGRO Moll. Taxable in household of George Chancey, Jr., Spesutia Lower Hundred, 1775.
NEGRO Moll. Taxable on plantation of James Phillips, Spesutia Lower Hundred, 1775.
NEGRO Moll. Taxable at William Paca's Quarters, Spesutia Lower Hundred, 1775.
NEGRO Moll. Taxable at William Smith's Quarters, Spesutia Lower Hundred, 1775.
NEGRO Moll. Taxable in the household of James Osborn, Jr., Spesutia Lower Hundred, 1775.
NEGRO Moll. Taxable in the household of Edward Hall, Spesutia Lower Hundred, 1775.
NEGRO Moll. Taxable in household of Hester Johnson, Spesutia Upper Hundred, 1775.
NEGRO Moll. Taxable in household of John Barton, Bush River Upper Hundred, 1775.
NEGRO Moll. Taxable in household of Joshua Miles, Bush River Upper Hundred, 1775.
NEGRO Moll. Taxable on plantation of Stephen Jay, Deer Creek Lower Hundred, 1775.
NEGRO Moll. Taxable in household of John Hawkins, Deer Creek Lower Hundred, 1775.
NEGRO Moll. Taxable in household of Ignatius Wheeler, Jr., Deer Creek Upper Hundred, 1775.
NEGRO Moll. Taxable in household of John Brown, Spesutia Lower Hundred, 1776.
NEGRO Moll. Taxable on plantation of Thomas Gash, Spesutia Lower Hundred, 1776.
NEGRO Moll. Taxable in household of Richard Garrettson, Spesutia Lower Hundred, 1776.
NEGRO Moll. Taxable on plantation of William Smith, Jr., Spesutia Lower Hundred, 1776.
NEGRO Montros. Taxable in household of Josias Carvel Hall, Spesutia Lower Hundred, 1775.
NEGRO Montross. Taxable on plantation of Hannah Hall, Spesutia Lower Hundred, 1776.
NEGRO Montsleer. Taxable on plantation of Philip Gover, Susquehanna Hundred, 1776.
NEGRO Mora. Taxable in household of Benedict Edward Hall, Spesutia Lower Hundred, 1776.
NEGRO Morey. Taxable at Richard Dallam's Quarters at Romney, Spesutia Lower Hundred, 1775.
NEGRO Morey. Taxable in the household of Benedict Edward Hall, Spesutia Lower Hundred, 1775.
NEGRO Mory. Taxable in household of John Diemer, Spesutia Lower Hundred, 1775.
NEGRO Mosa. Taxable in household of Samuel Dooley, Spesutia Lower Hundred, 1776.
NEGRO Moses. Taxable in household of Rachel Thorp, Bush River Lower Hundred, 1775.
NEGRO Mounan. Taxable in household of Philip Gover, Susquehanna Hundred, 1775.
NEGRO Mudlin. Taxable in household of Alexander Cowen, Gunpowder Lower Hundred, 1775.
NEGRO Mumah. Taxable at Jacob Bond's Quarters, Gunpowder Lower Hundred, 1775.
NEGRO Murrier. Taxable in household of Sarah Brown, Spesutia Lower Hundred, 1776.
NEGRO Murrier. Taxable on plantation of Thomas Gash, Spesutia Lower Hundred, 1776.
NEGRO Nace. Taxable on plantation of Ignatious Wheler, Spesutia Upper Hundred, 1775.
NEGRO Naise. Taxable at Dr. Henry Stephenson's Quarters, Spesutia Lower Hundred, 1775.
NEGRO Nan. Taxable in household of Thomas Waltham, Gunpowder Lower Hundred, 1775.
NEGRO Nan. Taxable in household of Thomas Taylor, Gunpowder Lower Hundred, 1775.
NEGRO Nan. Taxable in household of John Day (son of Edward), Gunpowder Lower Hundred, 1775.
NEGRO Nan. Taxable in household of Ephraim Andrews, Susquehanna Hundred, 1775.
NEGRO Nan. Taxable in household of William Horner, Susquehanna Hundred, 1775.
NEGRO Nan. Taxable at Samuel Thomas' Quarters, Susquehanna Hundred, 1775.
NEGRO Nan. Taxable in household of John Rumsey, Susquehanna Hundred, 1775.
NEGRO Nan. Taxable in household of John Wilson (merchant), Susquehanna Hundred, 1775.
NEGRO Nan. Taxable in household of George Ford,

EARLY HARFORD COUNTIANS: Supplement

Spesutia Lower Hundred, 1775.
NEGRO Nan. Taxable in household of Jacob Forward, Spesutia Lower Hundred, 1775.
NEGRO Nan. Taxable in household of John Diemer, Spesutia Lower Hundred, 1775.
NEGRO Nan. Taxable in household of Thomas Peregrin Frisby, Spesutia Lower Hundred, 1775.
NEGRO Nan. Taxable in household of Thomas Johnson, Sr., Spesutia Upper Hundred, 1775.
NEGRO Nan. Taxable in household of John Love, Spesutia Upper Hundred, 1775.
NEGRO Nan. Taxable in household of George Bradford, Spesutia Upper Hundred, 1775.
NEGRO Nan. Taxable in household of Benjaman Wheler, Spesutia Upper Hundred, 1775.
NEGRO Nan. Taxable on plantation of Ignatious Wheler, Spesutia Upper Hundred, 1775.
NEGRO Nan. Taxable in household of Robert Briarly, Bush River Upper Hundred, 1775.
NEGRO Nan. Taxable on plantation of William Smith, Sr, Bush River Upper Hundred, 1775.
NEGRO Nan. Taxable on plantation of James Lee, Deer Creek Lower Hundred, 1775.
NEGRO Nan. Taxable in household of Elizabeth Gover, Deer Creek Lower Hundred, 1775.
NEGRO Nan. Taxable in household of Joseph Hopkins, Deer Creek Lower Hundred, 1775.
NEGRO Nan. Taxable in household of John Wilson, Deer Creek Upper Hundred, 1775.
NEGRO Nan. Taxable in household of William Morgan, Deer Creek Upper Hundred, 1775.
NEGRO Nan. Taxable in household of William Horner, Susquehanna Hundred, 1776.
NEGRO Nann. Taxable at Clark Young's Quarters, Spesutia Lower Hundred, 1775.
NEGRO Nann. Taxable at Jacob Forward's Quarters, Spesutia Lower Hundred, 1776.
NEGRO Nann. Taxable on plantation of George Ford, Spesutia Lower Hundred, 1776.
NEGRO Nann. Taxable on plantation of John Lee Webster, Spesutia Lower Hundred, 1776.
NEGRO Nann. Taxable on plantation of Ephrem Andres, Susquehanna Hundred, 1776.
NEGRO Nann. Taxable in household of John Rumsey, Susquehanna Hundred, 1776.
NEGRO Nann. Taxable at Samuel Thomas' Quarters, Susquehanna Hundred, 1776.
NEGRO Nanney. Taxable in household of James Rigbie, Deer Creek Lower Hundred, 1775.
NEGRO Nanney. Taxables on plantation of William Hopkins, Deer Creek Lower Hundred, 1775.
NEGRO Nase. Taxable on plantation of William Webb, Deer Creek Upper Hundred, 1775.
NEGRO Nat. Taxable at Clark Young's Quarters, Spesutia Lower Hundred, 1775.
NEGRO Nathan. Taxable in household of Nathaniel Howard, Gunpowder Lower Hundred, 1775.
NEGRO Nathan. Taxable on plantation of Edward Carvel Tolley, Spesutia Lower Hundred, 1776.
NEGRO Ned. Taxable in household of Buckler Bond, Bush River Lower Hundred, 1775.
NEGRO Ned. Taxable in household of John Wain, Bush River Lower Hundred, 1775.
NEGRO Ned. Taxable in household of Nicholas Alender, Gunpowder Lower Hundred, 1775.
NEGRO Ned. Taxable at Thomas Harrison's Quarters, Susquehanna Hundred, 1775.
NEGRO Ned. Taxable in household of George Copland, Spesutia Lower Hundred, 1775.
NEGRO Ned. Taxable at William Wilson's Quarter, Susquehanna Hundred, 1775.
NEGRO Ned. Taxable in household of Benjamin Ford, Spesutia Lower Hundred, 1775.
NEGRO Ned. Taxable in the household of James Taylor, Spesutia Lower Hundred, 1775.
NEGRO Ned. Taxable on plantation of Aquila Hall, Spesutia Lower Hundred, 1775.
NEGRO Ned. Taxable on plantation of Aquila Hall, Spesutia Lower Hundred, 1775.
NEGRO Ned. Taxable in household of Danniel Robinson, Spesutia Upper Hundred, 1775.
NEGRO Ned. Taxable in household of Thomas Wheler, Spesutia Upper Hundred, 1775.
NEGRO Ned. Taxable in household of Thomas Bond, Jr., Bush River Upper Hundred, 1775.
NEGRO Ned. Taxable in household of Joseph Wilson, Jr., Deer Creek Lower Hundred, 1775.
NEGRO Ned. Taxable in household of Samuel Wilson, Deer Creek Lower Hundred, 1775.
NEGRO Ned. Taxable in household of Samuel Morgan, Deer Creek Upper Hundred, 1775.
NEGRO Ned. Taxable at Aquila Hall's Quarters, Spesutia Lower Hundred, 1776.
NEGRO Ned. Taxable on plantation of George Ford, Spesutia Lower Hundred, 1776.
NEGRO Ned. Taxable in household of Elizabeth Barns, Susquehanna Hundred, 1776.
NEGRO Ned. Taxable on plantation of William Smith, Jr., Spesutia Lower Hundred, 1776.
NEGRO Ned. Taxable in household of James Taylor, Jr., Spesutia Lower Hundred, 1776.
NEGRO Ned. Taxable at Thomas Harrison's Quarters, Susquehanna Hundred, 1776.
NEGRO Ned. Taxable in household of William Wilson (overseer), Susquehanna Hundred, 1776.
NEGRO Ned. Taxables on plantation of William Hopkins, Deer Creek Lower Hundred, 1775.
NEGRO Nedd. Taxable in Bush River Lower Hundred,

1775, with Benjamin Howard as security.

NEGRO Nel. Taxable in household of James Death, Susquehanna Hundred, 1776.

NEGRO Nell. Taxable in household of Burgess Chaney, Bush River Lower Hundred, 1775.

NEGRO Nell. Taxable in household of James Death, Susquehanna Hundred, 1775.

NEGRO Nell. Taxable in household of Mary Griffith, Spesutia Lower Hundred, 1775.

NEGRO Nell. Taxable in the household of Benjamin Hanson, Spesutia Lower Hundred, 1775.

NEGRO Nell. Taxable on plantation of John Lee Webster, Spesutia Lower Hundred, 1775.

NEGRO Nell. Taxable at William Smith's Quarters, Spesutia Lower Hundred, 1775.

NEGRO Nell. Taxable in household of Edmond Bull, Spesutia Upper Hundred, 1775.

NEGRO Nell. Taxable in household of Henry Waters, Spesutia Upper Hundred, 1775.

NEGRO Nell. Taxable in household of Danniel Richardson, Spesutia Upper Hundred, 1775.

NEGRO Nell. Taxable in household of Richard Willmot, Spesutia Upper Hundred, 1775.

NEGRO Nell. Taxable in household of Josiah Lee, Deer Creek Upper Hundred, 1775.

NEGRO Nell. Taxable in household of Ignatius Wheeler, Jr., Deer Creek Upper Hundred, 1775.

NEGRO Nell. Taxable on plantation of Samuel Griffith, Spesutia Lower Hundred, 1776.

NEGRO Nell. Taxable at Dr. Henry Stephenson's Quarters, Spesutia Lower Hundred, 1776.

NEGRO Nelly. Taxable on plantation of John Lee Webster, Spesutia Lower Hundred, 1776.

NEGRO Neptune. Taxables on plantation of William Hopkins, Deer Creek Lower Hundred, 1775.

NEGRO Nero. Taxable in household of Nicklaus Amoss, Bush River Upper Hundred, 1775.

NEGRO Nero. Taxable at Giles & Smith's Rock Run Plantation, Susquehanna Hundred, 1776.

NEGRO Nicholas. Taxable in household of Robbert Bishop, Gunpowder Lower Hundred, 1775.

NEGRO Nicholas. Taxable at William Paca's Quarters, Spesutia Upper Hundred, 1775.

NEGRO --nkey Tom. Taxable at Cumberland Forge, Deer Creek Lower Hundred, 1775.

NEGRO Noah. Taxable in household of James Amoss, Bush River Upper Hundred, 1775.

NEGRO Nob. Taxable on plantation of John Matthews, Spesutia Lower Hundred, 1775.

NEGRO Nobb. Taxable on plantation of Capt. John Mathews, Spesutia Lower Hundred, 1776.

NEGRO Norsay. Taxable at Thomas Gash's Quarters, Spesutia Upper Hundred, 1775.

NEGRO Old Dinah. Taxable on plantation of Aquila Hall, Spesutia Lower Hundred, 1775.

NEGRO Old George. Taxable on plantation of John Matthews, Spesutia Lower Hundred, 1775.

NEGRO Old Toney. Taxable in household of John Brown, Spesutia Lower Hundred, 1775.

NEGRO Oliver. Taxable in household of Jacob Bull, Sr. Bush River Lower Hundred, 1775.

NEGRO Oliver. Taxable in household of Sarah Norris, Bush River Lower Hundred, 1775.

NEGRO Ollerver. Taxable in household of Freeborn Brown, Susquehanna Hundred, 1776.

NEGRO Ollever. Taxable in household of Francis Downing, Deer Creek Lower Hundred, 1775.

NEGRO Orange. Taxable in the household of William Smith, Spesutia Lower Hundred, 1775.

NEGRO Orange. Taxable on plantation of Josias William Dallam, Spesutia Lower Hundred, 1776.

NEGRO Orange. Taxable at Aquila Hall's Quarters, Spesutia Lower Hundred, 1776.

NEGRO Orange. Taxable on plantation of William Smith, Jr., Spesutia Lower Hundred, 1776.

NEGRO Oringe. Taxable on plantation of Aquila Hall, Spesutia Lower Hundred, 1775.

NEGRO Orras. Taxable at Thomas Harrison's Quarters, Susquehanna Hundred, 1776.

NEGRO Oval. Taxable on the plantation of Amos Garrett, Spesutia Lower Hundred, 1775.

NEGRO Oval. Taxable on plantation of Amos Garrett, Spesutia Lower Hundred, 1776.

NEGRO P----. Taxable in household of Robert Morgan, Deer Creek Lower Hundred, 1775.

NEGRO Pack. Taxable in household of Martha Presbury, Gunpowder Lower Hundred, 1775.

NEGRO Pain. Taxable on plantation of Jacob Giles, Susquehanna Hundred, 1776.

NEGRO Pam. Taxable in household of Thomas James, Bush River Upper Hundred, 1775.

NEGRO Paraway. Taxable in household of Josiah Lee, Deer Creek Upper Hundred, 1775.

NEGRO Parina. Taxable in household of John Rumsey, Susquehanna Hundred, 1775.

NEGRO Parraway. Taxable on plantation of William Webb, Deer Creek Upper Hundred, 1775.

NEGRO Pat. Taxable in household of James Chancey, Spesutia Lower Hundred, 1775.

NEGRO Patience. Taxable on the plantation of Amos Garrett, Spesutia Lower Hundred, 1775.

NEGRO Patience. Taxable on plantation of Hannah Hall, Spesutia Lower Hundred, 1775.

NEGRO Patience. Taxable on plantation of Hannah Hall, Spesutia Lower Hundred, 1776.

NEGRO Patience. Taxable on plantation of Amos Garrett, Spesutia Lower Hundred, 1776.

NEGRO Patt. Taxable in household of Greenberry

EARLY HARFORD COUNTIANS: Supplement

Dorsey, Spesutia Lower Hundred, 1775.
NEGRO Patt. Taxable on plantation of Josias William Dallam, Spesutia Lower Hundred, 1776.
NEGRO Patt. Taxable in household of Greenberry Dorsey, Spesutia Lower Hundred, 1776.
NEGRO Paul. Taxable in household of John Patrick, Deer Creek Lower Hundred, 1775.
NEGRO Paul. Taxable in household of Samuel Worthington, Deer Creek Lower Hundred, 1775.
NEGRO Peg. Taxable in household of Micah Gilbert, Susquehanna Hundred, 1775.
NEGRO Peg. Taxable in household of Ephraim Andrews, Susquehanna Hundred, 1775.
NEGRO Peg. Taxable in household of Henery Stump, Susquehanna Hundred, 1775.
NEGRO Peg. Taxable in household of William Hall, Spesutia Lower Hundred, 1775.
NEGRO Peg. Taxable in household of George Ford, Spesutia Lower Hundred, 1775.
NEGRO Peg. Taxable in the household of Benedict Edward Hall, Spesutia Lower Hundred, 1775.
NEGRO Peg. Taxable in household of David Durham, Bush River Upper Hundred, 1775.
NEGRO Peg. Taxable in household of John Peacock, Deer Creek Lower Hundred, 1775.
NEGRO Peg. Taxable in household of Joseph Wilson, Deer Creek Lower Hundred, 1775.
NEGRO Peg. Taxable at Aquila Hall's Quarters, Spesutia Lower Hundred, 1776.
NEGRO Peg. Taxable in household of Micah Gilbert, Susquehanna Hundred, 1776.
NEGRO Peg. Taxable in household of Henry Stump, Susquehanna Hundred, 1776.
NEGRO Peg. Taxables on plantation of William Hopkins, Deer Creek Lower Hundred, 1775.
NEGRO Pegg. Taxable in household of Mordicai Amos, Bush River Lower Hundred, 1775.
NEGRO Pegg. Taxable in household of Alexander McComas, Bush River Lower Hundred, 1775.
NEGRO Pegg. Taxable in household of Richard Willmot, Spesutia Upper Hundred, 1775.
NEGRO Pegg. Taxable at Isaac Whiteker's Quarters, Spesutia Upper Hundred, 1775.
NEGRO Pegg. Taxable in household of Benedict Edward Hall, Spesutia Lower Hundred, 1776.
NEGRO Pegg. Taxable on plantation of Ephrem Andres, Susquehanna Hundred, 1776.
NEGRO Pen. Taxable in household of J. Beale Boadley, Gunpowder Lower Hundred, 1775.
NEGRO Pen. Taxable in household of John Hodges Taylor, Gunpowder Lower Hundred, 1775.
NEGRO Perina. Taxable on the plantation of Amos Garrett, Spesutia Lower Hundred, 1775.
NEGRO Perina. Taxable on plantation of Amos Garrett, Spesutia Lower Hundred, 1776.
NEGRO Perinah. Taxable on plantation of Edward Carvel Tolley, Spesutia Lower Hundred, 1776.
NEGRO Perriner. Taxable in household of John Rumsey, Susquehanna Hundred, 1776.
NEGRO Perry. Taxable at Thomas Harrison's Quarters, Susquehanna Hundred, 1775.
NEGRO Perry. Taxable on plantation of Capt. John Hall, Spesutia Lower Hundred, 1775.
NEGRO Pet. Taxable in household of William Fisher, Jr., Deer Creek Upper Hundred, 1775.
NEGRO Peter. Taxable in household of Joseph Renshaw, Sr., Bush River Lower Hundred, 1775.
NEGRO Peter. Taxable in household of Samuel Ricketts, Gunpowder Lower Hundred, 1775.
NEGRO Peter. Taxable in household of Lambert Wilmer, Gunpowder Lower Hundred, 1775.
NEGRO Peter. Taxable in household of John Day (son of Edward), Gunpowder Lower Hundred, 1775.
NEGRO Peter. Taxable in household of Martha Presbury, Gunpowder Lower Hundred, 1775.
NEGRO Peter. Taxable at Thomas Harrison's Quarters, Susquehanna Hundred, 1775.
NEGRO Peter. Taxable at Richard Dallam's Quarters at Swan Creek, Spesutia Lower Hundred, 1775.
NEGRO Peter. Taxable at Thomas Frisby Henderson's Quarters, Spesutia Lower Hundred, 1775.
NEGRO Peter. Taxable at Jacob Giles' Quarters at Romney, Spesutia Lower Hundred, 1775.
NEGRO Peter. Taxable on plantation of Aquila Hall, Spesutia Lower Hundred, 1775.
NEGRO Peter. Taxable in the household of James Osborn, Jr., Spesutia Lower Hundred, 1775.
NEGRO Peter. Taxable in the household of William Smith, Spesutia Lower Hundred, 1775.
NEGRO Peter. Taxable in household of Richard Willmot, Spesutia Upper Hundred, 1775.
NEGRO Peter. Taxable in household of Nathan Scott, Bush River Upper Hundred, 1775.
NEGRO Peter. Taxable in household of Thomas Hawkins, Deer Creek Lower Hundred, 1775.
NEGRO Peter. Taxable in household of Casandra Sheridine (widow), Deer Creek Lower Hundred, 1775.
NEGRO Peter. Taxable in household of Mary Renshaw, Deer Creek Upper Hundred, 1775.
NEGRO Peter. Taxable on plantation of William Smith, Jr., Spesutia Lower Hundred, 1776.
NEGRO Peter. Taxable at Thomas Harrison's Quarters, Susquehanna Hundred, 1776.
NEGRO Phebe. Taxable in household of Ellender Durham, Bush River Lower Hundred, 1775.
NEGRO Phebe. Taxable in household of Ann Norris, Bush River Lower Hundred, 1775.

NEGRO Phebe. Taxable in household of Martha McComas, Bush River Lower Hundred, 1775.
NEGRO Pheby. Taxable in household of John Rutledge, Bush River Upper Hundred, 1775.
NEGRO Phil. Taxable in the household of William Smith, Spesutia Lower Hundred, 1775.
NEGRO Phil. Taxable on plantation of John Lee Webster, Spesutia Lower Hundred, 1775.
NEGRO Phil. Taxable in household of William Morgan, Deer Creek Upper Hundred, 1775.
NEGRO Philis. Taxable in household of Henry Scarff, Bush River Upper Hundred, 1775.
NEGRO Phill. Taxable on plantation of Aquila Hall, Spesutia Lower Hundred, 1775.
NEGRO Phill. Taxable at Aquila Hall's Quarters, Spesutia Lower Hundred, 1776.
NEGRO Phill. Taxable on plantation of John Lee Webster, Spesutia Lower Hundred, 1776.
NEGRO Phillis. Taxable in household of Ellender Durham, Bush River Lower Hundred, 1775.
NEGRO Phillis. Taxable in household of William Amos, Sr., Bush River Lower Hundred, 1775.
NEGRO Phillis. Taxable in household of James Scott, Bush River Lower Hundred, 1775.
NEGRO Phillis. Taxable in household of Jacob Bond, Sr., Bush River Lower Hundred, 1775.
NEGRO Phillis. Taxable in household of Elizabeth Davis, Bush River Lower Hundred, 1775.
NEGRO Phillis. Taxable in household of Ann Scott, Bush River Lower Hundred, 1775.
NEGRO Phillis. Taxable in household of Ann Norris, Bush River Lower Hundred, 1775.
NEGRO Phillis. Taxable at Benjamin Howard's Quarters, Gunpowder Lower Hundred, 1775.
NEGRO Phillis. Taxable in household of Henery Wetherell, Gunpowder Lower Hundred, 1775.
NEGRO Phillis. Taxable in household of Uphan Debrular, Gunpowder Lower Hundred, 1775.
NEGRO Phillis. Taxable in household of Samuel Griffith, Spesutia Lower Hundred, 1775.
NEGRO Phillis. Taxable in the household of Leven Matthews, Spesutia Lower Hundred, 1775.
NEGRO Phillis. Taxable in the household of John Ruff, Spesutia Lower Hundred, 1775.
NEGRO Phillis. Taxable on plantation of Hannah Hall, Spesutia Lower Hundred, 1775.
NEGRO Phillis. Taxable in household of Richard Wells, Jr., Deer Creek Lower Hundred, 1775.
NEGRO Phillis. Taxable in household of Henry Crooks, Deer Creek Upper Hundred, 1775.
NEGRO Phillis. Taxable on plantation of Hannah Hall, Spesutia Lower Hundred, 1776.
NEGRO Phillis. Taxable on plantation of Samuel Griffith, Spesutia Lower Hundred, 1776.
NEGRO Phillis. Taxable in household of Leven Mathews, Spesutia Lower Hundred, 1776.
NEGRO Phoebe. Taxable in household of William Chapel, Susquehanna Hundred, 1775.
NEGRO Phoebe. Taxable in household of Henery Stump, Susquehanna Hundred, 1775.
NEGRO Phy. Taxable in household of Capt. James Maxwell, Gunpowder Lower Hundred, 1775.
NEGRO Pimon. Taxable in household of Richard Willmot, Spesutia Upper Hundred, 1775.
NEGRO Pip. Taxable in household of Mary Waters, Gunpowder Lower Hundred, 1775.
NEGRO Pitt. Taxable in household of Josias William Dallam, Spesutia Lower Hundred, 1775.
NEGRO Pitt. Taxable in household of James Webster, Spesutia Upper Hundred, 1775.
NEGRO Plez. Taxable on plantation of William Smith, Sr, Bush River Upper Hundred, 1775.
NEGRO Pol. Taxable in household of James Lytle, Gunpowder Lower Hundred, 1775.
NEGRO Pol. Taxable in household of Henry Stump, Susquehanna Hundred, 1776.
NEGRO Pol. Taxables on plantation of Col. Thomas White, Susquehanna Hundred, 1776.
NEGRO Polador. Taxable in household of John Ellis, Spesutia Upper Hundred, 1775.
NEGRO Poladore. Taxable at Giles & Smith's Rock Run Plantation, Susquehanna Hundred, 1776.
NEGRO Poledor. Taxable in household of Joseph Hopkins, Deer Creek Lower Hundred, 1775.
NEGRO Polidore. Taxable in household of John Rumsey, Susquehanna Hundred, 1775.
NEGRO Polidore. Taxable at William Smith's Quarters, Susquehanna Hundred, 1775.
NEGRO Polipus. Taxable in household of Benedict Edward Hall, Spesutia Lower Hundred, 1776.
NEGRO Poll. Taxable in household of Jacob Bond, Sr., Bush River Lower Hundred, 1775.
NEGRO Poll. Taxable in household of Daniel Durbin, Susquehanna Hundred, 1775.
NEGRO Poll. Taxable on plantation of James Phillips, Spesutia Lower Hundred, 1775.
NEGRO Poll. Taxable on plantation of Thomas Gash, Spesutia Lower Hundred, 1776.
NEGRO Poll. Taxable in household of Robert Stokes, Spesutia Lower Hundred, 1776.
NEGRO Polledore. Taxable in household of Negro Thomas (a free negro), Susquehanna Hundred, 1776.
NEGRO Pollipus. Taxable in the household of Benedict Edward Hall, Spesutia Lower Hundred, 1775.
NEGRO Polly. Taxable on plantation of William Smith, Sr, Bush River Upper Hundred, 1775.
NEGRO Polydore. Taxable in household of Richard Johns, Susquehanna Hundred, 1775.

EARLY HARFORD COUNTIANS: Supplement

NEGRO Pomp. Taxable in household of Ann Bond, Bush River Lower Hundred, 1775.

NEGRO Pomp. Taxable in household of Moses Ruth, Sr., Spesutia Upper Hundred, 1775.

NEGRO Pomp. Taxable in household of Sarrah McCommos (widdow), Bush River Upper Hundred, 1775.

NEGRO Pompey. Taxable in household of Stephen Waters, Gunpowder Lower Hundred, 1775.

NEGRO Pompey. Taxable in household of Jacob Giles, Susquehanna Hundred, 1775.

NEGRO Pompey. Taxable in household of John Worthington, Deer Creek Lower Hundred, 1775.

NEGRO Pompey. Taxable in Deer Creek Lower Hundred, 1775. [The actual entry stated "Pompey, free negro, set free by James Rigbie"].

NEGRO Pompey. Taxable on plantation of Jacob Giles, Susquehanna Hundred, 1776.

NEGRO Pompey. Taxable at Giles & Smith's Rock Run Plantation, Susquehanna Hundred, 1776.

NEGRO Pompey. Taxables on plantation of William Hopkins, Deer Creek Lower Hundred, 1775.

NEGRO Pompy. Taxable on the plantation of Amos Garrett, Spesutia Lower Hundred, 1775.

NEGRO Pompy. Taxable on plantation of George Ford, Spesutia Lower Hundred, 1776.

NEGRO Pompy. Taxable on plantation of Amos Garrett, Spesutia Lower Hundred, 1776.

NEGRO Pool. Taxable in household of Daniel Durbin, Spesutia Lower Hundred, 1776.

NEGRO Press. Taxable in household of Danniel Richardson, Spesutia Upper Hundred, 1775.

NEGRO Primos. Taxable in household of John Archer, Spesutia Upper Hundred, 1775.

NEGRO Primus. Taxable in household of John Taylor, Bush River Lower Hundred, 1775.

NEGRO Primus. Taxable on plantation of Capt. John Hall, Spesutia Lower Hundred, 1775.

NEGRO Primus. Taxable in the household of James Stewart, Spesutia Lower Hundred, 1775.

NEGRO Primus. Taxable in household of James Stewart, Spesutia Lower Hundred, 1776.

NEGRO Prince. Taxable in household of Capt. James Maxwell, Gunpowder Lower Hundred, 1775.

NEGRO Prince. Taxable on plantation of Stephen Jay, Deer Creek Lower Hundred, 1775.

NEGRO Pris. Taxable in household of Joseph Presbury, Gunpowder Lower Hundred, 1775.

NEGRO Priscilla. Taxable in the household of Rev. William West, Spesutia Lower Hundred, 1775.

NEGRO Priss. Taxable in household of John Chancey, Spesutia Lower Hundred, 1775.

NEGRO Priss. Taxable in household of Benjamin Ford, Spesutia Lower Hundred, 1775.

NEGRO Priss. Taxable at William Paca's Quarters, Spesutia Lower Hundred, 1775.

NEGRO Priss. Taxable in the household of William Osborn, Jr., Spesutia Lower Hundred, 1775.

NEGRO Priss. Taxable in household of Henry Cooper, Spesutia Upper Hundred, 1775.

NEGRO Priss. Taxable in household of Christon Baker, Spesutia Upper Hundred, 1775.

NEGRO Priss. Taxable in household of Samuel Webster, Jr., Spesutia Upper Hundred, 1775.

NEGRO Priss. Taxable in household of Elizabeth Morgan, Deer Creek Lower Hundred, 1775.

NEGRO Priss. Taxable on plantation of Thomas Gash, Spesutia Lower Hundred, 1776.

NEGRO Priss. Taxable on plantation of George Ford, Spesutia Lower Hundred, 1776.

NEGRO Priss. Taxable on plantation of Dr. Josias Carvell Hall, Spesutia Lower Hundred, 1776.

NEGRO Prissa. Taxable in the household of George Little, Spesutia Lower Hundred, 1775.

NEGRO Prudy. Taxable in household of Jacob Bond, Sr., Bush River Lower Hundred, 1775.

NEGRO Prue. Taxable in household of John Love, Spesutia Upper Hundred, 1775.

NEGRO Prye. Taxable in household of Josias Carvel Hall, Spesutia Lower Hundred, 1775.

NEGRO Pug. Taxable in household of Kent Mitchel, Susquehanna Hundred, 1775.

NEGRO Pug. Taxable in household of John Chancey, Spesutia Lower Hundred, 1775.

NEGRO Pug. Taxable in the household of Benjamin Hanson, Spesutia Lower Hundred, 1775.

NEGRO Pug. Taxable on plantation of James Phillips, Spesutia Lower Hundred, 1775.

NEGRO Pug. Taxable in household of Robert Clerk, Sr., Deer Creek Upper Hundred, 1775.

NEGRO Pugg. Taxable in household of Peter Bond, Bush River Lower Hundred, 1775.

NEGRO Pugg. Taxable in household of Walter Billingsley, Spesutia Upper Hundred, 1775.

NEGRO Pugg. Taxable in household of Thomas Johnson, Sr., Spesutia Upper Hundred, 1775.

NEGRO Pugg. Taxable at Joseph Presbury's Quarters, Spesutia Upper Hundred, 1775.

NEGRO Pugg. Taxable in household of Barnard Preston, Spesutia Upper Hundred, 1775.

NEGRO Puggaty. Taxable in household of Godfrey Waters, Susquehanna Hundred, 1775.

NEGRO Rachael (of Sarah). Taxable on plantation of Aquila Hall, Spesutia Lower Hundred, 1775.

NEGRO Rachael. Taxable in household of Milkey Lusby, Gunpowder Lower Hundred, 1775.

NEGRO Rachael. Taxable in household of Charles Gilbert, Susquehanna Hundred, 1775.

NEGRO Rachael. Taxable in household of Joseph Everest, Spesutia Lower Hundred, 1775.
NEGRO Rachael. Taxable in household of Col. Thomas White, Susquehanna Hundred, 1775.
NEGRO Rachael. Taxable on plantation of James Phillips, Spesutia Lower Hundred, 1775.
NEGRO Rachael. Taxable on plantation of John Matthews, Spesutia Lower Hundred, 1775.
NEGRO Rachael. Taxable in the household of William Smith, Spesutia Lower Hundred, 1775.
NEGRO Rachael. Taxable in household of Joseph Everest, Spesutia Lower Hundred, 1776.
NEGRO Rachael. Taxable on plantation of Hannah Hall, Spesutia Lower Hundred, 1776.
NEGRO Rachael. Taxable on plantation of Capt. John Mathews, Spesutia Lower Hundred, 1776.
NEGRO Rachael. Taxable on plantation of William Smith, Jr., Spesutia Lower Hundred, 1776.
NEGRO Rache. Taxable in household of John Craton, Spesutia Upper Hundred, 1775.
NEGRO Rachel. Taxable in household of Ann Bond, Bush River Lower Hundred, 1775.
NEGRO Rachel. Taxable on plantation of Aquila Hall, Spesutia Lower Hundred, 1775.
NEGRO Rachel. Taxable in household of Benjamin Green, Spesutia Upper Hundred, 1775.
NEGRO Rachel. Taxable in household of Thaddeus Juett, Spesutia Upper Hundred, 1775.
NEGRO Rachel. Taxable in household of Thomas Wheler, Spesutia Upper Hundred, 1775.
NEGRO Rachel. Taxable in household of Ruth Billingsly, Deer Creek Upper Hundred, 1775.
NEGRO Rachel. Taxable on plantation of Jacob Giles, Jr., Susquehanna Hundred, 1776.
NEGRO Rachel. Taxable in household of Michel Gilbert (son of Charles), Susquehanna Hundred, 1776.
NEGRO Rachel. Taxable at Thomas Harrison's Quarters, Susquehanna Hundred, 1776.
NEGRO Rachel. Taxables on plantation of Col. Thomas White, Susquehanna Hundred, 1776.
NEGRO Raggue. Taxable at Thomas Harrison's Quarters, Susquehanna Hundred, 1776.
NEGRO Ragoo. Taxable at Thomas Harrison's Quarters, Susquehanna Hundred, 1775.
NEGRO Raphael. See "Milkey Lusby," q.v.
NEGRO Rene. Taxable in household of Jonathan Woodland, Gunpowder Lower Hundred, 1775.
NEGRO Reubin. Taxable at Dr. Henry Stephenson's Quarters, Spesutia Lower Hundred, 1775.
NEGRO Reubin. Taxable at Dr. Henry Stephenson's Quarters, Spesutia Lower Hundred, 1776.
NEGRO Reynor. Taxable in household of Benjamin Rumsey, Gunpowder Lower Hundred, 1775.
NEGRO Rich. Taxable in household of Micheal Hannor, Spesutia Upper Hundred, 1775.
NEGRO Robert. Taxable in household of Aquila Paca, Jr., Spesutia Lower Hundred, 1776.
NEGRO Robin. Taxable on plantation of Ignatious Wheler, Spesutia Upper Hundred, 1775.
NEGRO Roger. Taxable in household of Jacob Bond, Sr., Bush River Lower Hundred, 1775.
NEGRO Roger. Taxable in household of Joseph Presbury, Gunpowder Lower Hundred, 1775.
NEGRO Roger. Taxable at Joseph Presbury's Quarters, Spesutia Upper Hundred, 1775.
NEGRO Rosa. Taxable in household of William Ensor, Gunpowder Lower Hundred, 1775.
NEGRO Rose. Taxable in household of William Smithson, Bush River Lower Hundred, 1775.
NEGRO Rose. Taxable in household of Robbert Bishop, Gunpowder Lower Hundred, 1775.
NEGRO Rose. Taxable in household of George Chancey, Sr., Spesutia Lower Hundred, 1775.
NEGRO Rose. Taxable at William Smith's Quarters, Susquehanna Hundred, 1775.
NEGRO Rose. Taxable in household of John Craton, Spesutia Upper Hundred, 1775.
NEGRO Rose. Taxable in household of James Mores, Spesutia Upper Hundred, 1775.
NEGRO Rose. Taxable at William Paca's Quarters, Spesutia Upper Hundred, 1775.
NEGRO Rute. Taxable in household of Moses Ruth, Sr., Spesutia Upper Hundred, 1775.
NEGRO Ruth. Taxable in household of Martha Presbury, Gunpowder Lower Hundred, 1775.
NEGRO Ruth. Taxable in household of Francis Garland, Spesutia Lower Hundred, 1775.
NEGRO Ruth. Taxable in household of Robert Nelson, Bush River Upper Hundred, 1775.
NEGRO Ruth. Taxable in household of John Peacock, Deer Creek Lower Hundred, 1775.
NEGRO S--- [illegible]. Taxable in household of Isaac Webster, Spesutia Upper Hundred, 1775.
NEGRO Sabra. Taxable in household of Philip Gover, Susquehanna Hundred, 1775.
NEGRO Sabra. Taxable on plantation of Philip Gover, Susquehanna Hundred, 1776.
NEGRO Sagg. Taxable in household of Joseph Butler, Spesutia Upper Hundred, 1775.
NEGRO Sal. Taxable in household of Lambert Wilmer, Gunpowder Lower Hundred, 1775.
NEGRO Sal. Taxable in household of Capt. James Maxwell, Gunpowder Lower Hundred, 1775.
NEGRO Sal. Taxable at William Paca's Quarters, Spesutia Upper Hundred, 1775.
NEGRO Sal. Taxable in household of James Mitchel (weaver), Susquehanna Hundred, 1776.
NEGRO Sal. Taxable on plantation of Philip Gover,

EARLY HARFORD COUNTIANS: Supplement

Susquehanna Hundred, 1776.
NEGRO Sall. Taxable in household of James Carroll, Bush River Lower Hundred, 1775.
NEGRO Sall. Taxable in household of Benjamin Scott, Bush River Lower Hundred, 1775.
NEGRO Sall. Taxable in household of William Smithson, Bush River Lower Hundred, 1775.
NEGRO Sall. Taxable in household of Alexander McComas, Bush River Lower Hundred, 1775.
NEGRO Sall. Taxable in household of Balcher Michael, Susquehanna Hundred, 1775.
NEGRO Sall. Taxable in household of George Copland, Spesutia Lower Hundred, 1775.
NEGRO Sall. Taxable at Richard Dallam's Quarters at Romney, Spesutia Lower Hundred, 1775.
NEGRO Sall. Taxable in household of Mary Griffith, Spesutia Lower Hundred, 1775.
NEGRO Sall. Taxable on plantation of John Lee Webster, Spesutia Lower Hundred, 1775.
NEGRO Sall. Taxable at William Paca's Quarters, Spesutia Lower Hundred, 1775.
NEGRO Sall. Taxable in household of Christon Baker, Spesutia Upper Hundred, 1775.
NEGRO Sall. Taxable in household of John Hays, Sr., Spesutia Upper Hundred, 1775.
NEGRO Sall. Taxable on plantation of Ignatious Wheler, Spesutia Upper Hundred, 1775.
NEGRO Sall. Taxable in household of Ann Preston, Spesutia Upper Hundred, 1775.
NEGRO Sall. Taxable in household of James Lee, Jr., Spesutia Upper Hundred, 1775.
NEGRO Sall. Taxable on plantation of Stephen Jay, Deer Creek Lower Hundred, 1775.
NEGRO Sall. Taxable in household of Charles Worthington, Deer Creek Lower Hundred, 1775.
NEGRO Sall. Taxable in household of Samuel Morgan, Deer Creek Upper Hundred, 1775.
NEGRO Sall. Taxable on plantation of Thomas Gash, Spesutia Lower Hundred, 1776.
NEGRO Sall. Taxable on plantation of George Ford, Spesutia Lower Hundred, 1776.
NEGRO Sall. Taxable in household of George Dougherty, Spesutia Lower Hundred, 1776.
NEGRO Sall. Taxable in household of Samuel Dooley, Spesutia Lower Hundred, 1776.
NEGRO Sall. Taxable on plantation of John Lee Webster, Spesutia Lower Hundred, 1776.
NEGRO Sam. Taxable in household of James Scott, Bush River Lower Hundred, 1775.
NEGRO Sam. Taxable in household of Lemuel Howard, Bush River Lower Hundred, 1775.
NEGRO Sam. Taxable in household of Thomas Bond, Sr., Bush River Lower Hundred, 1775.
NEGRO Sam. Taxable in household of Aquila Scott, Bush River Lower Hundred, 1775.
NEGRO Sam. Taxable in household of Samuel Ricketts, Gunpowder Lower Hundred, 1775.
NEGRO Sam. Taxable in household of Aaburella Smith, Gunpowder Lower Hundred, 1775.
NEGRO Sam. Taxable in household of Capt. James Maxwell, Gunpowder Lower Hundred, 1775.
NEGRO Sam. Taxable in household of John Brown, Spesutia Lower Hundred, 1775.
NEGRO Sam. Taxable in household of Col. Thomas White, Susquehanna Hundred, 1775.
NEGRO Sam. Taxable at Amos Garrett's Quarters, Spesutia Lower Hundred, 1775.
NEGRO Sam. Taxable on plantation of James Phillips, Spesutia Lower Hundred, 1775.
NEGRO Sam. Taxable on plantation of Hannah Hall, Spesutia Lower Hundred, 1775.
NEGRO Sam. Taxable in household of Moses Ruth, Sr., Spesutia Upper Hundred, 1775.
NEGRO Sam. Taxable on plantation of Ignatious Wheler, Spesutia Upper Hundred, 1775.
NEGRO Sam. Taxable in household of Mary Chalk (widow), Bush River Upper Hundred, 1775.
NEGRO Sam. Taxable in household of Robert Nelson, Bush River Upper Hundred, 1775.
NEGRO Sam. Taxable in household of John Rutledge, Bush River Upper Hundred, 1775.
NEGRO Sam. Taxable in household of William Coal, Deer Creek Lower Hundred, 1775.
NEGRO Sam. Taxable in household of John Rutlage, Bush River Upper Hundred, 1775.
NEGRO Sam. Taxable in Deer Creek Lower Hundred, 1775. [The actual entry stated "Sam, free negro, set free by William Husbands"].
NEGRO Sam. Taxable in household of Elizabeth Husbands (widow), Deer Creek Lower Hundred, 1775.
NEGRO Sam. Taxable on plantation of James Lee, Deer Creek Lower Hundred, 1775.
NEGRO Sam. Taxable in household of John Brown, Spesutia Lower Hundred, 1776.
NEGRO Sam. Taxable in household of Daniel Durbin, Spesutia Lower Hundred, 1776.
NEGRO Sam. Taxable in household of Thomas Giles, Spesutia Lower Hundred, 1776.
NEGRO Sam. Taxable on plantation of Amos Garrett, Spesutia Lower Hundred, 1776.
NEGRO Sam. Taxable on plantation of Hannah Hall, Spesutia Lower Hundred, 1776.
NEGRO Sam. Taxable in household of Robert Stokes, Spesutia Lower Hundred, 1776.
NEGRO Sam. Taxables on plantation of Col. Thomas White, Susquehanna Hundred, 1776.
NEGRO Sambo. Taxable in household of Benjamin

Rumsey, Gunpowder Lower Hundred, 1775.
NEGRO Sambo. Taxable in household of Peter Laughlan, Susquehanna Hundred, 1775.
NEGRO Sambo. Taxable in household of Amos Hollis, Spesutia Lower Hundred, 1775.
NEGRO Sambo. Taxable in household of Walter Billingsley, Spesutia Upper Hundred, 1775.
NEGRO Samma. Taxable in household of Asell Hitchcock, Bush River Upper Hundred, 1775.
NEGRO Samp. Taxable on plantation of Stephen Jay, Deer Creek Lower Hundred, 1775.
NEGRO Sampson. Taxable in household of Peter Potee, Bush River Lower Hundred, 1775.
NEGRO Sampson. Taxable in household of William Vertchworth, Susquehanna Hundred, 1775.
NEGRO Sampson. Taxable in the household of Samuel Kimble, Spesutia Lower Hundred, 1775.
NEGRO Sampson. Taxable in the household of Edward Hall, Spesutia Lower Hundred, 1775.
NEGRO Sampson. Taxable in household of Samuel Kimble, Spesutia Lower Hundred, 1776.
NEGRO Samson. Taxable in household of Jacob Bond, Sr., Bush River Lower Hundred, 1775.
NEGRO Samson. Taxable in household of Martha McComas, Bush River Lower Hundred, 1775.
NEGRO Samson. Taxable in household of William Robinson, Sr., Bush River Lower Hundred, 1775.
NEGRO Samson. Taxable in household of John McComas, Bush River Lower Hundred, 1775.
NEGRO Samson. Taxable in household of John Barton, Bush River Upper Hundred, 1775.
NEGRO Samson. Taxable in household of James Scott, Bush River Upper Hundred, 1775.
NEGRO Samson. Taxable in household of Peter Loghlon, Susquehanna Hundred, 1776.
NEGRO Samson. Taxable in household of Samuel Howel, Susquehanna Hundred, 1776.
NEGRO Sandey. Taxable on plantation of Stephen Jay, Deer Creek Lower Hundred, 1775.
NEGRO Santy. Taxable in household of Benjamin Rumsey, Gunpowder Lower Hundred, 1775.
NEGRO Santy. Taxable in household of Mordika Amoss, Bush River Upper Hundred, 1775.
NEGRO Sarah. Taxable in household of John Green, Bush River Lower Hundred, 1775.
NEGRO Sarah. Taxable in household of John Peca, Bush River Lower Hundred, 1775.
NEGRO Sarah. Taxable in household of George Daugherty, Spesutia Lower Hundred, 1775.
NEGRO Sarah. Taxable in household of William Hall, Spesutia Lower Hundred, 1775.
NEGRO Sarah. Taxable in household of George Ford, Spesutia Lower Hundred, 1775.
NEGRO Sarah. Taxable on plantation of James Phillips, Spesutia Lower Hundred, 1775.
NEGRO Sarah. Taxable in the household of Edward Carvel Tolley, Spesutia Lower Hundred, 1775.
NEGRO Sarah. Taxable on plantation of Hannah Hall, Spesutia Lower Hundred, 1775.
NEGRO Sarah. Taxable in household of Robert Young, Spesutia Upper Hundred, 1775.
NEGRO Sarah. Taxable in household of Joseph Wheler, Spesutia Upper Hundred, 1775.
NEGRO Sarah. Taxable in household of Clemonsy Preston, Spesutia Upper Hundred, 1775.
NEGRO Sarah. Taxable in household of John Linch, Spesutia Upper Hundred, 1775.
NEGRO Sarah. Taxable in household of Joseph Wilson, Deer Creek Lower Hundred, 1775.
NEGRO Sarah. Taxable on plantation of Hannah Hall, Spesutia Lower Hundred, 1776.
NEGRO Sarah's Rachael. Taxable on plantation of Aquila Hall, Spesutia Lower Hundred, 1775.
NEGRO Sary (a free negro). Head of household in Susquehanna Hundred, 1776.
NEGRO Sary. Taxable on plantation of Philip Gover, Susquehanna Hundred, 1776.
NEGRO Sass. Taxable in household of Norris Lester, Spesutia Lower Hundred, 1776.
NEGRO Sate. Taxable in household of Judy Ligoe, Gunpowder Lower Hundred, 1775.
NEGRO Saul. Taxable on plantation of Thomas Gash, Spesutia Lower Hundred, 1776.
NEGRO Saunty. Taxable on the plantation of Amos Garrett, Spesutia Lower Hundred, 1775.
NEGRO Saunty. Taxable on plantation of Aquila Hall, Spesutia Lower Hundred, 1775.
NEGRO Saunty. Taxable on plantation of Amos Garrett, Spesutia Lower Hundred, 1776.
NEGRO Sawney. Taxable at Thomas Harrison's Quarters, Susquehanna Hundred, 1775.
NEGRO Scipio. Taxable in household of Benjamin Rumsey, Gunpowder Lower Hundred, 1775.
NEGRO Sedippo. Taxable in household of George Garretson, Spesutia Lower Hundred, 1775.
NEGRO Sepeo. Taxable at Giles & Smith's Rock Run Plantation, Susquehanna Hundred, 1776.
NEGRO Sesa. Taxable in household of George Patterson, Susquehanna Hundred, 1776.
NEGRO Shade. Taxable at Dr. Henry Stephenson's Quarters, Spesutia Lower Hundred, 1775.
NEGRO Shag. Taxable on plantation of Edward Carvel Tolley, Spesutia Lower Hundred, 1776.
NEGRO Shambo. Taxable in household of George Paterson, Susquehanna Hundred, 1775.
NEGRO Shambo. Taxable in household of George Patterson, Susquehanna Hundred, 1776.
NEGRO Sharper. Taxable in household of William

Vertchworth, Susquehanna Hundred, 1775.

NEGRO Sharper. Taxable in household of George Chancey, Jr., Spesutia Lower Hundred, 1775.

NEGRO Sharper. Taxable on plantation of Capt. John Hall, Spesutia Lower Hundred, 1775.

NEGRO Sharper. Taxable on plantation of John Matthews, Spesutia Lower Hundred, 1775.

NEGRO Sharper. Taxable in household of Bennett Matthews, Spesutia Upper Hundred, 1775.

NEGRO Sharper. Taxable in household of Joseph Hopkins, Deer Creek Lower Hundred, 1775.

NEGRO Sharper. Taxable in household of William Verchworth, Susquehanna Hundred, 1776.

NEGRO Shedrick. Taxable at Dr. Henry Stephenson's Quarters, Spesutia Lower Hundred, 1776.

NEGRO Shiloh. Taxable on plantation of William Webb, Deer Creek Upper Hundred, 1775.

NEGRO Sig. Taxable in household of Skipwith Coal, Deer Creek Lower Hundred, 1775.

NEGRO Silence. Taxable on plantation of Hannah Hall, Spesutia Lower Hundred, 1775.

NEGRO Silence. Taxable on plantation of Hannah Hall, Spesutia Lower Hundred, 1776.

NEGRO Silues. Taxable in household of Richard Willmot, Spesutia Upper Hundred, 1775.

NEGRO Silvey. Taxable in the household of William Young, Spesutia Lower Hundred, 1775.

NEGRO Silvia. Taxable in household of Garret Garretson, Spesutia Lower Hundred, 1775.

NEGRO Silvia. Taxable in household of Garrett Garrettson (son of James), Spesutia Lower Hundred, 1776.

NEGRO Sim. Taxable on plantation of James Phillips, Spesutia Lower Hundred, 1775.

NEGRO Simon. Taxable at Samuel Thomas' Quarters, Susquehanna Hundred, 1775.

NEGRO Simon. Taxable in household of George Chancey, Jr., Spesutia Lower Hundred, 1775.

NEGRO Simon. Taxable in household of Richard Willmot, Spesutia Upper Hundred, 1775.

NEGRO Simon. Taxable at Samuel Thomas' Quarters, Susquehanna Hundred, 1776.

NEGRO Sip. Taxable in the household of Leven Matthews, Spesutia Lower Hundred, 1775.

NEGRO Sip. Taxable on plantation of Stephen Jay, Deer Creek Lower Hundred, 1775.

NEGRO Sip. Taxable in household of Leven Mathews, Spesutia Lower Hundred, 1776.

NEGRO Sipo. Taxable in household of George Paterson, Susquehanna Hundred, 1775.

NEGRO Sipp. Taxable in household of Josias William Dallam, Spesutia Lower Hundred, 1775.

NEGRO Sirues. Taxable in household of Richard Willmot, Spesutia Upper Hundred, 1775.

NEGRO Sis. Taxable in household of Clemonsy Preston, Spesutia Upper Hundred, 1775.

NEGRO Sitop. Taxable on plantation of Josias William Dallam, Spesutia Lower Hundred, 1776.

NEGRO Smug. Taxable in household of Kent Mitchel, Susquehanna Hundred, 1776.

NEGRO Sofe. Taxable in household of Grace Wallace, Deer Creek Lower Hundred, 1775.

NEGRO Soldier. Taxable in household of Capt. James Maxwell, Gunpowder Lower Hundred, 1775.

NEGRO Solomon. Taxable in household of Peter Bond, Bush River Lower Hundred, 1775.

NEGRO Solomon. Taxable at William Paca's Quarters, Spesutia Lower Hundred, 1775.

NEGRO Soney. Taxable at Thomas Harrison's Quarters, Susquehanna Hundred, 1776.

NEGRO Sook. Taxable at William Paca's Quarters, Spesutia Upper Hundred, 1775.

NEGRO Stephney. Taxable on plantation of Dr. Josias Carvell Hall, Spesutia Lower Hundred, 1776.

NEGRO Stepney. Taxable on plantation of Capt. John Hall, Spesutia Lower Hundred, 1775.

NEGRO Stepney. Taxable on plantation of Hannah Hall, Spesutia Lower Hundred, 1775.

NEGRO Suck. Taxable in household of Thomas James, Bush River Upper Hundred, 1775.

NEGRO Suck. Taxable in household of Nathan Scott, Bush River Upper Hundred, 1775.

NEGRO Suck. Taxable on plantation of William Smith, Sr, Bush River Upper Hundred, 1775.

NEGRO Suck. Taxable in household of Thomas Chew, Deer Creek Lower Hundred, 1775.

NEGRO Suck. Taxable in household of Grace Wallace, Deer Creek Lower Hundred, 1775.

NEGRO Suck. Taxable in household of James Clerk, Deer Creek Upper Hundred, 1775.

NEGRO Suck. Taxable in household of John Jolley, Deer Creek Lower Hundred, 1775.

NEGRO Sucks. Taxable in household of Josiah Lee, Deer Creek Upper Hundred, 1775.

NEGRO Sue. Taxable in household of Henry Wilson, Sr., Bush River Lower Hundred, 1775.

NEGRO Sue. Taxable in household of Thomas Waltham, Gunpowder Lower Hundred, 1775.

NEGRO Sue. Taxable in household of Joseph Lisby, Gunpowder Lower Hundred, 1775.

NEGRO Sue. Taxable in household of Greenberry Dorsey, Spesutia Lower Hundred, 1775.

NEGRO Sue. Taxable in household of Abraham Andrews, Spesutia Upper Hundred, 1775.

NEGRO Sue. Taxable in household of James Lee, Jr., Spesutia Upper Hundred, 1775.

NEGRO Sue. Taxable in household of Greenberry Dorsey, Spesutia Lower Hundred, 1776.

NEGRO Suke. Taxable in household of Alexander Cowen, Gunpowder Lower Hundred, 1775.
NEGRO Sukey. Taxable on plantation of Capt. John Hall, Spesutia Lower Hundred, 1775.
NEGRO Tamar. Taxable in household of Sarrah McCommos (widdow), Bush River Upper Hundred, 1775.
NEGRO Tamer. Taxable in household of Elizabeth Davis, Bush River Lower Hundred, 1775.
NEGRO Tamer. Taxable in household of Ann Norris, Bush River Lower Hundred, 1775.
NEGRO Tamer. Taxable at Samuel Thomas' Quarters, Susquehanna Hundred, 1775.
NEGRO Tamer. Taxable on plantation of James Lee, Deer Creek Lower Hundred, 1775.
NEGRO Teeney. Taxable on plantation of Dr. Josias Carvell Hall, Spesutia Lower Hundred, 1776.
NEGRO Temer. Taxable in household of Jonathan Woodland, Gunpowder Lower Hundred, 1775.
NEGRO Thomas (a free negro). Taxable in Susquehanna Hundred, 1776, with taxables Affey, Mingo, William, George, Polledore, and Tower listed in his household, and Richard Johns was their security.
NEGRO Thomas. Taxable in household of Rachel Thorp, Bush River Lower Hundred, 1775.
NEGRO Thomas. Taxable in household of William Ditto, Bush River Upper Hundred, 1775.
NEGRO Thomasine. Taxable on plantation of Capt. John Mathews, Spesutia Lower Hundred, 1776.
NEGRO Tiney. Taxable at Amos Garrett's Quarters, Spesutia Lower Hundred, 1775.
NEGRO Toby. Taxable in household of Henery Wetherell, Gunpowder Lower Hundred, 1775.
NEGRO Toby. Taxable in household of William Clark, Spesutia Upper Hundred, 1775.
NEGRO Tom. Taxable in household of Lemuel Howard, Bush River Lower Hundred, 1775.
NEGRO Tom. Taxable in household of Ellender Durham, Bush River Lower Hundred, 1775.
NEGRO Tom. Taxable in Bush River Lower Hundred, 1775, with Henry Wilson, Sr. as his security.
NEGRO Tom. Taxable in household of Henry Wilson, Jr., Bush River Lower Hundred, 1775.
NEGRO Tom. Taxable in household of Joseph Presbury, Gunpowder Lower Hundred, 1775.
NEGRO Tom. Taxable at Jacob Bond's Quarters, Gunpowder Lower Hundred, 1775.
NEGRO Tom. Taxable in household of Richard Johns, Susquehanna Hundred, 1775.
NEGRO Tom. Taxable in household of Edward Mitchel, Susquehanna Hundred, 1775.
NEGRO Tom. Taxable in household of William Horten, Susquehanna Hundred, 1775.
NEGRO Tom. Taxable in household of George Chancey, Sr., Spesutia Lower Hundred, 1775.
NEGRO Tom. Taxable on the plantation of Amos Garrett, Spesutia Lower Hundred, 1775.
NEGRO Tom. Taxable in the household of William Smith, Spesutia Lower Hundred, 1775.
NEGRO Tom. Taxable in household of Edmond Bull, Spesutia Upper Hundred, 1775.
NEGRO Tom. Taxable in household of Sarah Grafton, Spesutia Upper Hundred, 1775.
NEGRO Tom. Taxable in household of Benjaman Wheler, Spesutia Upper Hundred, 1775.
NEGRO Tom. Taxable in household of Henry Ruff, Spesutia Upper Hundred, 1775.
NEGRO Tom. Taxable on plantation of Ignatious Wheler, Spesutia Upper Hundred, 1775.
NEGRO Tom. Taxable in household of Jonathan Lyon, Bush River Upper Hundred, 1775.
NEGRO Tom. Taxable in household of William Morgan, Deer Creek Upper Hundred, 1775.
NEGRO Tom. Taxable in household of Ignatius Wheeler, Jr., Deer Creek Upper Hundred, 1775.
NEGRO Tom. Taxable in household of Francis Holland, Spesutia Lower Hundred, 1776.
NEGRO Tom. Taxable on plantation of Amos Garrett, Spesutia Lower Hundred, 1776.
NEGRO Tom. Taxable in household of William Barns, Susquehanna Hundred, 1776.
NEGRO Tom. Taxable on plantation of John Lee Webster, Spesutia Lower Hundred, 1776.
NEGRO Tom. Taxable at Giles & Smith's Rock Run Plantation, Susquehanna Hundred, 1776.
NEGRO Tom. Taxable on plantation of Jacob Giles, Susquehanna Hundred, 1776.
NEGRO Tom. Taxable in household of William Horten, Susquehanna Hundred, 1776.
NEGRO Tom. Taxable in household of Edward Mitchel, Susquehanna Hundred, 1776.
NEGRO Tom. Taxables on plantation of William Hopkins, Deer Creek Lower Hundred, 1775.
NEGRO Tomey. Taxable in household of Micaja Mitchel, Susquehanna Hundred, 1775.
NEGRO Tomson. Taxable on plantation of John Matthews, Spesutia Lower Hundred, 1775.
NEGRO Toney. Taxable in household of Jacob Bond, Sr., Bush River Lower Hundred, 1775.
NEGRO Toney. Taxable in household of James McComas, Bush River Lower Hundred, 1775.
NEGRO Toney. Taxable in household of Peter Potee, Bush River Lower Hundred, 1775.
NEGRO Toney. Taxable in household of Elizabeth Lytle, Gunpowder Lower Hundred, 1775.
NEGRO Toney. Taxable in household of John Brown, Spesutia Lower Hundred, 1775.
NEGRO Toney. Taxable in household of George Ford,

Spesutia Lower Hundred, 1775.

NEGRO Toney. Taxable at Thomas Frisby Henderson's Quarters, Spesutia Lower Hundred, 1775.

NEGRO Toney. Taxable in the household of William Hollis, Sr., Spesutia Lower Hundred, 1775.

NEGRO Toney. Taxable on plantation of Aquila Hall, Spesutia Lower Hundred, 1775.

NEGRO Toney. Taxable in household of James Mores, Spesutia Upper Hundred, 1775.

NEGRO Toney. Taxable in household of James Fisher, Deer Creek Lower Hundred, 1775.

NEGRO Toney. Taxable in household of Samuel Gover, Deer Creek Lower Hundred, 1775.

NEGRO Toney. Taxable in household of John Brown, Spesutia Lower Hundred, 1776.

NEGRO Toney. Taxable in household of Ann Johnson (widow), Deer Creek Upper Hundred, 1775.

NEGRO Toney. Taxable in household of Francis Holland, Spesutia Lower Hundred, 1776.

NEGRO Toney. Taxable in household of Micajh [Micajah] Mitchel, Susquehanna Hundred, 1776.

NEGRO Tony. Taxable in household of Thomas Wheler, Spesutia Upper Hundred, 1775.

NEGRO Tower (a free negro). Head of household in Susquehanna Hundred, 1776, with Giddean Pervale as his security.

NEGRO Tower. Taxable in household of Henry Wilson, Sr., Bush River Lower Hundred, 1775.

NEGRO Tower. Taxable in household of Josias William Dallam, Spesutia Lower Hundred, 1775.

NEGRO Tower. Taxable in household of James Rigbie, Deer Creek Lower Hundred, 1775.

NEGRO Tower. Taxable in household of Elizabeth Gover, Deer Creek Lower Hundred, 1775.

NEGRO Tower. Taxable on plantation of Josias William Dallam, Spesutia Lower Hundred, 1776.

NEGRO Tower. Taxable in household of Negro Thomas (a free negro), Susquehanna Hundred, 1776.

NEGRO Tower. Taxables on plantation of Samuel Harris, Deer Creek Lower Hundred, 1775.

NEGRO Tral. Taxable in household of Nicholas Alender, Gunpowder Lower Hundred, 1775.

NEGRO Triall. Taxable in household of Daniel McComas, Bush River Lower Hundred, 1775.

NEGRO Val. Taxable in the household of Edward Carvel Tolley, Spesutia Lower Hundred, 1775.

NEGRO Valentine. Taxable in household of Jacob Giles, Susquehanna Hundred, 1775.

NEGRO Venus. Taxable in household of George Paterson, Susquehanna Hundred, 1775.

NEGRO Venus. Taxable in household of Danniel Robinson, Spesutia Upper Hundred, 1775.

NEGRO Venus. Taxable in household of George Patterson, Susquehanna Hundred, 1776.

NEGRO Vilet. Taxable in household of Nicholas Alender, Gunpowder Lower Hundred, 1775.

NEGRO Vilet. Taxable in household of Thomas Foster, Deer Creek Upper Hundred, 1775.

NEGRO Vilet. Taxable in household of William Morgan, Deer Creek Upper Hundred, 1775.

NEGRO Vingo. Taxable in household of George Copland, Spesutia Lower Hundred, 1775.

NEGRO Violet. Taxable in household of RObert Brown, Spesutia Lower Hundred, 1775.

NEGRO Violet. Taxable in household of John Diemer, Spesutia Lower Hundred, 1775.

NEGRO Violet. Taxable in household of Francis Holland, Spesutia Lower Hundred, 1776.

NEGRO Voll. Taxable in household of Freeborn Brown, Spesutia Lower Hundred, 1775.

NEGRO Vollentine. Taxable on plantation of Jacob Giles, Susquehanna Hundred, 1776.

NEGRO Voluntine. Taxable in household of Thomas Bond, Sr., Bush River Lower Hundred, 1775.

NEGRO Voluntine. Taxable in household of Joseph Norris, Bush River Lower Hundred, 1775.

NEGRO Walton. Taxable in the household of William Smith, Spesutia Lower Hundred, 1775.

NEGRO Wapping. Taxable at Thomas Harrison's Quarters, Susquehanna Hundred, 1775.

NEGRO Well. Taxable in household of Henry Green, Spesutia Upper Hundred, 1775.

NEGRO Welton. Taxable in household of John Diemer, Spesutia Lower Hundred, 1775.

NEGRO Welton. Taxable in the household of William Smith, Spesutia Lower Hundred, 1775.

NEGRO Welton. Taxable on plantation of William Smith, Jr., Spesutia Lower Hundred, 1776.

NEGRO Wench. Taxable in household of James Scott (son of Aquila), Bush River Lower Hundred, 1775.

NEGRO Wench. Taxable in household of James Finly, Bush River Upper Hundred, 1775.

NEGRO Wench. Taxable in household of John Barrett, Bush River Upper Hundred, 1775.

NEGRO Whopen. Taxable at Thomas Harrison's Quarters, Susquehanna Hundred, 1776.

NEGRO Wil. Taxable at Benjamin Howard's Quarters, Gunpowder Lower Hundred, 1775.

NEGRO Wil. Taxable at William Buchanan's Quarters, Gunpowder Lower Hundred, 1775.

NEGRO Wil. Taxable in household of Richard Johns, Susquehanna Hundred, 1775.

NEGRO Will Gwinn. Taxable on plantation of William Hall, Spesutia Lower Hundred, 1776.

NEGRO Will Jr. Taxable on plantation of William Smith, Sr, Bush River Upper Hundred, 1775.

NEGRO Will. Taxable in household of Lambert Wilmer, Gunpowder Lower Hundred, 1775.

NEGRO Will. Taxable in household of Ephraim Andrews, Susquehanna Hundred, 1775.
NEGRO Will. Taxable at Samuel Thomas' Quarters, Susquehanna Hundred, 1775.
NEGRO Will. Taxable on the plantation of Amos Garrett, Spesutia Lower Hundred, 1775.
NEGRO Will. Taxable in household of Samuel Griffith, Spesutia Lower Hundred, 1775.
NEGRO Will. Taxable in household of William Hall, Spesutia Lower Hundred, 1775.
NEGRO Will. Taxable at Luke Griffin's Quarters, Spesutia Lower Hundred, 1775.
NEGRO Will. Taxable on plantation of John Lee Webster, Spesutia Lower Hundred, 1775.
NEGRO Will. Taxable on plantation of John Matthews, Spesutia Lower Hundred, 1775.
NEGRO Will. Taxable in the household of James Kimble, Spesutia Lower Hundred, 1775.
NEGRO Will. Taxable in household of Lenard Green, Spesutia Upper Hundred, 1775.
NEGRO Will. Taxable in the household of Rev. William West, Spesutia Lower Hundred, 1775.
NEGRO Will. Taxable at Dr. Henry Stephenson's Quarters, Spesutia Lower Hundred, 1775.
NEGRO Will. Taxable in household of Isaac Webster, Spesutia Upper Hundred, 1775.
NEGRO Will. Taxable in household of Richard Ruff, Spesutia Upper Hundred, 1775.
NEGRO Will. Taxable on plantation of Ignatious Wheler, Spesutia Upper Hundred, 1775.
NEGRO Will. Taxable in Spesutia Upper Hundred, 1775.
NEGRO Will. Taxable on plantation of William Smith, Sr, Bush River Upper Hundred, 1775.
NEGRO Will. Taxable in household of Elizabeth Gover, Deer Creek Lower Hundred, 1775.
NEGRO Will. Taxable in household of Grace Wallace, Deer Creek Lower Hundred, 1775.
NEGRO Will. Taxable at Luke Griffith's Quarters, Spesutia Lower Hundred, 1776.
NEGRO Will. Taxable on plantation of William Hall, Spesutia Lower Hundred, 1776.
NEGRO Will. Taxable on plantation of Amos Garrett, Spesutia Lower Hundred, 1776.
NEGRO Will. Taxable on plantation of Ephrem Andres, Susquehanna Hundred, 1776.
NEGRO Will. Taxable on plantation of Jacob Giles, Jr., Susquehanna Hundred, 1776.
NEGRO Will. Taxable on plantation of John Lee Webster, Spesutia Lower Hundred, 1776.
NEGRO Will. Taxable on plantation of Jacob Giles, Susquehanna Hundred, 1776.
NEGRO Will. Taxable at Samuel Thomas' Quarters, Susquehanna Hundred, 1776.
NEGRO Will. Taxables on plantation of William Hopkins, Deer Creek Lower Hundred, 1775.
NEGRO William. Taxable in household of James Kimble, Spesutia Lower Hundred, 1776.
NEGRO William. Taxable in household of Negro Thomas (a free negro), Susquehanna Hundred, 1776.
NEGRO York. Taxable in household of Hannah Norris, Bush River Lower Hundred, 1775.
NEGRO York. Taxable in household of Francis Downing, Deer Creek Lower Hundred, 1775.
NEGRO Young Tom. Taxable at Giles & Smith's Rock Run Plantation, Susquehanna Hundred, 1776.
NEGRO Zeb. Taxable in household of William Hall, Spesutia Lower Hundred, 1775.
NEGRO Zedor. Taxable in household of Capt. James Maxwell, Gunpowder Lower Hundred, 1775.
NEGRO ---- [illegible]. Taxable in the household of William Young, Spesutia Lower Hundred, 1775.
NEGRO ---- [illegible]. Taxable in household of Mordika Amoss, Bush River Upper Hundred, 1775.
NEGRO ---- [illegible]. Taxable in household of Benjamin Biddel, Bush River Upper Hundred, 1775.
NELSON, Robert. Taxable in Bush River Upper Hundred, 1775, with taxables Sam, Levi, and Ruth listed in his household.
NELSON, Thomas. Taxable in household of Archibald Beaty, Spesutia Lower Hundred, 1776.
NERGO Lucy. Taxable in the household of Benedict Edward Hall, Spesutia Lower Hundred, 1775.
NEVEL, Philip. Taxable (servant) in household of Andrew Howlet, Deer Creek Lower Hundred, 1775.
NEVIL, William. Taxable in Spesutia Lower Hundred, 1775.
NEVIN, Patrick. Taxable in household of James Horner, Susquehanna Hundred, 1775.
NICHELS, Joseph. Taxable in household of Samuel Webster, Jr., Spesutia Upper Hundred, 1775.
NICOLET, David. Taxable in the household of Edward Hall, Spesutia Lower Hundred, 1775.
NIGHT, William. Taxable in household of Nathan McClura (McCluna?), Bush River Upper Hundred, 1775.
NIPPER, George. Taxable on the plantation of Amos Garrett, Spesutia Lower Hundred, 1775.
NIVANS, Hugh. Taxable in Bush River Upper Hundred, 1775, with taxable servant James Lasarus listed in his household.
NOFORD, Richard. Taxable in Bush River Lower Hundred, 1775.
NOLLY, Peter. Taxable in household of John Wilson (merchant), Susquehanna Hundred, 1775.
NORINGTO [sic], John. Taxable in Spesutia Upper Hundred, 1775.
NORRID, William. Taxable in household of Thomas Ellet, Bush River Upper Hundred, 1775.

EARLY HARFORD COUNTIANS: Supplement

NORRINGTON, Francis. Taxable in Bush River Lower Hundred, 1775.

NORRINGTONE, John Jr. Taxable in Bush River Upper Hundred, 1775. [The constable entered his name on the tax list and then lined it out; no reason given].

NORRIS, Abrm. Taxable in household of William Kitely, Bush River Lower Hundred, 1775.

NORRIS, Alexander. Bush River Upper Hundred, 1775.

NORRIS, Andrew. Taxable in Bush River Upper Hundred, 1775, with taxable negro Joe listed in his household.

NORRIS, Ann. Head of household in Bush River Lower Hundred, 1775, with taxable negroes Isibiler, Phillis, Phebe, Mingo, and Tamer listed in her household.

NORRIS, Aquila (son of Edward). Taxable in Bush River Lower Hundred, 1775.

NORRIS, Aquila (son of Thomas). Taxable in Bush River Lower Hundred, 1775.

NORRIS, Benjamin. Taxable in Bush River Lower Hundred, 1775, with taxable servant Andrew Jacklin and negro Ben listed in his household.

NORRIS, Benjamin. Taxable in Bush River Lower Hundred, 1775, with taxable Robert Coal listed in his household.

NORRIS, Daniel (son of Edward). Taxable in Bush River Lower Hundred, 1775, with taxable Richard Herbert listed in his household.

NORRIS, Edward (son of Edward). Taxable in Bush River Lower Hundred, 1775.

NORRIS, Edward (son of Joseph). See "William McMullen" and "Samuel McMullen," q.v.

NORRIS, Edward (son of Joseph). Taxable in Bush River Lower Hundred, 1775.

NORRIS, Edward. Taxable in Bush River Upper Hundred, 1775.

NORRIS, Edward. Taxable in Deer Creek Upper Hundred, 1775, with taxable men Rowlan Capen and Thomas Varley (servants) listed in his household.

NORRIS, Hannah. Head of household in Bush River Lower Hundred, 1775, with taxable negro York listed in her household.

NORRIS, Jacob. Taxable in Bush River Lower Hundred, 1775.

NORRIS, James (sadler). Taxable in Bush River Upper Hundred, 1775. [The constable's scribbled handwriting makes the name appear to be "Jones Sodlen Norris" but it actually is "James Norris, sadler" as shown an another tax list].

NORRIS, James (son of James). Taxable in Bush River Lower Hundred, 1775.

NORRIS, James (son of William). Taxable in household of his father William Norris, Bush River Upper Hundred, 1775.

NORRIS, James. Taxable in household of Joseph Norris (son of Edward), Bush River Lower Hundred, 1775.

NORRIS, James. Taxable in Bush River Lower Hundred, 1775, with taxable negro Eff listed in his household.

NORRIS, John (son of William). Taxable in Bush River Lower Hundred, 1775.

NORRIS, John. Taxable in Bush River Lower Hundred, 1775, with taxables Thomas Norris and John Andrews listed in his household.

NORRIS, Joseph (son of Edward). Taxable in Bush River Lower Hundred, 1775, with taxables James Norris and William Norris listed in his household.

NORRIS, Joseph. Taxable in Bush River Lower Hundred, 1775, with Jonathan ---- and Stephen ---- (no last names given) and negro Voluntine listed in his household.

NORRIS, Richard. Taxable in Bush River Lower Hundred, 1775.

NORRIS, Sarah. Head of household in Bush River Lower Hundred, 1775, with taxable negroes Oliver and Jone listed in her household.

NORRIS, Thomas (son of Edward). Taxable in Bush River Lower Hundred, 1775.

NORRIS, Thomas. Taxable in household of John Norris, Bush River Lower Hundred, 1775.

NORRIS, Thomas. Taxable in Bush River Upper Hundred, 1775.

NORRIS, William. Taxable in household of Joseph Norris (son of Edward), Bush River Lower Hundred, 1775.

NORRIS, William. Taxable in Spesutia Upper Hundred, 1775.

NORRIS, William. Taxable in Bush River Upper Hundred, 1775, with taxables James Norris (son), Rinhard (Richard?) Jourdan (servant), and negroes Derry and Dina listed in his household.

NORVER, James. Taxable in Bush River Lower Hundred, 1775.

NOULON, Thomas. Taxable in household of James McCrackin, Spesutia Lower Hundred, 1776.

NOWLAN, William. Taxable in household of Patrick Creighton, Susquehanna Hundred, 1775.

NOWLEN, Thomas. Taxable in the household of James McCrackin, Spesutia Lower Hundred, 1775.

NUTAWELL, Daniel. Taxable in Susquehanna Hundred, 1776, with taxable negro Antinoy listed in his household.

NUTH, Thomas. Taxable in household of Henry Enlowes, Bush River Upper Hundred, 1775.

NUTTERWELL, Daniel. Taxable in Spesutia Lower Hundred, 1776.

NUTWELL, David. Taxable in Gunpowder Lower Hundred, 1775. His name (among others) was listed on the back of the tax list.

O'DANIEL, James. Taxable in Bush River Upper

Hundred, 1775. [The constable's scribbled handwriting makes the name appear to be "Jones Odanile" but it is actually "James O'Daniel" as shown on another tax list].

O'DANIEL, John. Taxable in Bush River Lower Hundred, 1775.

O'DELL, Talbot. Taxable in the household of Rev. William West, Spesutia Lower Hundred, 1775.

OBRICON, Roger. Taxable in household of Francis Holland, Spesutia Lower Hundred, 1776.

OEAL, George. Taxable servant in household of Edward Bull (son of Jacob), Bush River Lower Hundred, 1775.

OGALBE, James. Taxable in Bush River Upper Hundred, 1775.

OLDHAM, Henry. Taxable in household of Edward Talbott, Bush River Lower Hundred, 1775.

OLIVER, James Jr. Taxable in the household of James Oliver, Spesutia Lower Hundred, 1775.

OLIVER, James Sr. Taxable in Spesutia Lower Hundred, 1776.

OLIVER, James. Taxable in Spesutia Lower Hundred, 1775, with taxable James Oliver, Jr. listed in his household.

ONION, Zacheus' Quarters. Bush River Upper Hundred, 1775, with taxable Jacob Davis and two slaves (no names given) listed at these quarters.

OR, James. Taxable in Gunpowder Lower Hundred, 1775, with Benjamin Meed as his security.

ORE, John. Taxable in household of Peter Fort, Susquehanna Hundred, 1776.

ORR, James. Taxable in Bush River Upper Hundred, 1775. [The constable's scribbled handwriting makes the name appear to be "Jones Orr" but it is actally "James Orr" as shown on another tax list].

ORR, John. Taxable (servant) in household of John McClan, Bush River Upper Hundred, 1775.

ORR, Joseph. Taxable in Bush River Upper Hundred, 1775.

ORSBORN, John. Taxable in Susquehanna Hundred, 1776.

OSBORN, Benjamin. Taxable in Spesutia Lower Hundred, 1775, with taxable James ---- (Osborn?) listed in his household. [James' name on tax list is very dark and illegible].

OSBORN, Cyrus. Taxable in Spesutia Lower Hundred, 1775, with taxable slaves Esther and Jacob listed in his household.

OSBORN, Cyrus. Taxable in Spesutia Lower Hundred, 1776.

OSBORN, James Jr. Taxable in Spesutia Lower Hundred, 1775, with taxables Thomas Sutton and slaves Peter, Moll, Hagar, Dell, and Isaac listed in his household.

OSBORN, James Sr. Taxable in Spesutia Lower Hundred, 1775.

OSBORN, William Jr. See "Stephen Crouch," q.v.

OSBORN, William Jr. Taxable in Spesutia Lower Hundred, 1775, with taxable slaves Harry and Priss listed in his household.

OSBORN, William Sr. Taxable in Spesutia Lower Hundred, 1775, with taxable slave Dinah listed in his household.

OSBORN(?), James. Taxable in the household of Benjamin Osborn, Spesutia Lower Hundred, 1775.

OSBURN, John. Taxable in Susquehanna Hundred, 1775.

OSBURN, Samuel Groome. Taxable in Gunpowder Lower Hundred, 1775.

OSBURN, William. Taxable in Gunpowder Lower Hundred, 1775.

OWEN, John. Taxable in household of William Megill, Susquehanna Hundred, 1776.

OWENS, Arther. Taxable in Susquehanna Hundred, 1776.

P----, Hugh [page torn]. Taxable in Spesutia Upper Hundred, 1775, with John ---- [page torn] as his security.

P----, James [page torn]. Taxable in Bush River Lower Hundred, 1775.

PACA, Aquila Jr. Taxable in Spesutia Lower Hundred, 1775, with taxable slaves Bob, Bett, Grace, and Jack listed in his household. See "Thomas Pritchard," q.v.

PACA, Aquila Jr. Taxable in Spesutia Lower Hundred, 1776, with taxable negroes Robert, Jack, Bess, and Grace listed in his household.

PACA, Aquilla. Taxable in Gunpowder Lower Hundred, 1775, with taxable slaves Joe and Hago listed in his household.

PACA, John. See "John Peca," q.v.

PACA, William. Taxable in household of John Wilson (merchant), Susquehanna Hundred, 1775. [The actual entry looks like "William Paea"].

PACA, William's Quarters. Spesutia Lower Hundred, 1775, with taxables Thomas Gash and slaves Dick, David, Ben, Solomon, Priss, Moll, Mary, Moll 2nd, Sall, Agnus, Dinah, Jeremiah, Cate, and Maria listed at his quarters.

PACA, William's Quarters. Spesutia Upper Hundred, 1775, with taxable negroes Nicholas, Sook, Easter, Rose, and Sal listed at these quarters.

PAGE, Christopher. Taxable in Susquehanna Hundred, 1775.

PAGE, Cristopher. Taxable in Susquehanna Hundred, 1776.

PAGE, John. Taxable (servant) in household of Dannil Tridaway, Bush River Upper Hundred, 1775.

PARIS, William. Taxable in Bush River Lower Hundred, 1775.

PARKER, Martenie. Taxable in Bush River Upper

EARLY HARFORD COUNTIANS: Supplement

Hundred, 1775, with taxables Quillu [sic] Parker and servant men Mike and Ros [sic] listed in his household.

PARKER, Quillu. Taxable in household of Martenie Parker, Bush River Upper Hundred, 1775.

PARKER, William. Taxable in Bush River Upper Hundred, 1775.

PARKS, James. Taxable in Deer Creek Lower Hundred, 1775, with taxable man John Kelley (servant) listed in his household.

PARSON, Isaac. Taxable in Bush River Upper Hundred, 1775.

PARSON, John. Taxable in Bush River Upper Hundred, 1775.

PARSONS, John. Taxable in Bush River Lower Hundred, 1775.

PARSONS, Joseph. Taxable in Bush River Lower Hundred, 1775.

PATERSON, Alexander. See "George Paterson," q.v.

PATERSON, George. Taxable in Susquehanna Hundred, 1775, with taxable negroes Sipo, Shambo, and Venus, plus the name Alexander which was preceded by the word "negroe" but the word "negroe" was lined out; thus, it is unclear whether this was a slave, a servant, or a son named Alexander Paterson).

PATERSON, John. Taxable in Susquehanna Hundred, 1775.

PATERSON, Samuel. Taxable in Bush River Upper Hundred, 1775.

PATERSON, William. Taxable in Bush River Upper Hundred, 1775.

PATRICK, George. Taxable man in the household of Joseph Stokes, Deer Creek Upper Hundred, 1775.

PATRICK, John. Taxable in Deer Creek Lower Hundred, 1775, with taxables Nathan Litle and negro Paul listed in his household.

PATTERSON, George. Taxable in Susquehanna Hundred, 1776, with taxables Allexander Gardner and negroes Sesa, Shambo, and Venus listed in his household.

PAUL, John. Taxable in Bush River Lower Hundred, 1775.

PEACOCK, John. Taxable in Deer Creek Lower Hundred, 1775, with taxable negroes Peg, Ruth, and Dick listed in his household.

PEACOCK, Luke. Taxable in Deer Creek Upper Hundred, 1775, with taxable Samuel Peacock (son) listed in his household.

PEACOCK, Samuel (son of Luke). Taxable in household of his father Luke Peacock, Deer Creek Upper Hundred, 1775.

PEARSON, Able. Taxable in Deer Creek Lower Hundred, 1775.

PECA, John. Taxable in Bush River Lower Hundred, 1775, with taxable negroes Dick, Harry, Adam, Bob, Fanney, Hannah, Long Fanney, Sarah, and Lewshore listed in his household.

PEDLAR, Lewis. Taxable in household of George Drew, Spesutia Lower Hundred, 1775.

PEERY, James. Taxable in household of Ephraim Biars, Susquehanna Hundred, 1775.

PEIRCE, Richard. Taxable at Amos Garrett's Quarters, Spesutia Lower Hundred, 1775.

PEMBRICK(?), Thomas. Taxable in household of Ignatius Wheeler, Jr., Deer Creek Upper Hundred, 1775.

PENDERGAST, Thomas Jr. Taxable in household of Thomas Pendergast, Bush River Lower Hundred, 1775.

PENDERGAST, Thomas. Taxable in Bush River Lower Hundred, 1775, with Thomas Pendergast, Jr. listed in his household.

PENICKS, John. Taxable in Deer Creek Lower Hundred, 1775.

PENNICK, Thomas. Taxable in Spesutia Upper Hundred, 1775.

PENNIN, Jacob. Taxable (son-in-law) in household of James Brewer, Susquehanna Hundred, 1775.

PENROSE, Isaac. Taxable on plantation of Amos Garrett, Spesutia Lower Hundred, 1776.

PEREMON, John. Taxable in Susquehanna Hundred, 1776, with taxable Thomas Durbin listed in his household.

PEREY, William. Taxable in Susquehanna Hundred, 1776.

PERIMAN, John. Taxable in Susquehanna Hundred, 1775, with taxable Thomas Durbin listed in his household.

PERINE, James. Taxable in Bush River Upper Hundred, 1775, with taxable Peter Perine (son) listed in his household.

PERINE, Peter. Taxable in household of his father James Perine, Bush River Upper Hundred, 1775.

PERKINS, John. Taxable in Susquehanna Hundred, 1775.

PERKINS, John. Taxable in Susquehanna Hundred, 1776.

PERKINS, Richard. Taxable in household of John Mitchel, Susquehanna Hundred, 1776.

PERKINS, William. See "William Knight," q.v.

PERKINS, William. Taxable in Susquehanna Hundred, 1775.

PERKINS, William. Taxable in Susquehanna Hundred, 1776.

PERKINSON, Dinis. Taxable in household of William Ashmore, Deer Creek Upper Hundred, 1775.

PERRY, Edward. Taxable in Gunpowder Lower Hundred, 1775.

PERRY, John. Taxable at Richard Dallam's Quarters at Swan Creek, Spesutia Lower Hundred, 1775.
PERRY, Thomas. Taxable in Deer Creek Upper Hundred, 1775.
PERRY, William (son of William). Taxable in Susquehanna Hundred, 1775.
PERRYMAN, John. See "John Periman," q.v.
PERRYMAN, John. See "John Peremon," q.v.
PERVALE, Geddean. Taxable in Susquehanna Hundred, 1776, with taxable Samuel Harris listed in his household. See "Negro Tower (a free negro)," q.v.
PERY, John. Taxable in Bush River Upper Hundred, 1775.
PERY, William. Taxable in Bush River Upper Hundred, 1775.
PEW, Daniel. Taxable in Susquehanna Hundred, 1775, with taxable Daniel Pue [sic] listed in his household.
PHILIPS, James. Taxable in Deer Creek Upper Hundred, 1775.
PHILLIPS, James. See "William Mooberry," q.v.
PHILLIPS, James. Taxable in Spesutia Lower Hundred, 1775, with taxable slaves Harry, Cato, Jack, Charles, Sim, Jacob, Sam, Joe, Cleetus, Sarah, Pug, Poll, Hannah, Jane, Moll, Moll 2nd, Rachael, Esther, and Dinah listed on his plantation.
PICHPATRIK, Michal. See "George Ford" and "Benjamin Ford," q.v.
PIERCE, Richard. Taxable on plantation of Amos Garrett, Spesutia Lower Hundred, 1776.
PIKE, Andrew. Taxable in Spesutia Lower Hundred, 1775.
PILES, Ralph (son of Ralph). Taxable in household of his father Ralph Piles, Spesutia Upper Hundred, 1775.
PILES, Ralph. Taxable in Spesutia Upper Hundred, 1775, with taxables Ralph Piles (son) and Thomas Loyad listed in his household.
PITT, Francis. Taxable "at Rach Gallion's" in Spesutia Lower Hundred, 1775.
PITT, William. Taxable in household of Richard Ruff, Spesutia Upper Hundred, 1775.
PLANT, Stephen. Taxable in Bush River Upper Hundred, 1775, with Aquila Samson as his security.
PLASTER, Charles. Taxable in household of Jacob Giles, Susquehanna Hundred, 1775.
PLOWMAN, Edward. Taxable on plantation of Edward Carvel Tolley, Spesutia Lower Hundred, 1776.
PLUNKET, Michael. Taxable on plantation of George Ford, Spesutia Lower Hundred, 1776.
POAKE, Samuel. Taxable in household of Robert Gordon, Deer Creek Upper Hundred, 1775.
POCOCK, Daniel (son of Daniel). Taxable in household of his father Daniel Pocock, Bush River Upper Hundred, 1775.
POCOCK, Daniel. Taxable in Bush River Upper Hundred, 1775, with taxable Daniel Pocock (son) listed in his household. [The constable's scribbled handwriting makes the name appears to be "Donnill Pointer" but it is actually "Daniel Pocock" as shown on another tax list].
PORE, Neclus. Taxable in Susquehanna Hundred, 1776.
PORTER, James. Taxable in Susquehanna Hundred, 1775.
PORTOR, William. Taxable in Susquehanna Hundred, 1776.
POTEE, Peter. Taxable in Bush River Lower Hundred, 1775, with taxable negroes Toney, Sampson, and Dinah listed in his household.
POTEET, Thomas (son of John). Taxable in Bush River Upper Hundred, 1775.
POTEET, Thomas Jr. Taxable in Spesutia Upper Hundred, 1775.
POTEET, Thomas Jr. Taxable in Bush River Upper Hundred, 1775.
POTEET, Thomas Sr. Taxable in Bush River Upper Hundred, 1775.
POTS, Rinord. Taxable in Susquehanna Hundred, 1776.
POTTS, John Reynard. Taxable in Susquehanna Hundred, 1775.
POTTS, Reynard. See "John Reynard Potts," q.v.
POULSON, John. Taxable in Bush River Lower Hundred, 1775.
POUND, John. Taxable (servant) in household of William Hitchcock, Bush River Upper Hundred, 1775.
POWER, John. Taxable in Spesutia Lower Hundred, 1775, with John Cox as his security.
POWER, Nicholas. Taxable in Spesutia Upper Hundred, 1775.
PRALL, Edward. See "Edward Prawl," q.v.
PRAWL, Edward. Taxable in Susquehanna Hundred, 1775. [The tax list is dark and partially torn, but this is undoubtedly Edward Prall, sometimes written Edward Praul, who served in the Revolutionary War and was a county magistrate].
PRESBURY, Joseph. Taxable in Gunpowder Lower Hundred, 1775, with taxables Joseph ---- (no last name given) and slaves Roger, Darby, Tom, Hago, and Pris listed in his household.
PRESBURY, Joseph's Quarters. Spesutia Upper Hundred, 1775, with taxable negroes Roger [page torn, but other tax lists indicate his name was Roger], Darby, and Pugg listed at these quarters.
PRESBURY, Martha. Head of household in Gunpowder Lower Hundred, 1775, with taxables Anthony Knowlman and slaves Peter, Jack, Pack, Dinah, Hanna, Ruth, and Eve listed in her household.
PRESBURY, Thomas. Taxable in Gunpowder Lower Hundred, 1775, with taxables John White and Thomas

Fox listed in his household.

PRESTON, Ann. Head of household in Spesutia Upper Hundred, 1775, with taxable negro Sall listed in her household.

PRESTON, Barnard (son of Dan). Taxable in Bush River Lower Hundred, 1775.

PRESTON, Barnard (son of Barnard). Taxable in Spesutia Upper Hundred, 1775. [His name was listed out of alphabetical order at the end of the R's].

PRESTON, Barnard (son of Clemonsy). Taxable in household of his mother Clemonsy Preston, Spesutia Upper Hundred, 1775.

PRESTON, Barnard. Taxable in Spesutia Upper Hundred, 1775, with taxable negroes Jack and Pugg listed in his household.

PRESTON, Clemonsy. Head of household in SPesutia Upper Hundred, 1775, with taxables Barnard Preston (son) and negroes Bobb, Sarah and Sis listed in her household.

PRESTON, Danniel. Taxable in Spesutia Upper Hundred, 1775, with taxable negro Ceazer listed in his household.

PRESTON, Grafton. Taxable in Spesutia Upper Hundred, 1775.

PRESTON, James. Taxable in Spesutia Upper Hundred, 1775, with taxable Henry Rowland listed in his household.

PRESTON, Martin. Taxable in Spesutia Upper Hundred, 1775, with taxable negro Addam listed in his household.

PRICE, Daniel. Taxable in Deer Creek Lower Hundred, 1775, with Martha Smith as his security.

PRICE, James. Taxable in Gunpowder Lower Hundred, 1775.

PRICE, John. Taxable (servant) in household of Thomas Bond, Jr., Bush River Upper Hundred, 1775.

PRICE, Nathaniel. Taxable in household of William Jenkens, Bush River Lower Hundred, 1775.

PRICE, Robert. Taxable in Bush River Lower Hundred, 1775.

PRICE, William. Taxable in Gunpowder Lower Hundred, 1775.

PRICE, William. Taxable in household of James Mitchel, Susquehanna Hundred, 1776.

PRICHARD (PRITCHARDS), James. Taxable in Susquehanna Hundred, 1776, with taxable Harmon Prichard listed in his household. [The constable spelled James' last name as "Pritchards" while Harmon's and others on the list were spelled as "Prichard"].

PRICHARD, Harmon. Taxable in household of James Prichard, Susquehanna Hundred, 1776.

PRICHARD, James Jr. Taxable in Susquehanna Hundred, 1776.

PRICHARD, Jessee. See "Martain Scarf," q.v.

PRICHARD, Jessee. Taxable in Bush River Upper Hundred, 1775.

PRICHARD, John. Taxable in Bush River Upper Hundred, 1775.

PRICHARD, Obediah. Taxable in Susquehanna Hundred, 1776.

PRIGG, Edward. Taxable in Spesutia Upper Hundred, 1775.

PRIGG, William Jr. Taxable in Spesutia Upper Hundred, 1775.

PRIGG, William Sr. Taxable in Spesutia Upper Hundred, 1775, with taxable negroes George, Hannah, and Judy listed in his household. [His last name is torn from the page, but research shows it to be Prigg based on the names of his slaves on other tax lists].

PRINER, Edward. Taxable in household of Joseph Astin, Bush River Lower Hundred, 1775.

PRITCHARD, Charles. Taxable in the household of Samuel Pritchard, Spesutia Lower Hundred, 1775.

PRITCHARD, Eleazer. Taxable in Susquehanna Hundred, 1775.

PRITCHARD, Harman. Taxable in household of James Pritchard, Susquehanna Hundred, 1775.

PRITCHARD, James. Taxable in Susquehanna Hundred, 1775, with taxable Harman Pritchard listed in his household.

PRITCHARD, James. Taxable in Susquehanna Hundred, 1775.

PRITCHARD, Obadiah. Taxable in Susquehanna Hundred, 1775.

PRITCHARD, Obediah. Taxable in Spesutia Lower Hundred, 1775.

PRITCHARD, Obediah. Taxable in Spesutia Lower Hundred, 1775.

PRITCHARD, Samuel. Taxable in Spesutia Lower Hundred, 1775, with taxable Charles Pritchard listed in his household.

PRITCHARD, Thomas. Taxable in Spesutia Lower Hundred, 1775, with Aquila Paca, Jr. as his security.

PUE, Daniel. Taxable in household of Daniel Pew [sic], Susquehanna Hundred, 1775.

PUNTNEY, Joseph. Taxable in Spesutia Lower Hundred, 1775, with slaves James and Maria listed in his household.

QUEEN, James. Taxable in Deer Creek Upper Hundred, 1775.

QUINLAN, James (son of Phillip). Taxable in household of his father Phillip Quinlan, Spesutia Upper Hundred, 1775.

QUINLAN, James. Taxable in Spesutia Upper Hundred, 1775.

QUINLAN, Phillip. Taxable in Spesutia Upper Hundred, 1775, with taxables James Quinlan (son) and John

Ellis listed in his household.

RAMPLEY, James. Taxable in Deer Creek Upper Hundred, 1775.

RAMSEY, Andra. Taxable in household of William Ramsey, Susquehanna Hundred, 1776.

RAMSEY, Andrew. Taxable in household of William Ramsey, Susquehanna Hundred, 1775.

RAMSEY, William. Taxable in Susquehanna Hundred, 1775, with taxable Andrew Ramsey listed in his household.

RAMSEY, William. Taxable in Susquehanna Hundred, 1776, with taxable Andra Ramsey listed in his household.

RANN, William. Taxable in Spesutia Lower Hundred, 1776.

RATLIFF & Servant [sic]. Taxables in Bush River Lower Hundred, 1775 (no first name given for Ratliff, nor his servant's name).

RAY, George. Taxable in Susquehanna Hundred, 1775.

RAY, George. Taxable in Susquehanna Hundred, 1776.

RAY, James. Taxable on plantation of William Webb, Deer Creek Upper Hundred, 1775.

READING, Harry. Taxable servant in household of Nicklaus Amoss, Bush River Upper Hundred, 1775.

READING, William. Taxable in Spesutia Lower Hundred, 1775, with taxables James Brown and Thomas Dunn listed in his household.

REARDON, Josias. Taxable in Spesutia Lower Hundred, 1775.

REARDON, Osias. Taxable in Spesutia Lower Hundred, 1776.

REDMAN, James. Taxable in Spesutia Lower Hundred, 1775, with Michael Kermaid as his security.

REED, David. Taxable in Susquehanna Hundred, 1776.

REED, H. Taxable (servant) in household of Benjamin Jones, Deer Creek Upper Hundred, 1775.

REED, Patrick. Taxable in Deer Creek Upper Hundred, 1775.

REES, Abraham. Taxable in Susquehanna Hundred, 1776.

REES, John Taxable in household of John Rees, Susquehanna Hundred, 1776.

REES, John. Taxable in Deer Creek Lower Hundred, 1775.

REES, John. Taxable in Susquehanna Hundred, 1776, with taxable John Rees listed in his household.

REES, Robert. Taxable on plantation of Jacob Giles, Jr., Susquehanna Hundred, 1776.

REES, Solomon. Taxable in Susquehanna Hundred, 1776.

REES, William. Taxable in Deer Creek Lower Hundred, 1775.

REESE, Abraham. Taxable in Susquehanna Hundred, 1775.

REESE, Joseph. Taxable in Susquehanna Hundred, 1775.

REESE, Solomon. Taxable in Susquehanna Hundred, 1775.

REILDING, James. Taxable in Spesutia Lower Hundred, 1776.

REILEY, John. Taxable in household of James Hutchinson, Deer Creek Upper Hundred, 1775.

RELFROCK, John. Taxable (servant) in household of Thomas Thompson, Bush River Lower Hundred, 1775.

RENSHAW, John. Taxable in Bush River Lower Hundred, 1775.

RENSHAW, John. Taxable in Bush River Upper Hundred, 1775.

RENSHAW, Joseph Jr. Taxable in Bush River Lower Hundred, 1775, with Joseph Renshaw, Sr. as his security.

RENSHAW, Joseph Sr. Taxable in Bush River Lower Hundred, 1775, with taxables Thomas Renshaw, Philip Renshaw, and slaves Peter, Moll, and Doll listed in his household.

RENSHAW, Mary. Head of household in Deer Creek Upper Hundred, 1775, with taxable negroes Peter, George, and Diniah listed in her household.

RENSHAW, Philip. Taxable in household of Joseph Renshaw, Sr., Bush River Lower Hundred, 1775.

RENSHAW, Robert. Taxable in Deer Creek Upper Hundred, 1775.

RENSHAW, Thomas Jr. Taxable in Deer Creek Upper Hundred, 1775.

RENSHAW, Thomas. Taxable in household of Joseph Renshaw, Sr., Bush River Lower Hundred, 1775.

REVES, Josias. Taxable in Gunpowder Lower Hundred, 1775, with one taxable negro, no name given, listed in his household. His name was not included with the R's but was added as "Josias Reves & Negro" at the end of the tax list.

RICHARDS, John. Taxable in the household of Robert Megay, Spesutia Lower Hundred, 1775.

RICHARDSON, Benjamin. Taxable in Deer Creek Upper Hundred, 1775, with taxable man Thomas Arlat (servant) listed in his household.

RICHARDSON, Danniel. Taxable in Spesutia Upper Hundred, 1775, with taxable negroes Harry, Press, Jain, and Nell listed in his household.

RICHARDSON, Samuel. Taxable in Susquehanna Hundred, 1775. [His name on the tax list was written "Richardson, Saml. Taylor" which would indicate either he had a middle name of Taylor or his occupation was a tailor].

RICHARDSON, Samuel. Taxable in Deer Creek Upper Hundred, 1775, with taxable man James Ridgway (servant) listed in his household.

RICHARDSON, Thomas Jr. Taxable in Bush River

EARLY HARFORD COUNTIANS: Supplement

Lower Hundred, 1775.

RICHARDSON, Thomas Sr. Taxable in Bush River Lower Hundred, 1775, with taxable negroes Jack, Jude, and Holliday listed in his household.

RICHARDSON, Vincent. Taxable in Bush River Lower Hundred, 1775.

RICHARDSON, William. Taxable in Bush River Lower Hundred, 1775, with taxable negro Bob listed in his household.

RICHESON, Roberts. Taxable in Deer Creek Upper Hundred, 1775.

RICHEY, John. Taxable (servant) in household of John Bruce, Deer Creek Lower Hundred, 1775.

RICKETTS, Edward. Taxable in household of Samuel Ricketts, Gunpowder Lower Hundred, 1775.

RICKETTS, Samuel. Taxable in Gunpowder Lower Hundred, 1775, with taxables Edward Ricketts and slaves Peter, Sam, Dick and Bet listed in his household.

RIDDAL, John. Taxable in Spesutia Lower Hundred, 1775, with taxable William Blackmore listed in his household.

RIDDALL, John. Taxable in Spesutia Lower Hundred, 1776, with taxable William Blackman listed in his household.

RIDGDON, Charls. Taxable in Susquehanna Hundred, 1776.

RIDGWAY, James. Taxable (servant) in household of Samuel Richardson, Deer Creek Upper Hundred, 1775.

RIELY, Barnard. Taxable in Bush River Lower Hundred, 1775, with taxables John Tool and servant John Knight listed in his household.

RIGBIE, Isaac (son of James). Taxable in household of his father James Rigbie, Deer Creek Lower Hundred, 1775.

RIGBIE, James (son of James). Taxable in household of his father James Rigbie, Deer Creek Lower Hundred, 1775.

RIGBIE, James. See "Negro Pompey," q.v.

RIGBIE, James. Taxable in Deer Creek Lower Hundred, 1775, with taxables James Rigbie (son), Isaac Rigbie (son), and negroes Tower, Jacob, Nanney, and Dido listed in his household.

RIGBIE, Nathaniel. Taxable in Deer Creek Lower Hundred, 1775, with taxables Henry Harrod and negroes Cloe, Leah, and Bachus listed in his household.

RIGDON, Alexander. Taxable in Deer Creek Upper Hundred, 1775, with taxable man Michael Mathew (servant) listed in his household.

RIGDON, Baker. Taxable in Deer Creek Upper Hundred, 1775, with taxable man David Crata (servant) listed in his household.

RIGDON, Charles. Taxable in Susquehanna Hundred, 1775. See "John Sulivan" and "Patrick Terry," q.v.

RIGDON, George. Taxable in Spesutia Upper Hundred, 1775.

RIGDON, Stephen (son of Thomas). Taxable in household of his father Thomas Baker Rigdon, Deer Creek Upper Hundred, 1775.

RIGDON, Thomas Baker. Taxable in Deer Creek Upper Hundred, 1775, with taxables Stephen Rigdon (son) and negroes Mingoe, Cloe, John, and Kimish listed in his household.

RIGDON, William. Taxable in Deer Creek Upper Hundred, 1775.

RIGHT (KIGHT?), John. Taxable in household of John Carlile, Spesutia Lower Hundred, 1775.

RILEY, Matthew. Taxable in Susquehanna Hundred, 1775.

ROADS, Benjamin. Taxable in household of John Roads, Bush River Lower Hundred, 1775.

ROADS, John. Taxable in Bush River Lower Hundred, 1775, with taxables Benjamin Roads and Thomas Roads listed in his household.

ROADS, Thomas. Taxable in household of John Roads, Bush River Lower Hundred, 1775.

ROBBERTS, Billingsly. Taxable in Gunpowder Lower Hundred, 1775.

ROBERSON, Abraham. Taxable in Susquehanna Hundred, 1776.

ROBERT, John. Taxable in Gunpowder Lower Hundred, 1775. His name (among others) was listed on the back of the tax list.

ROBERTS, Billingsly. Constable in Gunpower Lower Hundred, 1775.

ROBERTSON, Abraham. Taxable in Susquehanna Hundred, 1775.

ROBESON, Edward. Taxable in Bush River Upper Hundred, 1775, with taxable Richard Robeson (son) and Richard Moulder or Moulden (servant) listed in his household.

ROBESON, Richard. Taxable in household of his father Edward Robeson, Bush River Upper Hundred, 1775.

ROBINSON, Arch. Taxable in household of William Robinson, Sr., Bush River Lower Hundred, 1775.

ROBINSON, Danniel. Taxable in Spesutia Upper Hundred, 1775, with taxable negroes Ned and Venus listed in his household.

ROBINSON, John. Taxable at Jacob Giles' mill at Bush, Spesutia Lower Hundred, 1775.

ROBINSON, John. Taxable in Spesutia Upper Hundred, 1775.

ROBINSON, Joseph. Taxable in Spesutia Upper Hundred, 1775.

ROBINSON, William Jr. Taxable in Bush River Lower Hundred, 1775.

ROBINSON, William Sr. Taxable in Bush River Lower Hundred, 1775, with taxables Arch Robinson and negroes Samson and Grace listed in his household.

ROBSON, William (mason). Taxable in Deer Creek Upper Hundred, 1775.

ROCK RUN. See "Giles & Smith's Rock Run Plantation," q.v.

ROCKHOLD, Charles. Taxable in Bush River Lower Hundred, 1775.

ROCKHOLD, Jacob. Taxable in Bush River Lower Hundred, 1775.

ROCKHOLD, John Jr. Taxable in Bush River Upper Hundred, 1775.

ROCKHOLD, Thomas. Taxable in Bush River Lower Hundred, 1775.

ROGERS, Alexander. Taxable in Bush River Upper Hundred, 1775, with Margret Akens as his security.

ROGERS, Benjaman. Taxable in Deer Creek Lower Hundred, 1775.

ROGERS, John (son of Owen). Taxable in household of his father Owen Rogers, Bush River Upper Hundred, 1775.

ROGERS, John. Taxable in Susquehanna Hundred, 1776. [The constable listed the name without the "s" at the end of "Rogers"].

ROGERS, Joseph. Taxable in Deer Creek Lower Hundred, 1775.

ROGERS, Joseph. Taxable (servant) in household of Sias Billingsly, Deer Creek Upper Hundred, 1775.

ROGERS, Owen. Taxable in Bush River Upper Hundred, 1775, with taxable John Rogers (son) listed in his household.

ROGERS, Samuel. Taxable in Deer Creek Lower Hundred, 1775.

ROLES, Joseph. Taxable in Susquehanna Hundred, 1775.

ROLES, Joseph. Taxable in Susquehanna Hundred, 1776.

RONEY, John. Taxable in Susquehanna Hundred, 1776.

ROOT, Daniel. Taxable in Susquehanna Hundred, 1775, with taxable Daniel Root listed in his household.

ROOT, Daniel. Taxable in household of Daniel Root, Susquehanna Hundred, 1775.

ROOT, Daniel. Taxable in household of Daniel Root, Susquehanna Hundred, 1776.

ROOT, Daniel. Taxable in Susquehanna Hundred, 1776, with taxables Daniel Root and John Root listed in his household.

ROOT, John. Taxable in household of Daniel Root, Susquehanna Hundred, 1776.

RORK, Patrick. Taxable in Bush River Upper Hundred, 1775, with taxable servant Robert ---- (no last name given) listed in his household.

RORKE, Michael. Taxable in household of John Wood, Spesutia Lower Hundred, 1776.

ROSE, Edward. See "William Rose," q.v.

ROSE, Isaac. Taxable in Bush River Lower Hundred, 1775.

ROSE, Joseph. Taxable in Bush River Lower Hundred, 1775, with 3 taxables in his household, but only his name was given.

ROSE, William. Taxable in Deer Creek Upper Hundred, 1775, with Edward Rose as his security.

ROUKE, Michael. Taxable in the household of John Wood, Spesutia Lower Hundred, 1775.

ROUNDTREE, Thomas. Taxable in Susquehanna Hundred, 1775.

ROW, William. Taxable in Bush River Upper Hundred, 1775.

ROWLAND, Henry. Taxable in household of James Preston, Spesutia Upper Hundred, 1775.

RUCHMAN, Thomas. Taxable in Deer Creek Upper Hundred, 1775, with taxable Able Martin listed in his household.

RUFF, Henry Jr. Taxable in household of James Mores, Spesutia Upper Hundred, 1775.

RUFF, Henry. Taxable in Spesutia Upper Hundred, 1775, with taxable negroes Jim and Tom listed in his household.

RUFF, John. Taxable in Spesutia Lower Hundred, 1775, with taxable slaves Ham, Gambowel, and Phillis listed in his household.

RUFF, Richard. Taxable in Spesutia Upper Hundred, 1775, with taxables William Pitt, James Murray, and negro Will listed in his household.

RUMSEY, Benjamin. Taxable in Gunpowder Lower Hundred, 1775, with taxable servant Thomas ---- (no last name given) and slaves Sambo, London, Scipio, Cesar, Santy, Cook, Jula, Betty, Reynor, and Bridget listed in his household.

RUMSEY, John. Taxable in Susquehanna Hundred, 1775, with taxable negroes Polidore, Caesar, Melford, Nan, Parina, and Beatrice listed in his household.

RUMSEY, John. Taxable in Susquehanna Hundred, 1776, with taxable negroes Ceaser, Learles, Milford, Nann, Perriner, and Batrice listed in his household.

RUSSELL, Robert. Taxable in Bush River Upper Hundred, 1775, with taxable servant man (no name given) listed in his household. [The constable entered this information on the tax list and then lined it out; no reason given].

RUTH, Jacob. Taxable in Deer Creek Upper Hundred, 1775.

RUTH, Joseph. Taxable in Spesutia Lower Hundred, 1775.

RUTH, Joseph. Taxable in Spesutia Upper Hundred, 1775.

RUTH, Moses Jr. Taxable in Spesutia Upper Hundred, 1775, with taxable negroes Abraham and Fillis. Taxable in Spesutia Upper Hundred, 1775.

RUTH, Moses Sr. Taxable in Spesutia Upper Hundred, 1775, with taxable negroes Sam, Pomp, and Rute listed in his household.

RUTLAGE, John. Taxable in Bush River Upper Hundred, 1775, with taxables Barney Cubing (servant) and negroes Sam and Fiby listed in his household.

RUTLAGE, Michal. Taxable in Bush River Upper Hundred, 1775.

RUTLAGE, William. Taxable in Bush River Upper Hundred, 1775.

RUTLEDGE, John. Taxable in Bush River Upper Hundred, 1775, with taxable negroes Sam and Pheby listed in his household.

RUTTER, Richard. Taxable in Susquehanna Hundred, 1775.

RUTTER, Richard. Taxable in Susquehanna Hundred, 1776

SADLER, John. Taxable in household of Jacob Bond, Sr., Bush River Lower Hundred, 1775.

SAMSON, Aquila. See "Stephen Plant," q.v.

SAUNDERS, James. Taxable in Bush River Lower Hundred, 1775.

SAUNDERS, John. Taxable in household of Thomas Saunders (miller), Bush River Lower Hundred, 1775.

SAUNDERS, Joseph. Taxable in Bush River Lower Hundred, 1775.

SAUNDERS, Joshua. Taxable in Bush River Lower Hundred, 1775.

SAUNDERS, Thomas (miller). Taxable in Bush River Lower Hundred, 1775, with taxable John Saunders listed in his household.

SAUNDERS, Thomas. Taxable in Bush River Lower Hundred, 1775.

SAUNDERS, William. Taxable in Bush River Lower Hundred, 1775.

SAUNDERS, William. Taxable at Asel Gittings' Quarters, Gunpowder Lower Hundred, 1775.

SAVAGE, George. Taxable in household of Benjamin Harbet, Susquehanna Hundred, 1775. See "George Sevege," q.v.

SAVAGE, John. Taxable in household of James Cole, Susquehanna Hundred, 1775.

SCANTLING, John. Taxable in Deer Creek Lower Hundred, 1775.

SCANTLON, John. Taxable in Susquehanna Hundred, 1776.

SCARF, Martain. Taxable in Bush River Upper Hundred, 1775, with Jessee Prichard as his security.

SCARFF, Henry. Taxable in Bush River Upper Hundred, 1775, with taxable negro Philis listed in his household.

SCARFF, John. See "John Skaff," q.v.

SCARFF, John. See "John Skarff," q.v.

SCARFORD, John. Taxable in household of David Tate, Bush River Upper Hundred, 1775.

SCHARBROUGH, John. Taxable in Deer Creek Upper Hundred, 1775. See "Stephen Murford," q.v.

SCHARBROUGH, Joseph. Taxable in Deer Creek Upper Hundred, 1775. See "Isaac Thomas," q.v.

SCIVINGTON, James. Taxable in Bush River Upper Hundred, 1775, with a taxable sercant man (no name given) listed in his household.

SCOT, Robbert (son of Robbert). Taxable in household of his father Robbert Scot, Sr., Gunpowder Lower Hundred, 1775.

SCOT, Robbert Sr. Taxable in Gunpowder Lower Hundred, 1775, with taxable Robbert Scot (son) listed in his household.

SCOTT, Ann. Head of household in Bush River Lower Hundred, 1775, with taxables Aquila Scott and negroes Jack and Phillis listed in her household.

SCOTT, Aquila. Taxable in household of Ann Scott, Bush River Lower Hundred, 1775.

SCOTT, Aquila. Taxable in Bush River Lower Hundred, 1775, with taxable negroes Sam and Jacob listed in his household.

SCOTT, Benjamin. Taxable in Bush River Lower Hundred, 1775, with taxable negro Sall listed in his household.

SCOTT, Daniel (son of James). Taxable in Bush River Upper Hundred, 1775.

SCOTT, Daniel. Taxable in Bush River Lower Hundred, 1775, with taxables negro Jack and servant Patrick ---- (no last name given) listed in his household.

SCOTT, James (son of Aquila). Taxable in Bush River Lower Hundred, 1775, with one taxable negro Wench and two taxable servants in his household (no names given).

SCOTT, James. Security for Winston Goldsmith, 1775.

SCOTT, James. Taxable in Bush River Lower Hundred, 1775, with taxable negroes Phillis and Sam listed in his household. [It should be noted that this James Scott is listed at the end of the E's and not with the S's in the tax list. The name is clearly Scott, not Evett, as one might assume alphabetically].

SCOTT, James. Taxable in Bush River Lower Hundred, 1775.

SCOTT, James. Taxable in Bush River Upper Hundred, 1775, with taxable servant Benjamin ---- (no last name given) and negroes Samson, Feby, and Felis listed in his household.

SCOTT, Joseph. Taxable in household of William Bradford, Spesutia Upper Hundred, 1775.

SCOTT, Mary. Head of household in Gunpowder Lower Hundred, 1775, with taxable slaves DIna and Emy listed in her household.

SCOTT, Nathan. Taxable in Bush River Upper Hundred,

1775, with taxable negroes Peter and Suck listed in hise household.

SCOTT, Robert. See "Robbert Scot, Sr.," q.v.

SCROGE, Francis. Taxable on plantation of Capt. John Hall, Spesutia Lower Hundred, 1775.

SEALS, James. Taxable in Susquehanna Hundred, 1775.

SERVANT ---- (name illegible). Taxable in household of Robert Cannaday, Deer Creek Upper Hundred, 1775.

SERVANT ---- (no name given). See "James Scott (son of Aquila)," q.v.

SERVANT ---- (no name given). Taxable in household of Mr. Ratliff, Bush River Lower Hundred, 1775.

SERVANT ---- (no name given). Taxable in household of William Magill, Susquehanna Hundred, 1775.

SERVANT ---- (no name given). Taxable in household of Joseph Husband, Susquehanna Hundred, 1775.

SERVANT ---- (no name given). See "Abraham Taylor," q.v.

SERVANT ---- (no name given). See "Robert Taylor," q.v.

SERVANT ---- (no name given). Taxable in household of Samuel Ashmore, Bush River Upper Hundred, 1775.

SERVANT ---- (no name given). Taxable in household of Zenas Hughes, Bush River Upper Hundred, 1775.

SERVANT ---- (no name given). Taxable in household of William James, Bush River Upper Hundred, 1775.

SERVANT ---- (no name given). Taxable in household of John Gray, Bush River Upper Hundred, 1775.

SERVANT ---- (no name given). Taxable in household of James Meads, Jr., Bush River Upper Hundred, 1775.

SERVANT ---- (no name given). Taxable in household of Curnelus McDonnel, Bush River Upper Hundred, 1775.

SERVANT ---- (no name given). Taxable in household of Adam McClung, Bush River Upper Hundred, 1775.

SERVANT ---- (no name given). Taxable in household of James Scivington, Bush River Upper Hundred, 1775.

SERVANT ---- (no name given). Taxable in household of Robert Russell, Bush River Upper Hundred, 1775.

SERVANT ---- (no name given). Taxable in household of John Whitekar, Bush River Upper Hundred, 1775.

SERVANT ---- (no name given). Taxable in household of James Vogan, Bush River Upper Hundred, 1775.

SERVANT Andrew Jacklin. Taxable in household of Benjamin Norris, Bush River Lower Hundred, 1775.

SERVANT Barnaby Dougherty. Taxable in household of Robert Craford, Deer Creek Lower Hundred, 1775.

SERVANT Barney Cubing. Taxable in household of John Rutlage, Bush River Upper Hundred, 1775.

SERVANT Benjamin ---- (no last name given). Taxable in household of James Scott, Bush River Upper Hundred, 1775.

SERVANT ---- Burningham. Taxable in household of Manessith Finney, Deer Creek Upper Hundred, 1775.

SERVANT Charles ---- (no last name given). Taxable in household of Alexander Cowen, Gunpowder Lower Hundred, 1775.

SERVANT Charles Celly. Taxable in household of Aquila Clark, Bush River Upper Hundred, 1775.

SERVANT Charles Martin. Taxable in household of William Jones, Deer Creek Upper Hundred, 1775.

SERVANT Daniel ---- (no last name given). Taxable in household of William Anderson, Bush River Lower Hundred, 1775.

SERVANT Darby Duyr [sic]. Taxable in household of James Mathers, Bush River Lower Hundred, 1775.

SERVANT David Crata. Taxable in the household of Baker Rigdon, Deer Creek Upper Hundred, 1775.

SERVANT Dick ---- (no last name given). Taxable in household of Joshua Durham, Bush River Lower Hundred, 1775.

SERVANT Edward Tomson. Taxable in household of Margret Akins, Bush River Upper Hundred, 1775.

SERVANT Esau Turk. Taxable in household of Isaac Whitaker, Bush River Lower Hundred, 1775.

SERVANT Francis Tipton. Taxable in household of Thomas Johnson, Deer Creek Lower Hundred, 1775.

SERVANT George ---- (no last name given). Taxable in household of Alexander Cowen, Gunpowder Lower Hundred, 1775.

SERVANT George ---- (no last name given). Taxable in household of Abram Whitekar, Bush River Upper Hundred, 1775.

SERVANT George Oeal [sic]. Taxable in household of Edward Bull (son of Jacob), Bush River Lower Hundred, 1775.

SERVANT H. Reed. Taxable in household of Benjamin Jones, Deer Creek Upper Hundred, 1775.

SERVANT Harry Ayrs. Taxable in household of William Bond (son of John), Bush River Lower Hundred, 1775.

SERVANT Harry Reading. Taxable in household of Nicklaus Amoss, Bush River Upper Hundred, 1775.

SERVANT Hugh Melone. Taxable in household of Samuel Calwell, Bush River Lower Hundred, 1775.

SERVANT J. Blanch. Taxable in household of James Hutcheson, Deer Creek Upper Hundred, 1775.

SERVANT James ---- (no last name given). Taxable in household of Hugh Kirkpatrick, Spesutia Upper Hundred, 1775.

SERVANT James ---- (no last name given). Taxable in household of John Vanclave, Spesutia Upper Hundred, 1775.

SERVANT James Jakelin(?). Taxable in household of William Beaty, Bush River Upper Hundred, 1775.

SERVANT James Lamford. Taxable on plantation of Stephen Jay, Deer Creek Lower Hundred, 1775.

SERVANT James Lasarus. Taxable in household of

EARLY HARFORD COUNTIANS: Supplement

Hugh Nivans, Bush River Upper Hundred, 1775.

SERVANT James Ridgway. Taxable in household of Samuel Richardson, Deer Creek Upper Hundred, 1775.

SERVANT James Stalkap (Stackap?). Taxable in household of Kid Wilson, Bush River Lower Hundred, 1775.

SERVANT John ---- (no last name given). Taxable in household of David Lee, Bush River Lower Hundred, 1775.

SERVANT John ---- (no last name given). Taxable in household of James Everett, Bush River Lower Hundred, 1775.

SERVANT John ---- (no last name given). Taxable in household of Thomas Denney, Spesutia Upper Hundred, 1775.

SERVANT John ---- (no last name given). Taxable in household of Robert Young, Spesutia Upper Hundred, 1775.

SERVANT John ---- (no last name given). Taxable in household of John Ward, Deer Creek Upper Hundred, 1775.

SERVANT John Gladden. Taxable in household of Robert McNair, Deer Creek Upper Hundred, 1775.

SERVANT John Johnson. Taxable in household of William Bradford, Bush River Lower Hundred, 1775.

SERVANT John Kelley. Taxable in household of James Parks, Deer Creek Lower Hundred, 1775.

SERVANT John Knight. Taxable in household of Barnard Riely, Bush River Lower Hundred, 1775.

SERVANT John Morris. Taxable in household of Charles Baker, Bush River Upper Hundred, 1775.

SERVANT John Orr. Taxable in household of John McClan, Bush River Upper Hundred, 1775.

SERVANT John Page. Taxable in household of Dannil Tridaway, Bush River Upper Hundred, 1775.

SERVANT John Pound. Taxable in household of William Hitchcock, Bush River Upper Hundred, 1775.

SERVANT John Price. Taxable in household of Thomas Bond, Jr., Bush River Upper Hundred, 1775.

SERVANT John Relfrock. Taxable in household of Thomas Thompson, Bush River Lower Hundred, 1775.

SERVANT John Richey. Taxable in household of John Bruce, Deer Creek Lower Hundred, 1775.

SERVANT Jonathan ---- (no last name given). Taxable in household of Robert Smith, Deer Creek Upper Hundred, 1775.

SERVANT Joseph Beall. Taxable in household of Samuel Calwell, Bush River Lower Hundred, 1775.

SERVANT Joseph Rogers. Taxable in household of Sias Billingsly, Deer Creek Upper Hundred, 1775.

SERVANT M. Kelly. Taxable man in household of John McFadden, Deer Creek Upper Hundred, 1775.

SERVANT Mart Carter. Taxable in household of Thomas Brice, Deer Creek Upper Hundred, 1775.

SERVANT ---- McGilton (no first name given). Taxable in household of Robert Hawkins, Deer Creek Upper Hundred, 1775.

SERVANT Michael Mathew. Taxable in household of Alexander Rigdon, Deer Creek Upper Hundred, 1775.

SERVANT Mike ---- (no last name given). Taxable in household of Martenie Parker, Bush River Upper Hundred, 1775.

SERVANT Owen Corkron. Taxable in household of James Brice, Deer Creek Lower Hundred, 1775.

SERVANT Patrick ---- (no last name given). Taxable in household of Daniel Scott, Bush River Lower Hundred, 1775.

SERVANT Patrick Ford. Taxable in household of Moses McComas, Bush River Lower Hundred, 1775.

SERVANT Peter ---- (no last name given). Taxable in household of Alexander Thompson, Spesutia Upper Hundred, 1775.

SERVANT Philip Nevel. Taxable in household of Andrew Howlet, Deer Creek Lower Hundred, 1775.

SERVANT Richard ---- (no last name given). Taxable in household of Thomas Streett, Bush River Upper Hundred, 1775.

SERVANT Richard Humphres. Taxable on plantation of Stephen Jay, Deer Creek Lower Hundred, 1775.

SERVANT Richard Moulder (Moulden?). Taxable in household of Edward Robeson, Bush River Upper Hundred, 1775.

SERVANT Rinhard (Richard?) Jourdan. Taxable in household of William Norris, Bush River Upper Hundred, 1775.

SERVANT Robert ---- (no last name given). Taxable in household of Patrick Rork, Bush River Upper Hundred, 1775.

SERVANT Ros ---- (no last name given). Taxable in household of Martenie Parker, Bush River Upper Hundred, 1775.

SERVANT Rowlan Capen. Taxable in household of Edward Norris, Deer Creek Upper Hundred, 1775.

SERVANT Samuel ---- (no last name given). Taxable in household of David Lee, Bush River Lower Hundred, 1775.

SERVANT Stephen Fell. Taxable in household of John Bond, Jr., Bush River Lower Hundred, 1775.

SERVANT Stephen Lockwood. Taxable in household of Sias Billingsly, Deer Creek Upper Hundred, 1775.

SERVANT Thomas ---- (no last name given). Taxable in household of John Taylor, Bush River Lower Hundred, 1775.

SERVANT Thomas ---- (no last name given). Taxable in household of Benjamin Rumsey, Gunpowder Lower Hundred, 1775.

SERVANT Thomas ---- (no last name given). Taxable in household of Joshua Chalk, Bush River Upper Hundred, 1775.
SERVANT Thomas Arlat. Taxable in the household of Benjamin Richardson, Deer Creek Upper Hundred, 1775.
SERVANT Thomas Sheredon. Taxable in household of James Holmes, Bush River Lower Hundred, 1775.
SERVANT Thomas Varley. Taxable in household of Edward Norris, Deer Creek Upper Hundred, 1775.
SERVANT Thomas Wright. Taxable in household of Edward Talbott, Bush River Lower Hundred, 1775.
SERVANT Will Tuder. Taxable in household of James Stevenson, Bush River Upper Hundred, 1775.
SERVANT William ---- (name illegible). Taxable in household of Robert Cannaday, Deer Creek Upper Hundred, 1775.
SERVANT William How. Taxable in household of John Montgomery, Deer Creek Lower Hundred, 1775.
SERVANT William Martin. Taxable in household of Benjamin Biddel, Bush River Upper Hundred, 1775.
SEVEGE, George. Taxable in household of Benjamin Harbet, Susquehanna Hundred, 1776. See "George Savage," q.v.
SEWELL, John. Taxable in Gunpowder Lower Hundred, 1775. His name (among others) was listed on the back of the tax list.
SHARP, John. Taxable in household of his father Thomas Sharp, Bush River Upper Hundred, 1775.
SHARP, Thomas. Taxable in Bush River Upper Hundred, 1775, with taxable John Sharp (son) listed in his household.
SHAVE, Richard. Taxable in Bush River Upper Hundred, 1775.
SHAVER, William. Taxable on plantation of Edward Carvel Tolley, Spesutia Lower Hundred, 1776.
SHEA, William. Taxable in Susquehanna Hundred, 1775.
SHEAPARD, William. Taxable in Spesutia Upper Hundred, 1775.
SHEARER, Thomas. Taxable in Susquehanna Hundred, 1775.
SHEARESWOOD, William. Taxable in Spesutia Upper Hundred, 1775.
SHEPHERD, ---- (first name illegible). Taxable in Bush River Lower Hundred, 1775.
SHEPHERD, Charles. Taxable in household of David Benfield, Bush River Lower Hundred, 1775.
SHEREDON, Thomas. Taxable (servant) in household of James Holmes, Bush River Lower Hundred, 1775.
SHERIDINE, Casandra (widow). Head of household in Deer Creek Lower Hundred, 1775, with taxable negroes Jacob, Jupiter, Peter, Mary, and Aaron listed in her household.
SHERIDINE, James. Taxable in Spesutia Upper Hundred, 1775.
SHEY, William. Taxable in Susquehanna Hundred, 1776.
SHINTON, John. Security for Thomas Hinks, 1775.
SHINTON, John. Taxable in Bush River Lower Hundred, 1775.
SHIPLEY, Richard. Taxable in Bush River Upper Hundred, 1775.
SHORT, Edward. Taxable in Spesutia Upper Hundred, 1775.
SILVER, Benjamin. Taxable in Susquehanna Hundred, 1775.
SILVER, Millison. Head of household in Susquehanna Hundred, 1775, with taxable William Silver listed in her household. [The actual entry is worded "Millison Silver, William Silver, Security"].
SILVER, William. Taxable in household of Millison Silver, Susquehanna Hundred, 1775.
SILVERS, Benjamin. Taxable in Susquehanna Hundred, 1776.
SILVERS, Millison. Head of household in Susquehanna Hundred, 1776, with taxable William Silvers listed in her household.
SILVERS, William. Taxable in household of Millison Silvers, Susquehanna Hundred, 1776.
SIMPERS, Thomas. Taxable on the plantation of Amos Garrett, Spesutia Lower Hundred, 1775.
SIMS, Ralf. Taxable in Deer Creek Lower Hundred, 1775.
SINCLEAR, James. Taxable in Bush River Upper Hundred, 1775.
SINCLEAR, Lister. Taxable in Bush River Upper Hundred, 1775.
SKAFF, John. Taxable in Bush River Lower Hundred, 1775, with taxable Thomas Curry listed in his household. [The name in all probability is "John Scarff"].
SKARFF, John. Taxable in Bush River Lower Hundred, 1775. [The name in all probability is "John Scarff"].
SKERRETT, Thomas. Taxable in Bush River Lower Hundred, 1775.
SLACK, John. Taxable in Spesutia Upper Hundred, 1775.
SLACK, Old. Taxable in household of Samuel Smith, Spesutia Upper Hundred, 1775. [The name "Old Slack" was written in at the end of this entry by the constable and the number of taxables was changed from 2 to 3. There was nothing to indicate whether this was a slave, a servant, or just an old man whose name was Slack].
SLADE, Ezikill. Taxable in household of, with taxable William Slade (son) listed in his household.
SLADE, William (son of Ezikill). Taxable in household of his father Ezikill Slade, Bush River Upper Hundred, 1775.

EARLY HARFORD COUNTIANS: Supplement

SLONE, John. Taxable in Susquehanna Hundred, 1776.
SMALL, John. Taxable in Susquehanna Hundred, 1775.
SMALL, John. Taxable in Susquehanna Hundred, 1776, with Robert Small as his security.
SMALL, Robert. Taxable in Susquehanna Hundred, 1775.
SMALL, Robert. Taxable in Susquehanna Hundred, 1776. See "John Small," q.v.
SMITH, Aaburella. Head of household in Gunpowder Lower Hundred, 1775, with taxable slaves Sam and Bet listed in her household.
SMITH, Amos. See "Emus Smith" and "William Smith," q.v.
SMITH, Basil. Taxable in Gunpowder Lower Hundred, 1775, with taxables William Ew and slave Jim listed in his household.
SMITH, Benjamin. Taxable in Susquehanna Hundred, 1775.
SMITH, Benjamin. Taxable in Susquehanna Hundred, 1776.
SMITH, Buchannon. Taxable in Susquehanna Hundred, 1775.
SMITH, David (son of Samuel). Taxable in household of his father Samuel Smith, Spesutia Upper Hundred, 1775.
SMITH, Dennis. Taxable in Bush River Upper Hundred, 1775, with Jos. Hitchcock (servant). [The actual entry is somewhat unclear: "Smith, Dennis Jos. Hitchcock servant" and the constable indicated just 1 taxable, not 2, in the household].
SMITH, Emus. Taxable in household of his father William Smith, Gunpowder Lower Hundred, 1775.
SMITH, Henry. Taxable in Bush River Lower Hundred, 1775.
SMITH, Hugh. Taxable in household of Thomas Smith, Susquehanna Hundred, 1776.
SMITH, Ichabud. Taxable in Susquehanna Hundred, 1775.
SMITH, Jabish. Taxable in Susquehanna Hundred, 1776.
SMITH, James. Taxable in Bush River Lower Hundred, 1775.
SMITH, James. Taxable in Bush River Upper Hundred, 1775.
SMITH, John (weaver). Taxable in Deer Creek Upper Hundred, 1775.
SMITH, John. Taxable in Bush River Lower Hundred, 1775, with taxable Joshua Smith listed in his household.
SMITH, John. Taxable in household of Isaac Webster, Spesutia Upper Hundred, 1775.
SMITH, John. Taxable in Bush River Upper Hundred, 1775.
SMITH, John. Taxable in Deer Creek Upper Hundred, 1775, with taxable Robert Smith (son) listed in his household.
SMITH, John. Taxable man in the household of Joseph Stokes, Deer Creek Upper Hundred, 1775.
SMITH, John. Taxable in Spesutia Lower Hundred, 1776.
SMITH, Joseph Sr. Taxable in Bush River Lower Hundred, 1775.
SMITH, Joshua. Taxable in household of John Smith, Bush River Lower Hundred, 1775.
SMITH, Josias. Taxable in Gunpowder Lower Hundred, 1775.
SMITH, Martha. Head of household in Deer Creek Lower Hundred, 1775, with taxables Ralf Smith (son), negro Ceaser, and a servant man (no name given) listed in her household. See "Daniel Harris" and "Daniel Price," q.v.
SMITH, Nathan. Taxable in household of William Smith, Sr, Bush River Upper Hundred, 1775.
SMITH, Nathaniel. Taxable in Deer Creek Upper Hundred, 1775.
SMITH, Partrigk [sic]. Taxable in Susquehanna Hundred, 1776.
SMITH, Patrick. Taxable in Susquehanna Hundred, 1775.
SMITH, Peter. Taxable in Bush River Upper Hundred, 1775.
SMITH, Ralf. Taxable in household of his mother Martha Smith, Deer Creek Lower Hundred, 1775.
SMITH, Robert (son of John). Taxable in household of his father John Smith, Deer Creek Upper Hundred, 1775.
SMITH, Robert Jr. Taxable in Deer Creek Upper Hundred, 1775.
SMITH, Robert. Taxable in Bush River Lower Hundred, 1775.
SMITH, Robert. Taxable in Susquehanna Hundred, 1775, with Robert Mills as his security.
SMITH, Robert. Taxable in Bush River Upper Hundred, 1775, with taxable William Smith (son) listed in his household.
SMITH, Robert. Taxable in Deer Creek Upper Hundred, 1775, with taxables William Smith (son) and man Jonathan ---- (servant) listed in his household.
SMITH, Samuel. Taxable in Susquehanna Hundred, 1775.
SMITH, Samuel. Taxable in Spesutia Upper Hundred, 1775, with taxables David Smith (son) and "Old Slack" listed in his household.
SMITH, Thomas. Taxable in Gunpowder Lower Hundred, 1775.
SMITH, Thomas. Taxable in Susquehanna Hundred, 1775, with taxable Hugh Smith and negro Jeff listed in his household.
SMITH, Thomas. Taxable in Susquehanna Hundred, 1776, with taxable Hugh Smith and Negro Jeffery listed in his household. [The constable entered the

names "Smith, Thomas, Hugh Smith, Jeffery ... 3" which indicated the three taxables were Thomas Smith, Hugh Smith, and a negro named Jeffery, as shown on other tax lists].

SMITH, William (son of Robert). Taxable in household of his father Robert Smith, Bush River Upper Hundred, 1775.

SMITH, William (son of Robert). Taxable in household of his father Robert Smith, Deer Creek Upper Hundred, 1775.

SMITH, William Jr. Taxable in household of William Smith, Sr, Bush River Upper Hundred, 1775.

SMITH, William Jr. Taxable in Spesutia Lower Hundred, 1776, with taxable negroes Harry, Orange, Welton, Peter, James, Ned, Moll, Dutchess, Rachael, Bett, and Hettey listed on his plantation.

SMITH, William Sr. Taxable in Bush River Upper Hundred, 1775, with taxables William Smith, Jr., Nathan Smith, and slaves James, Dundee, Plez, Will, Will Jr., Jack, Charles, Suck, Nan, and Polly listed on his plantation.

SMITH, William. Taxable in Gunpowder Lower Hundred, 1775, with taxables Emus Smith (son), Thomas Craggin, and slave Bob listed in his household.

SMITH, William. Taxable in Spesutia Lower Hundred, 1775, with taxable slaves Harry, Peter, Tom, Phil, Walton, Welton, Rachael, and Orange listed in his household, and taxable slaves James, Moll and Nell listed at his quarters.

SMITH, William. Taxable in household of Samuel Lenhard, Deer Creek Upper Hundred, 1775.

SMITH, William. Taxable in Spesutia Lower Hundred, 1776, with Greenberry Dorsey as his security.

SMITH, William's Quarters. Susquehanna Hundred, 1775, with taxable negroes Adam, Polidore, and Rose listed at these quarters.

SMITH, Winston. Taxable in Bush River Upper Hundred, 1775, with slaves Ben and Harry listed in his household.

SMITH. See "Giles & Smith's Rock Run Plantation," q.v.

SMITHSON, Avarilla. See "David Smithson," q.v.

SMITHSON, Daniel. Taxable in Bush River Lower Hundred, 1775.

SMITHSON, David (son of Avarilla). Taxable in Bush River Upper Hundred, 1775.

SMITHSON, Nathan. Taxable in household of Thomas Smithson, Sr., Bush River Lower Hundred, 1775.

SMITHSON, Thomas Sr. Taxable in Bush River Lower Hundred, 1775, with taxables Nathan Smithson and negroes Flora and Hannah listed in his household.

SMITHSON, William. Taxable in Bush River Lower Hundred, 1775, with taxable negroes Jack, Sall, and Rose listed in his household.

SNODGRASS, William. Taxable in Susquehanna Hundred, 1775.

SNOTGRASS, William. Taxable in Susquehanna Hundred, 1776.

SONE, Jos. Taxable in Bush River Lower Hundred, 1775.

SOWARD, Richard. Taxable in Susquehanna Hundred, 1775.

SPARKS, William. Taxable in Deer Creek Upper Hundred, 1775.

SPEAR, James. Taxable in Deer Creek Upper Hundred, 1775.

SPENCER, Able. Taxable in Bush River Lower Hundred, 1775.

SPENCER, Enoch. Taxable in Bush River Lower Hundred, 1775, with taxable George Williams listed in his household.

SPENCER, Henery. Taxable in Susquehanna Hundred, 1775, with taxables James Spencer and John Spencer listed in his household. [The entry actually shows the name of Henery Spencer first, followed by James Spencer and John Spencer, for a total of 3 taxables; however, Henery's name was lined out, but the number of taxables remained at 3 instead of being changed to 2].

SPENCER, Henry. Taxable in Susquehanna Hundred, 1776, with taxables James Spenser, John Spenser, and negro Abraham listed in his household. [The constable spelled Henry's last name as "Spencer" and yet spelled James and John's last name as "Spenser" on the same list].

SPENCER, James. Taxable in Gunpowder Lower Hundred, 1775.

SPENCER, James. Taxable in household of Henery Spencer, Susquehanna Hundred, 1775.

SPENCER, James. Taxable in household of Henry Spencer, Susquehanna Hundred, 1776.

SPENCER, Job. Taxable in Bush River Lower Hundred, 1775.

SPENCER, John. Taxable in household of Henery Spencer, Susquehanna Hundred, 1775.

SPENCER, John. Taxable in Deer Creek Upper Hundred, 1775.

SPENCER, John. Taxable in household of Henry Spencer, Susquehanna Hundred, 1776..

SPENCER, Richard. Taxable in household of Roland Spencer, Susquehanna Hundred, 1775.

SPENCER, Richard. Taxable in household of Rowland Spencer, Susquehanna Hundred, 1776.

SPENCER, Roland. Taxable in Susquehanna Hundred, 1775, with taxable Richard Spencer listed in his household.

SPENCER, Rowland. Taxable in Susquehanna Hundred, 1776, with taxable Richard Spencer listed in his household.

SPOTTER, Harice. Taxable in household of William Coal (carpenter), Deer Creek Lower Hundred, 1775.

STAFARD, Foster. Taxable in Bush River Upper Hundred, 1775, with Robert Amoss as his security.

STALKAP (STACKAP?), James. Taxable in household of Kid Wilson, Bush River Lower Hundred, 1775.

STALLINGS, Kent. Taxable in Spesutia Upper Hundred, 1775.

STANDIFORD, Aquilla. Taxable in Bush River Lower Hundred, 1775.

STANDIFORD, Samuel. Taxable in Bush River Lower Hundred, 1775.

STANDIFORD, William. Taxable in Bush River Upper Hundred, 1775.

STANDLEY, Francis. Taxable "lives with E. Hall" in Spesutia Lower Hundred, 1775.

STAPLETON, Joshua. Taxable in Deer Creek Lower Hundred, 1775.

STAR, William. Taxable in Bush River Lower Hundred, 1775.

STARRAT, Jonathan. Taxable in Deer Creek Lower Hundred, 1775, with Thomas McCullough as his security. Taxable in Deer Creek Lower Hundred, 1775

STEEAL, John. Taxable in Susquehanna Hundred, 1776.

STEELE, John. Taxable in Susquehanna Hundred, 1775.

STEELE, Joseph. Taxable in Susquehanna Hundred, 1775.

STENSON, John. Taxable in Susquehanna Hundred, 1775.

STEPHENSON, Henry's Quarters (doctor). Spesutia Lower Hundred, 1775, with taxables John Jones and slaves Joe, Shade, Naise, Jack, Will, Hannibal, Grace, Charity, and Reubin listed at these quarters. [The names appeared at the end of the "W's" on the tax list].

STEPHENSON, Henry's Quarters (doctor). Spesutia Lower Hundred, 1776, with taxable negroes Joe, Shedrick, Reubin, Jack, Nell, Grace, Amey, Hannah, and Hannah Jr. listed at these quarters.

STEPHENSON, Jonas. Taxable in Spesutia Lower Hundred, 1775.

STEPHENSON, Thomas. Taxable in Deer Creek Lower Hundred, 1775, with John Morgan as his security.

STEVENSON, Alexander. Taxable in household of James Clendenon, Spesutia Upper Hundred, 1775.

STEVENSON, Ann. Head of household in Spesutia Upper Hundred, 1775, with taxables William Allen and negro Dinnah listed in her household.

STEVENSON, James. Taxable in Bush River Upper Hundred, 1775, with taxable Will Tuder (servant) listed in his household.

STEVENSON, John (merchant). Taxable in Susquehanna Hundred, 1776.

STEVENSON, Jonas. Taxable at Jacob Giles' Quarters at Romney, Spesutia Lower Hundred, 1775.

STEWARD, Allexander. Taxable in Susquehanna Hundred, 1776.

STEWART, James. Taxable in Bush River Lower Hundred, 1775, with 2 taxables in his household, but only his name was given.

STEWART, James. Taxable in Spesutia Lower Hundred, 1775, with taxable slaves Mingo, Primus, and Dido listed in his household.

STEWART, James. Taxable in Spesutia Lower Hundred, 1776, with taxable negroes Mingo, Primus, and Dido listed in his household.

STEWART, William. Taxable in household of Maulden Amos, Bush River Lower Hundred, 1775.

STILES, Joseph. Taxable in Spesutia Upper Hundred, 1775, with taxables John Lamp, William Eavins, and negro Dinnah listed in his household.

STOKES, Joseph. Taxable in Deer Creek Upper Hundred, 1775, with taxable men Ouy (Aug?) Hart, John Smith, and George Patrick listed in his household.

STOKES, Robert. Taxable in Spesutia Lower Hundred, 1776, with taxable negroes Jerry, Poll, David, and Sam listed in his household.

STOUDER, Magnis. Taxable in Bush River Upper Hundred, 1775.

STRAW, Thomas (son of Thomas). Taxable in household of his father Thomas Straw, Spesutia Upper Hundred, 1775.

STRAW, Thomas. Taxable in Spesutia Upper Hundred, 1775, with taxable Thomas Straw (son) listed in his household.

STREETT, Thomas (son of Thomas). Taxable in household of his father Thomas Streett, Bush River Upper Hundred, 1775.

STREETT, Thomas. Taxable in Bush River Upper Hundred, 1775, with taxables Thomas Streett (son), servant Richard ---- (no last name given), and negroes Ben and Filis listed in his household. [The constable's scribbled handwriting makes the name appear to be "Jhos Strtt" but it is "Thomas Streett" as shown on another tax list].

STRICKLAND, Henery. Taxable in Gunpowder Lower Hundred, 1775.

STRONG, Thomas. Taxable in Gunpowder Lower Hundred, 1775.

STROUD, William. Taxable in Spesutia Upper Hundred, 1775.

STUART, Alexander. Taxable in Susquehanna Hundred, 1775.

STUART, John. Taxable in Gunpowder Lower Hundred, 1775.

STUART, John. Taxable in Bush River Upper Hundred, 1775, with William James as his security.

STUMP, Henery. Taxable in Susquehanna Hundred, 1775, with taxable negroes Jack, Joe, Peg, and Phoebe listed in his household.

STUMP, Henry. Taxable in Susquehanna Hundred, 1776, with taxables John Stump and negroes Jack, Peg, Joe, Feby, and Pol listed in his housheold.

STUMP, John. Taxable in household of John Wilson (merchant), Susquehanna Hundred, 1775.

STUMP, John. Taxable in household of Henry Stump, Susquehanna Hundred, 1776.

STURGEANT, William. Taxable in Bush River Upper Hundred, 1775.

SULIVAN, John. Taxable in Susquehanna Hundred, 1775, with Charles Rigdon as his security.

SUTTON, Edward. Taxable in household of Nathanel Balis, Susquehanna Hundred, 1776.

SUTTON, Oswin. Taxable in Spesutia Lower Hundred, 1775.

SUTTON, Oswin. Taxable in Spesutia Lower Hundred, 1776.

SUTTON, Reuben. Taxable in Spesutia Lower Hundred, 1775, with taxable William Denton listed in his household.

SUTTON, Reubin. Taxable in Spesutia Lower Hundred, 1776.

SUTTON, Samuel. Taxable in Spesutia Lower Hundred, 1775, with taxable James Neegle listed in his household.

SUTTON, Thomas. Taxable in the household of James Osborn, Jr., Spesutia Lower Hundred, 1775.

SWAIN, Gabriel. Taxable on the plantation of Amos Garrett, Spesutia Lower Hundred, 1775.

SWAIN, Gabriel. Taxable on plantation of Amos Garrett, Spesutia Lower Hundred, 1776.

SWAIN, Nathan. Taxable on the plantation of Amos Garrett, Spesutia Lower Hundred, 1775.

SWAN, Frederick. Taxable in Bush River Upper Hundred, 1775.

SWARTH, Samuel. Taxable in Susquehanna Hundred, 1775.

SWATH, Samuel. Taxable in Susquehanna Hundred, 1776.

SWATON, Peter. Taxable in Spesutia Upper Hundred, 1775, listed in same household with Job Key.

SWEANY, Matthew. Taxable in Spesutia Upper Hundred, 1775.

SWEENY (SWEENEY), David Jr. Taxable in Deer Creek Lower Hundred, 1775, with taxable negro Jeffrey listed in his household. See "William Tayler," q.v.

SWIFT, Luke. Taxable in Gunpowder Lower Hundred, 1775.

SWILOVEN, James. Taxable in household of Edward Thompson, Susquehanna Hundred, 1776. [The constable listed his name as "James Swilivn" on the tax list].

SWILOVEN, John. Taxable in Susquehanna Hundred, 1776.

TALBERT, John. Taxable in Spesutia Upper Hundred, 1775, with taxable negroes Will and Bett listed in his household.

TALBOTT, Edward. Taxable in Bush River Lower Hundred, 1775, with taxables Henry Oldham, servant Thomas Wright, and negroes Jocka and Hannah listed in his household.

TALBOTT, James. Taxable in Gunpowder Lower Hundred, 1775.

TALLEY, Walter. See "Walter Tolley," q.v.

TARNER (TORNER?), Philip. Taxable in Bush River Upper Hundred, 1775.

TATE, David. Taxable in Bush River Upper Hundred, 1775, with John Scarford listed in his household.

TATE, Timmothy. Taxable in Bush River Upper Hundred, 1775.

TAYLER, William. Taxable in Deer Creek Lower Hundred, 1775, with Davis Sweeney, Jr. as his security.

TAYLOR, Abraham. Taxable in Spesutia Lower Hundred, 1775, with one taxable servant in his household (no name given).

TAYLOR, Abraham. Taxable in Spesutia Lower Hundred, 1776.

TAYLOR, Amasa. Taxable in the household of James Taylor, Sr., Spesutia Lower Hundred, 1775.

TAYLOR, Asa. Taxable in Spesutia Lower Hundred, 1776.

TAYLOR, James Jr. Taxable in Spesutia Lower Hundred, 1776, with taxable negro Ned listed in his household.

TAYLOR, James Sr. Taxable in Spesutia Lower Hundred, 1775, with taxables Amasa Taylor, slave Alice, and an illegible name listed between them [page is dark and smudged].

TAYLOR, James Sr. Taxable in Spesutia Lower Hundred, 1776, with taxable negroes Alice and Caesar listed in his household.

TAYLOR, James. Taxable in Spesutia Lower Hundred, 1775, with taxable slave Ned listed in his household.

TAYLOR, John Hodges. Taxable in Gunpowder Lower Hundred, 1775, with taxable slave Pen listed in his household.

TAYLOR, John. Taxable in Bush River Lower Hundred, 1775, with taxable servant Thomas ---- (no last name given) and negroes Cato, Primus, and Jenny listed in his household.

TAYLOR, John. Taxable in Deer Creek Upper Hundred, 1775.

TAYLOR, Launcelot. Taxable on the plantation of Amos Garrett, Spesutia Lower Hundred, 1775.

TAYLOR, Robert. Taxable in Spesutia Lower Hundred, 1775, with one taxable servant in his household (no name given).

TAYLOR, Robert. Taxable in Spesutia Lower Hundred, 1776.

TAYLOR, Stephen. Taxable in Spesutia Lower Hundred, 1775, with Hannah Hall as his security.

TAYLOR, Stephen. Taxable in Spesutia Lower Hundred, 1776. [Name was listed at the end of the H's on the tax list].

TAYLOR, Thomas. Taxable in Gunpowder Lower Hundred, 1775, with taxable slave Nan listed in his household.

TAYLOR, Walter. Taxable in household of Mathew Alexander, Susquehanna Hundred, 1775.

TAYLOR, Walter. Taxable in household of Peter Fort, Susquehanna Hundred, 1776.

TAYLOR, William. Taxable in Deer Creek Upper Hundred, 1775.

TEAS, Andrews. Taxable in Bush River Upper Hundred, 1775.

TERRY, Patrick. Taxable in Susquehanna Hundred, 1775, with Charles Ridgon as his security.

THACKER, John. Taxable in Bush River Upper Hundred, 1775.

THOMAS, Daniel. Taxable in Bush River Lower Hundred, 1775.

THOMAS, David. Taxable in Spesutia Upper Hundred, 1775.

THOMAS, David. Taxable in Deer Creek Lower Hundred, 1775, with taxable sons John, James and Issac Thomas listed in his household.

THOMAS, Henry Jr. Taxable in Spesutia Upper Hundred, 1775, with taxable John Aspel listed in his household.

THOMAS, Henry Sr. Taxable in Spesutia Upper Hundred, 1775.

THOMAS, Isaac (son of David). Taxable in household of his father David Thomas, Deer Creek Lower Hundred, 1775.

THOMAS, Isaac. Taxable in Deer Creek Upper Hundred, 1775, with Joseph Scharbrough as his security.

THOMAS, James (son of David). Taxable in household of his father David Thomas, Deer Creek Lower Hundred, 1775.

THOMAS, James. Taxable in Spesutia Upper Hundred, 1775.

THOMAS, John (son of David). Taxable in household of his father David Thomas, Deer Creek Lower Hundred, 1775.

THOMAS, John. Taxable in Gunpowder Lower Hundred, 1775.

THOMAS, John. Taxable in Spesutia Lower Hundred, 1775.

THOMAS, John. Taxable in Spesutia Upper Hundred, 1775.

THOMAS, Joseph. Taxable in Bush River Upper Hundred, 1775, with taxable Robert Hannen (Hanner?) listed in his household.

THOMAS, Samuel's Quarters. Susquehanna Hundred, 1775, with taxable negroes Simon, Will, Jenny, Nan, Moll, and Tamer listed at these quarters.

THOMAS, Samuel's Quarters. Susquehanna Hundred, 1776, with taxable negroes Simon, Will, Jenney, Nann, and Mol listed at these quarters.

THOMAS, Thomas. Taxable in Bush River Upper Hundred, 1775.

THOMAS, William. Taxable in Gunpowder Lower Hundred, 1775.

THOMPSON, Alexander. Taxable in Spesutia Upper Hundred, 1775, with taxables Danniel Grafton and "man Peter ----" [servant, no last name given] listed in his household.

THOMPSON, Aquila. Taxable in Bush River Upper Hundred, 1775.

THOMPSON, Daniel. Taxable in Bush River Lower Hundred, 1775.

THOMPSON, David. Taxable in household of Mary Thompson, Susquehanna Hundred, 1775.

THOMPSON, David. Taxable in household of Mary Thompson, Susquehanna Hundred, 1776.

THOMPSON, Edward (son of William). Taxable in household of his father William Thompson, Spesutia Upper Hundred, 1775.

THOMPSON, Edward. Taxable in Susquehanna Hundred, 1776, with taxable James Swilivn [sic] listed in his household. See "Edward Tompson," q.v.

THOMPSON, James (son of John). Taxable in household of his father John Thompson, Spesutia Upper Hundred, 1775.

THOMPSON, James. Taxable in Spesutia Upper Hundred, 1775.

THOMPSON, John Jr. Taxable in Spesutia Upper Hundred, 1775.

THOMPSON, John. Taxable in Spesutia Upper Hundred, 1775, with taxable James Thompson (son) listed in his household.

THOMPSON, Mary. Head of household in Susquehanna Hundred, 1775, with taxable David Thompson listed in her household.

THOMPSON, Mary. Head of household in Susquehanna Hundred, 1776, with taxables David Thompson and Peto Bolin [sic] listed in her household.

THOMPSON, Nathan. Taxable in household of Thomas Everest, Spesutia Lower Hundred, 1776.

THOMPSON, Richard. Taxable in household of William

Boner, Jr., Susquehanna Hundred, 1775.

THOMPSON, Thomas. Taxable in Bush River Lower Hundred, 1775, with taxable servant John Relfrock listed in his household.

THOMPSON, William. Taxable in Spesutia Upper Hundred, 1775, with taxable Edward Thompson (son) listed in his household.

THOMSON, Richard. Taxable in household of William Bonar, Jr., Susquehanna Hundred, 1776.

THORN, John. Taxable in household of William Jenkens, Bush River Lower Hundred, 1775.

THOROMAN, William. Taxable in Deer Creek Upper Hundred, 1775.

THORP, Rachel. Head of household in Bush River Lower Hundred, 1775, with taxable negroes Thomas, James, Gin, and Moses, plus one more negro name not legible, listed in her household.

THRIFT, James. Taxable in Gunpowder Lower Hundred, 1775.

THRIFT, Richard. Taxable in Gunpowder Lower Hundred, 1775.

THURSTON, Thomas. Taxable in Bush River Lower Hundred, 1775.

TILBROOK, John. Taxable in household of James Holmes, Bush River Lower Hundred, 1775.

TIMMONS, John. Taxable in Gunpowder Lower Hundred, 1775.

TIPTON, Francis. Taxable (servant) in household of Thomas Johnson, Deer Creek Lower Hundred, 1775.

TODD, George. Taxable in household of Thomas Ayres, Spesutia Lower Hundred, 1776.

TOLBERT, Marthew. Taxable in Bush River Upper Hundred, 1775.

TOLLEY, Edward Carvel. Taxable in Spesutia Lower Hundred, 1775, with taxables Edward Dowley, Patrick Carker, and slaves Val, Cato, Sarah, Judy, and Bett listed in his household.

TOLLEY, Edward Carvel. Taxable in Spesutia Lower Hundred, 1776, with taxables William Shaver, Edward Plowman, Patrick Corker, and negroes Nathan, Cato, Bett, Juelia, Perinah, Shag, and Jenney listed on his plantation.

TOLLEY, Walter. Spesutie Lower Hundred, 1775, list stated tax was paid by "Walter Talley, Sr. for his slave at Mrs. Garrett's."

TOLLINGER, George. Taxable in Spesutia Upper Hundred, 1775.

TOMPSON, Edward. Taxable in Susquehanna Hundred, 1775.

TOMSON, Andrew. Taxable in Bush River Upper Hundred, 1775.

TOMSON, James. Taxable in Bush River Upper Hundred, 1775.

TOMSON, Nathan. Taxable in household of Thomas Everest, Spesutia Lower Hundred, 1775.

TOOL, John. Taxable in household of Barnard Riely, Bush River Lower Hundred, 1775.

TOOLE, Christian. Taxable in household of John Wilson (merchant), Susquehanna Hundred, 1775.

TORNER (TARNER?), Philip. Taxable in Bush River Upper Hundred, 1775.

TOUNSTRET(?), James. Taxable in Bush River Upper Hundred, 1775.

TOUSLAND, William. Taxable in Spesutia Lower Hundred, 1775.

TOUT, Abram. Taxable in Bush River Upper Hundred, 1775.

TOWNSEND, James. Taxable in household of Phillip Donoven, Susquehanna Hundred, 1775.

TOWNSLEY, John (son of John). Taxable in household of his father John Townsley, Spesutia Upper Hundred, 1775.

TOWNSLEY, John. Taxable in Spesutia Upper Hundred, 1775, with taxable John Townsley (son) listed in his household.

TRACEY, Usher. Taxable on plantation of Amos Garrett, Spesutia Lower Hundred, 1776.

TRADAWAY, Richard. Taxable in Susquehanna Hundred, 1775.

TRAVIS, Robert. Taxable in Bush River Lower Hundred, 1775.

TREADWAY, Daniel. See "Dannil Tridaway," q.v.

TRIDAWAY, Dannell (son of Dannil). Taxable in household of his father Dannil Tridaway, Bush River Upper Hundred, 1775.

TRIDAWAY, Dannil. Taxable in Bush River Upper Hundred, 1775, with taxable Dannell Tridaway (son) and John Page (servant) listed in his household.

TRIMBLE, Robert. Taxable in Bush River Lower Hundred, 1775.

TROTTER, Richard (son of William). Taxable in household of his father William Trotter, Deer Creek Upper Hundred, 1775.

TROTTER, William. Taxable in Deer Creek Upper Hundred, 1775, with taxable Richard Trotter (son) listed in his household.

TRUEBOUER, Mr. (no first name given). Taxable in household of Elizabeth Gallion, Spesutia Lower Hundred, 1776.

TRUELOCK, Moses. See "Moses Tulock," q.v.

TRUELOVE, Michael. Taxable in household of Elizabeth Gallion, Spesutia Lower Hundred, 1775.

TRULOCK, Isaac. Taxable in Gunpowder Lower Hundred, 1775, with taxables Mathew Dorsey and slave Jack listed in his household.

TUCKER, Seaborn. Taxable in Deer Creek Upper Hundred, 1775.

TUCKER, William. Taxable in Susquehanna Hundred,

1775.

TUDER, Will. Taxable (servant) in household of James Stevenson, Bush River Upper Hundred, 1775.

TULOCK, Isaac. Taxable in Spesutia Lower Hundred, 1776, with taxables Mathew Dawsey and negro Hannah listed in his household.

TULOCK, Moses. Taxable in Spesutia Lower Hundred, 1776.

TURK, Esau. Taxable (servant) in household of Isaac Whitaker, Bush River Lower Hundred, 1775.

TURNER, Allexander. Taxable in Bush River Upper Hundred, 1775, with John Clark as his security.

TURNER, Andrew. Taxable in Bush River Upper Hundred, 1775.

TURNER, Danniel. Taxable in Spesutia Upper Hundred, 1775.

TURNER, John. Taxable in household of Rev. John Davis, Bush River Upper Hundred, 1775.

TURNER, Sammul. Taxable in Bush River Upper Hundred, 1775.

TURNER, Thomas. Taxable in Bush River Upper Hundred, 1775.

TUSH, Samuel. Taxable on the plantation of Amos Garrett, Spesutia Lower Hundred, 1775.

TUSTY(?), James. Taxable in Bush River Upper Hundred, 1775, with taxable Nick Day listed in his household.

UMBLE, Isaac. Taxable in Susquehanna Hundred, 1775.

VAN, Edward. Taxable in Spesutia Upper Hundred, 1775.

VANCE, David (son of Sammuel). Taxable in household of his father Sammuel Vance, Gunpowder Lower Hundred, 1775.

VANCE, Sammuel. Taxable in Gunpowder Lower Hundred, 1775, with taxable David Vance (son) listed in his household.

VANCLAVE, John. Taxable in Spesutia Upper Hundred, 1775, with taxable "man James ----" [servant, no last name given] listed in his household.

VANDEGRIF, George. Taxable in Susquehanna Hundred, 1776.

VANDEGRIFF, George. Taxable in Susquehanna Hundred, 1775.

VANHORN, Ezekiel. See "Ezeakle Venhorn," q.v.

VANHORN, Gabriel. Taxable in Bush River Upper Hundred, 1775.

VANHORN, Richard. See "Richard Venhorne," q.v.

VANHORN, Richard. Taxable in household of James Walker, Susquehanna Hundred, 1775.

VANSICKLETON, Henry. Taxable in Spesutia Lower Hundred, 1775, with taxables John Cinnamon and slave Joe listed in his household.

VANSICKLETON, Henry. Taxable in Spesutia Lower Hundred, 1776, with taxables Michael Dorbey, John Churnman, and negroes Joe and Adam listed in his household.

VARLEY, Thomas. Taxable (servant) in household of Edward Norris, Deer Creek Upper Hundred, 1775.

VEATCH (ZEATCH?), Jacob. Taxable in household of Joseph Brownley, Spesutia Upper Hundred, 1775.

VENHORN, Ezeakle Taxable in Susquehanna Hundred, 1776.

VENHORNE, Richard. Taxable in household of James Worker, Susquehanna Hundred, 1776.

VERCHWORTH, William. Taxable in Susquehanna Hundred, 1776, with taxable negro Sharper listed in his household.

VERTCHWORTH, William. Taxable in Susquehanna Hundred, 1775, with taxable Samuel Howel and negroes Sampson, Sharper, and Meriah listed in his household.

VOGAN, George. Taxable in Bush River Upper Hundred, 1775, with taxable negroes Jim and Dina listed in his household.

VOGAN, James. Taxable in Bush River Upper Hundred, 1775, with one taxable servant (no name given).

WAIN, John. Taxable in Bush River Lower Hundred, 1775, with taxable negroes Ned and Jean listed in his household.

WAKELIN, John. Taxable in household of James Everett, Bush River Lower Hundred, 1775.

WALDROM, Richard. Taxable in Spesutia Upper Hundred, 1775.

WALKER, George. Taxable in Susquehanna Hundred, 1775.

WALKER, James. Taxable in Bush River Lower Hundred, 1775.

WALKER, James. Taxable in household of George Garretson, Bush River Lower Hundred, 1775.

WALKER, James. Taxable in Susquehanna Hundred, 1775, with taxables Richard Vanhorn and Jacob Henson listed in his household.

WALKER, John. Taxable on the plantation of Amos Garrett, Spesutia Lower Hundred, 1775.

WALKER, John. Taxable on plantation of Amos Garrett, Spesutia Lower Hundred, 1776.

WALKER, Thomas. Taxable in Spesutia Lower Hundred, 1775, with Josias Dallam as his security.

WALL, Edward. Taxable in household of William Chapel, Susquehanna Hundred, 1775.

WALLACE, Grace. Head of household in Deer Creek Lower Hundred, 1775. with taxable negroes Will, Ben, George, Dinah, Sofe, and Suck listed in her household.

WALTHAM, Charlton. Taxable in household of Thomas Waltham, Gunpowder Lower Hundred, 1775.

WALTHAM, Thomas. Taxable in Gunpowder Lower Hundred, 1775, with taxables Charlton Waltham,

William Waltham, servant Isaac Martin, and slaves Jack, Dick, Charles, Mike, Sue, Nan, Mol, and Gin listed in his household.

WALTHAM, William. Taxable in household of Thomas Waltham, Gunpowder Lower Hundred, 1775.

WARD (WEAD?), Joseph. Taxable in Bush River Upper Hundred, 1775.

WARD, Charles. Taxable in Bush River Upper Hundred, 1775.

WARD, Edward. Taxable in Spesutia Lower Hundred, 1775, with taxable slaves Hazard, Mingo, and Judy listed in his household.

WARD, Edward. Taxable in Deer Creek Lower Hundred, 1775, with taxables Richard Ward (son), George Hubbard, and negro Lida listed in his household.

WARD, Edward. Taxable in Spesutia Lower Hundred, 1776, with taxable negro Hazard listed in his household.

WARD, James. Taxable in Deer Creek Upper Hundred, 1775.

WARD, John. Taxable in Deer Creek Upper Hundred, 1775, with taxable man John ---- (servant, no last name given) listed in his household.

WARD, Joshua. Taxable in Deer Creek Upper Hundred, 1775.

WARD, Richard (son of Edward). Taxable in household of his father Edward Ward, Deer Creek Lower Hundred, 1775.

WARE(?), John. Taxable in household of his father Thomas Ware(?), Bush River Upper Hundred, 1775.

WARE(?), Thomas. Taxable in Bush River Upper Hundred, 1775, with taxable son John Ware(?) listed in his household.

WARMERGER, Thomas. Taxable in Susquehanna Hundred, 1775.

WARNER, Asiph. Taxable in household of his brother Cuthbert Warner, Deer Creek Lower Hundred, 1775.

WARNER, Benjamin. Taxable in Deer Creek Upper Hundred, 1775.

WARNER, Cuthbert. Taxable in Deer Creek Lower Hundred, 1775, with taxable Asiph Warner (brother) listed in his household.

WARNER, Joseph Jr. Taxable in household of Joseph Warner, Deer Creek Lower Hundred, 1775.

WARNER, Joseph. Taxable in Deer Creek Lower Hundred, 1775, with taxable Joseph Warner, Jr. listed in his household.

WATERS, Godfrey. Taxable in Susquehanna Hundred, 1775, with taxable negroes Adam and Puggaty listed in his household.

WATERS, Henry. Taxable in Spesutia Upper Hundred, 1775, with taxables Matthew Judd and negroes Charles and Nell listed in his household.

WATERS, Mary. Head of household in Gunpowder Lower Hundred, 1775, with taxable slaves Pip and Liddy listed in her household.

WATERS, Nicholous. Taxable in Spesutia Upper Hundred, 1775, with taxable negro Jenny listed in his household.

WATERS, Stephen. Taxable in Gunpowder Lower Hundred, 1775, with taxable slaves Pompey and Dick listed in his household.

WATERS, Thomas. Taxable in Bush River Upper Hundred, 1775.

WATERS, Walter. Taxable in Spesutia Upper Hundred, 1775.

WATKINS, John (son of John). Taxable in household of his father John Watkins, Deer Creek Upper Hundred, 1775.

WATKINS, John. Taxable in Spesutia Lower Hundred, 1775, with taxable William Birch listed in his household.

WATKINS, John. Taxable in Deer Creek Upper Hundred, 1775, with taxables Samuel Watkins (son) and John Watkins (son) listed in his household.

WATKINS, Samuel (son of John). Taxable in household of his father John Watkins, Deer Creek Upper Hundred, 1775.

WATSON, Donnill. Taxable in Bush River Upper Hundred, 1775.

WATT, John. Taxable in Deer Creek Upper Hundred, 1775.

WATTERS, Godfery. Taxable in Susquehanna Hundred, 1776, with taxable negroes Adam and Hager listed in his household.

WEAD (WARD?), Joseph. Taxable in Bush River Upper Hundred, 1775.

WEAKES, Dannill. Taxable in Bush River Upper Hundred, 1775.

WEATHERALL, James. Taxable in Spesutia Upper Hundred, 1775.

WEATHERALL, Jos. or Jas. See "Thomas Knight," q.v.

WEBB, Samuel Jr. Taxable in Deer Creek Upper Hundred, 1775.

WEBB, Samuel. Taxable in Deer Creek Upper Hundred, 1775.

WEBB, William. Taxable in Deer Creek Upper Hundred, 1775, with taxable men John Carral(?), James Ray, James Crawford, Realph Alison, John Miller and negroes Parraway, Nase, James, Shiloh, and Bett listed on his plantation.

WEBSTER, Isaac. Taxable in Spesutia Upper Hundred, 1775, with taxables John Smith and negroes Jo, Ben, Will, S--- [illegible], Bobb, Jim, and Bacheus listed in his household.

WEBSTER, James. Taxable in Spesutia Upper Hundred, 1775, with taxable negro Pitt listed in his household.

WEBSTER, John Lee. Taxable in Spesutia Lower

Hundred, 1775, with taxables George Williamson and slaves Dick, Will, Joe, Phil, Frank, Ben, George, Jupiter, David, Dido, Sall, Easther, Dinah, and Nell listed on his plantation.

WEBSTER, John Lee. Taxable in Spesutia Lower Hundred, 1776, with taxable negroes Dick, Will, Phill, Joe, George, Milbourn, Frank, Henry, Ben, David, Mingo, Danby, Tom, Dido, Sall, Esther, Kate, Nelly, Jane, and Nann listed on his plantation.

WEBSTER, Samuel Jr. Taxable in Spesutia Upper Hundred, 1775, with taxables Joseph Nichels and negro Priss listed in his hoousehold.

WEBSTER, Samuel Sr. Taxable in Spesutia Upper Hundred, 1775.

WELCH, James. Taxable in Spesutia Upper Hundred, 1775.

WELCH, John (son of William). Taxable in household of his father William Welch, Spesutia Upper Hundred, 1775.

WELCH, John. Taxable in Spesutia Upper Hundred, 1775.

WELCH, Thomas. Taxable in household of Henry Guspey, Deer Creek Lower Hundred, 1775.

WELCH, Thomas. Taxable in Susquehanna Hundred, 1776.

WELCH, William. Taxable in Spesutia Upper Hundred, 1775, with taxable John Welch (son) listed in his household.

WELCH, William. Taxable in Susquehanna Hundred, 1776, with taxable Rodger Cord listed in his household.

WELLS (WILLS?), William. Taxable in Bush River Upper Hundred, 1775.

WELLS, Richard Jr. Taxable in Deer Creek Lower Hundred, 1775, with taxable negro Phillis listed in his household.

WELLS, Richard. Taxable in Deer Creek Lower Hundred, 1775, with taxable negroes London and Isaac listed in his household.

WELLS, William. Taxable in Deer Creek Upper Hundred, 1775, with taxable negro Bachus listed in his household.

WEST, ----. See "Nathaniel West," q.v.

WEST, David. Taxable in Bush River Upper Hundred, 1775.

WEST, Enoch. Taxable in Susquehanna Hundred, 1775, with taxable Thomas West listed in his household.

WEST, Enoch. Taxable in Susquehanna Hundred, 1776, with taxable Thomas West listed in his household.

WEST, Isaac. Taxable in household of Samuel West, Bush River Upper Hundred, 1775.

WEST, James (Jr.?). Taxable in household of John Griffeth, Susquehanna Hundred, 1776.

WEST, John. Taxable in Spesutia Upper Hundred, 1775.

WEST, John. Taxable in Deer Creek Lower Hundred, 1775.

WEST, Jonathan (son of Jonathan). Taxable in household of his father Jonathan West, Spesutia Upper Hundred, 1775.

WEST, Jonathan. Taxable in Spesutia Upper Hundred, 1775, with taxable Jonathan West (son) listed in his household.

WEST, Joseph. Taxable in Deer Creek Upper Hundred, 1775.

WEST, Nathaniel. Taxable in Bush River Lower Hundred, 1775. "Nathaniel West" was security for Edward Freeman, 1775. Also, tax was paid by "Nathan West for his son" (name not given), 1775.

WEST, Robert. Taxable in Susquehanna Hundred, 1775.

WEST, Robert. Taxable in Susquehanna Hundred, 1776.

WEST, Samuel. Taxable in Bush River Upper Hundred, 1775, with taxables Thomas and Isaac listed in hise household.

WEST, Thomas. Taxable in Susquehanna Hundred, 1775.

WEST, Thomas. Taxable in household of ENoch West, Susquehanna Hundred, 1775.

WEST, Thomas. Taxable in Spesutia Lower Hundred, 1775.

WEST, Thomas. Taxable in household of Samuel West, Bush River Upper Hundred, 1775.

WEST, Thomas. Taxable in household of Enoch West, Susquehanna Hundred, 1776.

WEST, Thomas. Taxable in Susquehanna Hundred, 1776.

WEST, William (reverend). Spesutia Lower Hundred, 1775, with taxable slaves Priscilla, Will, and Fann listed in his household, and slaves Austin, Peter, Harry, Mary, and Davy listed "at ye glebe" [plus another name that is illegible due to the page being very dark and smudged, but it might be Talbot O'Dell who was listed with Rev. West in the 1774 tax list]. It should be noted that Rev. West himself was not a taxable (clergymen were exempted from being taxed).

WEST, William (reverend). See "Samuel Hanson," q.v.

WEST, William. Taxable in Susquehanna Hundred, 1775.

WESTFIELD, William. Taxable on the plantation of Amos Garrett, Spesutia Lower Hundred, 1775.

WETHERELL, Henery. Taxable in Gunpowder Lower Hundred, 1775, with taxable slaves Toby, Jim, and Phillis listed in his household.

WHEELER, Benjamin. See "Benjaman Wheler," q.v.

WHEELER, Elizabeth. See "Elizabeth Wheler," q.v.

WHEELER, Ignatius Jr. Taxable in Deer Creek Upper Hundred, 1775, with taxables Thomas Pembrick(?) and negroes Isaac, Tom, Bill, Jess, Moll, Marier, Nell, and Clove listed on his plantation.

WHEELER, Ignatius. See "Ignatious Wheler," q.v.

WHEELER, James. Taxable in Gunpowder Lower

Hundred, 1775, with James Butters as his security.

WHEELER, Joseph. See "Joseph Wheler," q.v.

WHEELER, Thomas. See "Thomas Wheler," q.v.

WHELAR, Jacob. Taxable in Bush River Upper Hundred, 1775.

WHELAR, Thomas. Taxable in Bush River Upper Hundred, 1775, with taxable negro Abram listed in his household.

WHELER, Benjaman. Taxable in Spesutia Upper Hundred, 1775, with taxable Thomas Wheler (son) and negroes Jack, Tom, Henny, and Nan listed in his household.

WHELER, Bennett. Taxable in household of Ignatious Wheler, Spesutia Upper Hundred, 1775.

WHELER, Elizabeth. Head of household in Spesutia Upper Hundred, 1775, with taxable negroes Jack and Cate listed in her household.

WHELER, Ignatious. Taxable in Spesutia Upper Hundred, 1775, with taxables Bennett Wheler, Joseph Wheler, and negroes Tom, Nace, Will, Robin, Sam, Jone, Hanary, Sall, Nan, Henny, Hester, and Nace or Nan [illegible] listed on his plantation.

WHELER, Joseph. Taxable in household of Ignatious Wheler, Spesutia Upper Hundred, 1775.

WHELER, Joseph. Taxable in Spesutia Upper Hundred, 1775, with taxable negroes Jim and Sarah listed in his household.

WHELER, Thomas (son of Benjaman). Taxable in household of his father Benjaman Wheler, Spesutia Upper Hundred, 1775.

WHELER, Thomas. Taxable in Spesutia Upper Hundred, 1775, with taxable negroes Abner, Ned, Jack, Tony, Cook, Darkish, Rachel, and Bett listed in his household.

WHITACRE's Quarters [sic]. Bush River Lower Hundred, 1775, with 5 taxables at these quarters (no names given).

WHITAKER, Hezekiah. Taxable in household of Thomas Fisher, Spesutia Lower Hundred, 1775.

WHITAKER, Isaac. Taxable in Bush River Lower Hundred, 1775, with servant Esau Turk listed in his household.

WHITAKER, Isaac. Taxable in household of Thomas Fisher, Spesutia Lower Hundred, 1775.

WHITE, Aaron. Taxable in household of Phillip Henderson, Spesutia Upper Hundred, 1775.

WHITE, Charles. Taxable on the plantation of Amos Garrett, Spesutia Lower Hundred, 1775.

WHITE, Charles. Taxable in Spesutia Lower Hundred, 1775.

WHITE, Charles. Taxable in Spesutia Lower Hundred, 1776.

WHITE, Grafton. Taxable in Bush River Lower Hundred, 1775.

WHITE, James. Taxable in Gunpowder Lower Hundred, 1775.

WHITE, John. Taxable in household of Thomas Presbury, Gunpowder Lower Hundred, 1775.

WHITE, Jonathan. Taxable in Spesutia Lower Hundred, 1776, with taxable Oliver Denney listed in his household.

WHITE, Richard. Taxable in Susquehanna Hundred, 1775.

WHITE, Richard. Taxable in Susquehanna Hundred, 1776.

WHITE, Stephen. Taxable in Bush River Lower Hundred, 1775.

WHITE, Thomas (colonel). Taxable in Susquehanna Hundred, 1775, with taxable William Wilson and negroes Sam, Medars, Jessee, Hanibal, Limpal, Rachael, and Esther listed in his household.

WHITE, Thomas (colonel). Taxable in Susquehanna Hundred, 1776, with taxable negroes Sam, Medary, Lin, Rachel, Jessey, Anneble, Eyester, and Pol listed on his plantation.

WHITEFORD, Hugh Jr. Taxable in Deer Creek Upper Hundred, 1775, with taxables William Bates and negro Grace listed in his household.

WHITEFORD, John. Taxable in Deer Creek Upper Hundred, 1775, with taxable men John Johnson and John McCall listed in his household.

WHITEFORD, William. Taxable in Deer Creek Upper Hundred, 1775.

WHITEKAR, Abram. Taxable in Bush River Upper Hundred, 1775, with taxable servant George ---- (no last name given) and negroes Mary and Dina listed in his household.

WHITEKAR, John. Taxable in the household of Leven Matthews, Spesutia Lower Hundred, 1775.

WHITEKAR, John. Taxable in Bush River Upper Hundred, 1775, with one taxable servant (no name given) listed in his household.

WHITEKER, Isaac's Quarters. Spesutia Upper Hundred, 1775, with taxable negroes Hary and Pegg listed at these quarters.

WIGGINGS, James. Taxable in Spesutia Lower Hundred, 1775.

WIGGINS, James. Taxable in Spesutia Lower Hundred, 1776.

WILES, John. Taxable in Bush River Lower Hundred, 1775.

WILEY, John. Taxable in household of Nathaniel Wiley, Deer Creek Lower Hundred, 1775.

WILEY, Nathaniel. Taxable in Deer Creek Lower Hundred, 1775, with taxable John Wiley listed in his household.

WILGUSS, James. Taxable in Bush River Upper Hundred, 1775.

EARLY HARFORD COUNTIANS: Supplement

WILKINSON, John. Taxable at Jacob Giles' mill at Bush, Spesutia Lower Hundred, 1775.

WILLIAMS, ---- (no first name). See "Jacob Botts," q.v.

WILLIAMS, Barnet. Taxable in household of William Williams, Susquehanna Hundred, 1776.

WILLIAMS, Barnett. Taxable in Susquehanna Hundred, 1775.

WILLIAMS, Daniel. Taxable in household of Jacob Giles, Susquehanna Hundred, 1775.

WILLIAMS, Daniel. Taxable in household of Thomas Giles, Spesutia Lower Hundred, 1776.

WILLIAMS, David. Taxable in Bush River Upper Hundred, 1775, with taxable Richard Williams (son) listed in his household.

WILLIAMS, Edward. Taxable in Susquehanna Hundred, 1775 [The name was entered on the tax list and then a line was drawn through it; no reason was given].

WILLIAMS, George. Taxable in household of Enoch Spencer, Bush River Lower Hundred, 1775.

WILLIAMS, James. Taxable in Susquehanna Hundred, 1775.

WILLIAMS, James. Taxable in Susquehanna Hundred, 1776.

WILLIAMS, John. Taxable in Susquehanna Hundred, 1775.

WILLIAMS, Morris. Taxable in Susquehanna Hundred, 1776. [The constable listed the name without the "s" at the end of "Williams"].

WILLIAMS, Richard. Taxable in household of his father David Williams, Bush River Upper Hundred, 1775.

WILLIAMS, Robert. Taxable in household of Jacob Giles, Jr., Susquehanna Hundred, 1775.

WILLIAMS, Thomas. Taxable at Jacob Giles' mill at Bush, Spesutia Lower Hundred, 1775.

WILLIAMS, William. Taxable in Susquehanna Hundred, 1775.

WILLIAMS, William. Taxable in Susquehanna Hundred, 1775, with taxable James Boner listed in his household.

WILLIAMS, William. Taxable in household of Bennett Matthews, Spesutia Upper Hundred, 1775.

WILLIAMS, William. Taxable in Susquehanna Hundred, 1776, with taxable Barnet Williams listed in his household.

WILLIAMSON, George. Taxable on plantation of John Lee Webster, Spesutia Lower Hundred, 1775.

WILLIAMSON, George. Taxable in Spesutia Lower Hundred, 1776.

WILLMOT, Richard (son of Richard). Taxable in household of his father Richard Willmot, Spesutia Upper Hundred, 1775.

WILLMOT, Richard. Taxable in Spesutia Upper Hundred, 1775, with taxables Richard Willmot (son) and negroes Pimon (Simon?), Sirues (Silues?), Peter, Mary, Beck, Hager, Debb, Pegg, and Nell listed in his household.

WILLMURTON, Joseph. Taxable in household of Benjamin Fleetwood, Susquehanna Hundred, 1776.

WILLS (WELLS?), William. Taxable in Bush River Upper Hundred, 1775.

WILLS, James. Taxable in household of Richard Cruise, Susquehanna Hundred, 1775.

WILLSON, Henry. Taxable in Spesutia Lower Hundred, 1776.

WILMER, Lambert. Taxable in Gunpowder Lower Hundred, 1775, with taxables Godfrey Gunrey and slaves Will, Peter, Fan, Dina, Sal, and Cloe listed in her household.

WILMOTT, Samuel. Taxable in Bush River Lower Hundred, 1775.

WILSON, Andrew. Taxable in Susquehanna Hundred, 1775, with taxable John Allet listed in his household.

WILSON, Andrey [sic]. Taxable in Susquehanna Hundred, 1776, with taxable John Hollit listed in his household.

WILSON, Benjaman. Taxable in Deer Creek Lower Hundred, 1775, with taxable negroes Hazard and Amey listed in his household.

WILSON, Henry Jr. Taxable in Bush River Lower Hundred, 1775, with taxable negroes Tom and Dyner listed in his household.

WILSON, Henry Sr. Taxable in Bush River Lower Hundred, 1775, with taxable negroes Tower and Sue listed in his household. Security for negroes Tom, Lyda, Affey, and Juda.

WILSON, Hugh (Glades). Taxable in Deer Creek Lower Hundred, 1775.

WILSON, Hugh. Taxable in Bush River Lower Hundred, 1775.

WILSON, James (Glades). Taxable in Deer Creek Lower Hundred, 1775.

WILSON, James Sr. Taxable in Gunpowder Lower Hundred, 1775, with taxable William Wilson listed in his household.

WILSON, John (Glades). Taxable in Deer Creek Lower Hundred, 1775.

WILSON, John (merchant). Taxable in Susquehanna Hundred, 1775, with taxables Peter Wilson, William Paea or Paca, John Stump, Christian Toole, and Negro Nan listed in his household.

WILSON, John (Rock Run). Taxable in Susquehanna Hundred, 1776.

WILSON, John Jr. (Glades). Taxable in Deer Creek Lower Hundred, 1775.

WILSON, John. Taxable in Bush River Lower Hundred, 1775, with taxable David Levey listed in his household.

WILSON, John. Taxable in Bush River Lower Hundred,

1775.

WILSON, John. Taxable in Deer Creek Lower Hundred, 1775, with taxable negro Hager listed in his household.

WILSON, John. Taxable in Deer Creek Upper Hundred, 1775.

WILSON, John. Taxable in Deer Creek Upper Hundred, 1775, with taxables Joseph Wilson (son) and negro Nan listed in his household.

WILSON, Joseph (son of John). Taxable in household of his father John Wilson, Deer Creek Upper Hundred, 1775.

WILSON, Joseph Jr. Taxable in Deer Creek Lower Hundred, 1775, with taxable negro Ned listed in his household.

WILSON, Joseph. Taxable in Deer Creek Lower Hundred, 1775, with taxable negroes Sarah and Peg listed in his household.

WILSON, Kid. Taxable in Bush River Lower Hundred, 1775, with taxable servant James Stalkap (Stackap?) listed in his household.

WILSON, Peter. Taxable in household of John Wilson (merchant), Susquehanna Hundred, 1775.

WILSON, Peter. Taxable in Susquehanna Hundred, 1776.

WILSON, Rachel. Head of household in Susquehanna Hundred, 1776, with taxable negroes Floro and Jane listed in her household.

WILSON, Samuel. Taxable in Deer Creek Lower Hundred, 1775, with taxable negro Ned listed in his household.

WILSON, Samuel. Taxable in Susquehanna Hundred, 1776, with taxable negroes Clem, Betty, and Cloe listed in his household.

WILSON, William (overseer). Taxable in Susquehanna Hundred, 1776, with taxable negroes Ned and Jemima listed in his household.

WILSON, William Jr. Taxable in Bush River Lower Hundred, 1775 (5 taxables, but only his name was given).

WILSON, William. Taxable in household of James Wilson, Sr., Gunpowder Lower Hundred, 1775.

WILSON, William. Taxable in Susquehanna Hundred, 1775, with taxable negroes Ned and Jemimah listed in his household. [The actual entry shows "William Wilson, Negroe Ned, Jemimah" and then "Negroe Quarter" and a total of "2" taxables].

WILSON, William. Taxable in Susquehanna Hundred, 1775, with taxable negroes Harry, Chloe, Jane, Betty, Flora, Ada, and Coleme listed in his household.

WILSON, William. Taxable in household of Col. Thomas White, Susquehanna Hundred, 1775.

WILSON, William. Taxable in Susquehanna Hundred, 1776, with taxable negroes Harry, Adam, and Cloe listed in his household.

WILTSHIRE, Samuel. Taxable in Spesutia Lower Hundred, 1775.

WINEMAN, John. Taxable in Deer Creek Lower Hundred, 1775.

WINKS, Joseph. Taxable in Bush River Lower Hundred, 1775.

WINNET, Thomas. Taxable in household of Thaddeus Juett, Spesutia Upper Hundred, 1775.

WOMMEGEM, Thomas. Taxable in Susquehanna Hundred, 1776.

WOOD, George. Taxable in household of John Crusson, Susquehanna Hundred, 1776.

WOOD, Isaac. Taxable in Susquehanna Hundred, 1775.

WOOD, James. Taxable in Susquehanna Hundred, 1775.

WOOD, James. Taxable in Susquehanna Hundred, 1776.

WOOD, John. Taxable in Spesutia Lower Hundred, 1775, with taxables Michael Rouke and Nathan Harris(?) listed in his household.

WOOD, John. Taxable in Spesutia Lower Hundred, 1776, with taxables Nathaniel Horner and Michael Rorke listed in his household.

WOOD, Joseph. See "Robert Briarly," q.v.

WOOD, Joshua. Taxable in Susquehanna Hundred, 1775.

WOOD, Joshua. Taxable in Susquehanna Hundred, 1776.

WOODLAND, Jonathan. Taxable in Gunpowder Lower Hundred, 1775, with taxable slaves Herculees, Rene, and Temer listed in his household.

WOODS, Henry. Taxable in Bush River Upper Hundred, 1775.

WOODWARD, Thomas. Taxable in Spesutia Lower Hundred, 1775.

WOODWARD, Thomas. Taxable in Spesutia Lower Hundred, 1776.

WOOLEY, Jacob. Taxable on the plantation of Amos Garrett, Spesutia Lower Hundred, 1775.

WOOLSY, Joseph. Taxable in Spesutia Upper Hundred, 1775, with taxable Patrick Butler listed in his household.

WOOLT, George. Taxable in household of John Cruise, Susquehanna Hundred, 1775.

WORKER, George. Taxable in Spesutia Lower Hundred, 1776.

WORKER, James. Taxable in Susquehanna Hundred, 1776, with taxables Richard Venhorne and Jacob Hanson listed in his household.

WORRILOW, William. Taxable in household of Thomas Ellet, Bush River Upper Hundred, 1775.

WORSLEY, George (reverend). See "William Lattimore," q.v.

WORSLEY, George. Taxable in Bush River Upper Hundred, 1775.

WORTHINGTON, Charles. Taxable in Deer Creek Lower Hundred, 1775, with taxable negroes Harrey and Sall listed in his household.

EARLY HARFORD COUNTIANS: Supplement

WORTHINGTON, John. Taxable in Deer Creek Lower Hundred, 1775, with taxable negroes Boatswain, Pompey, Jenney, Fanney, and Meriah listed in his household.

WORTHINGTON, Samuel. Taxable in Deer Creek Lower Hundred, 1775, with taxable negroes Davey, Ceaser, and Paul listed in his household.

WRAIN, William. Taxable in Spesutia Lower Hundred, 1775.

WRIGHT, Charles. Taxable in household of William Chapel, Susquehanna Hundred, 1775.

WRIGHT, Charles. Taxable in household of William Cox, Susquehanna Hundred, 1776.

WRIGHT, Daniel. Taxable in household of William Ady, Bush River Lower Hundred, 1775.

WRIGHT, John. Taxable in household of William Loney, Spesutia Lower Hundred, 1776.

WRIGHT, Thomas. Serveant (and taxable) in household of Edward Talbott, Bush River Lower Hundred, 1775.

WRIGHT, Thomas. Taxable in Bush River Lower Hundred, 1775, with taxable Christopher Clemen listed in his household.

YARDLEY, Nathaniel. Taxable in Bush River Lower Hundred, 1775.

YEAMON, Thomas. Taxable in Spesutia Upper Hundred, 1775.

YEATES, George. Taxable in Spesutia Upper Hundred, 1775.

YORK, George. Taxable in Gunpowder Lower Hundred, 1775.

YORK, James. Taxable in Gunpowder Lower Hundred, 1775.

YORK, Oliver. Taxable in Gunpowder Lower Hundred, 1775.

YOUNG, Clark's Quarters. Spesutia Lower Hundred, 1775, with taxables William Godsgrace and slaves Jerry, Jack, Nat, David, and Nann listed at these quarters.

YOUNG, George. Taxable in Spesutia Upper Hundred, 1775.

YOUNG, Robert. Taxable in Spesutia Upper Hundred, 1775, with taxable "man John ----" [servant] and negro Sarah listed in his household.

YOUNG, Thomas. Taxable on the plantation of Amos Garrett, Spesutia Lower Hundred, 1775.

YOUNG, Thomas. Taxable in household of Thomas Chisholm, Susquehanna Hundred, 1776.

YOUNG, William. Taxable in Spesutia Lower Hundred, 1775, with taxable servant Thomas McDornel or McDaniel(?) and two slaves, one named Silvey and the other name illegible. See "John Clark (schoolmaster)," q.v.

ZEATCH (YEATCH?), Jacob. Taxable in household of Joseph Brownley, Spesutia Upper Hundred, 1775.

----, Alexander. See "George Paterson," q.v.

----, Benjamin (no last name given). Taxable (servant) in household of James Scott, Bush River Upper Hundred, 1775.

----, Charles (no last name given). Taxable (servant) in household of Alexander Cowen, Gunpowder Lower Hundred, 1775.

----, Daniel (no last name given). Taxable (servant) in household of William Anderson, Bush River Lower Hundred, 1775.

----, Dick (no last name given). Taxable (servant) in household of Joshua Durham, Bush River Lower Hundred, 1775.

----, George (no last name given). Taxable (servant) in household of Alexander Cowen, Gunpowder Lower Hundred, 1775.

----, George (no last name given). Taxable (servant) in household of Abram Whitekar, Bush River Upper Hundred, 1775.

----, Hannah (no last name given). Free negro and head of household in Susquehanna Hundred, 1776.

----, James (no last name given). Taxable (servant) in household of Hugh Kirkpatrick, Spesutia Upper Hundred, 1775.

----, James (no last name given). Taxable (servant) in household of John Vanclave, Spesutia Upper Hundred, 1775.

----, Jehu (no last name given). See "Negro Jehu," q.v.

----, Jehue (no last name given). Free negro and head of household in Susquehanna Hundred, 1776. See "Negro Jehue," q.v.

----, John (no last name given). Taxable (servant) in household of David Lee, Bush River Lower Hundred, 1775.

----, John (no last name given). Taxable (servant) in the household of Thomas Denney, Spesutia Upper Hundred, 1775.

----, John (no last name given). Taxable (servant) in household of Robert Young, Spesutia Upper Hundred, 1775.

----, John (no last name given). Taxable (servant) in household of John Ward, Deer Creek Upper Hundred, 1775.

----, John. See "Hugh P----," q.v.

----, John. Servant (and taxable) in household of James Everett, Bush River Lower Hundred, 1775.

----, Jonathan (no last name given). Taxable in household of Joseph Norris, Bush River Lower Hundred, 1775.

----, Jonathan (no last name given). Taxable (servant) in household of Robert Smith, Deer Creek Upper Hundred, 1775.

----, Joseph (no last name given). Taxable in household of Joseph Presbury, Gunpowder Lower Hundred, 1775.

----, Joseph (no last name given). Taxable in household of

Robert Briarly, Bush River Upper Hundred, 1775.
- ----, Mike (no last name given). Taxable (servant) in household of Martenie Parker, Bush River Upper Hundred, 1775.
- ----, Patrick (no last name given). Taxable (servant) in household of Daniel Scott, Bush River Lower Hundred, 1775.
- ----, Perrey (no last name given). Taxable apprentice ("prentis boy") in household of Ephram Biards, Susquehanna Hundred, 1776.
- ----, Peter (no last name given). Taxable (servant) in household of Alexander Thompson, Spesutia Upper Hundred, 1775.
- ----, Pompey (no last name given). See "Negro Pompey," q.v.
- ----, RIchard (no last name given). Taxable (servant) in household of Thomas Streett, Bush River Upper Hundred, 1775.
- ----, Robert (no last name given). Taxable (servant) in household of Patrick Rork, Bush River Upper Hundred, 1775.
- ----, Ros (no last name given). Taxable (servant) in household of Martenie Parker, Bush River Upper Hundred, 1775.
- ----, Sam (no last name given). See "Negro Sam," q.v.
- ----, Samuel (no last name given). Taxable (servant) in household of David Lee, Bush River Lower Hundred, 1775.
- ----, Sary (no last name given). Free negro and head of household in Susquehanna Hundred, 1776.
- ----, Sauce or Samie(?). Taxable in household of Mary Griffith, Spcsutia Lower Hundred, 1775.
- ----, Stephen (no last name given). Taxable in household of Joseph Norris, Bush River Lower Hundred, 1775.
- ----, Thomas (no last name given). Taxable (servant) in household of John Taylor, Bush River Lower Hundred, 1775.
- ----, Thomas (no last name given). Servant (and taxable) in household of Benjamin Rumsey, Gunpowder Lower Hundred, 1775.
- ----, Thomas (no last name given). Taxable (servant) in the household of Joshua Chalk, Bush River Upper Hundred, 1775.
- ----, Thomas (no last name given). Free negro and head of household in Susquehanna Hundred, 1776. For other names, see "Negro Thomas (a free negro)," q.v.
- ----, Tower (no last name given). Free negro and head of household in Susquehanna Hundred, 1776, with Giddean Pervale as his security.
- ----, William (last name illegible). Taxable (servant) in household of Robert Cannaday, Deer Creek Upper Hundred, 1775.

Other Heritage Books by Henry C. Peden, Jr. :

A Closer Look at St. John's Parish Registers [Baltimore County, Maryland], 1701-1801

A Collection of Maryland Church Records

A Guide to Genealogical Research in Maryland: 5th Edition, Revised and Enlarged

Abstracts of the Ledgers and Accounts of the Bush Store and Rock Run Store, 1759-1771

Abstracts of the Orphans Court Proceedings of Harford County, 1778-1800

Abstracts of Wills, Harford County, Maryland, 1800-1805

Baltimore City [Maryland] Deaths and Burials, 1834-1840

Baltimore County, Maryland, Overseers of Roads, 1693-1793

Bastardy Cases in Baltimore County, Maryland, 1673-1783

Bastardy Cases in Harford County, Maryland, 1774-1844

Bible and Family Records of Harford County, Maryland Families: Volume V

Children of Harford County: Indentures and Guardianships, 1801-1830

Colonial Delaware Soldiers and Sailors, 1638-1776

*Colonial Families of the Eastern Shore of Maryland
Volumes 5, 6, 7, 8, 9, 11, 12, 13, 14, and 16*

Colonial Maryland Soldiers and Sailors, 1634-1734

Dr. John Archer's First Medical Ledger, 1767-1769, Annotated Abstracts

Early Anglican Records of Cecil County

*Early Harford Countians, Individuals Living in Harford County, Maryland in Its Formative Years
Volume 1: A to K, Volume 2: L to Z, and Volume 3: Supplement*

Harford County Taxpayers in 1870, 1872 and 1883

Harford County, Maryland Divorce Cases, 1827-1912: An Annotated Index

Heirs and Legatees of Harford County, Maryland, 1774-1802

Heirs and Legatees of Harford County, Maryland, 1802-1846

Inhabitants of Baltimore County, Maryland, 1763-1774

Inhabitants of Cecil County, Maryland, 1649-1774

Inhabitants of Harford County, Maryland, 1791-1800

Inhabitants of Kent County, Maryland, 1637-1787

*Joseph A. Pennington & Co., Havre De Grace, Maryland Funeral Home Records:
Volume II, 1877-1882, 1893-1900*

Maryland Bible Records, Volume 1: Baltimore and Harford Counties

Maryland Bible Records, Volume 2: Baltimore and Harford Counties

Maryland Bible Records, Volume 3: Carroll County

Maryland Bible Records, Volume 4: Eastern Shore

Maryland Deponents, 1634-1799

Maryland Deponents: Volume 3, 1634-1776

*Maryland Public Service Records, 1775-1783: A Compendium of Men and Women of
Maryland Who Rendered Aid in Support of the American Cause against
Great Britain during the Revolutionary War*

*Marylanders to Carolina: Migration of Marylanders to
North Carolina and South Carolina prior to 1800*

Marylanders to Kentucky, 1775-1825

Methodist Records of Baltimore City, Maryland: Volume 1, 1799-1829

Methodist Records of Baltimore City, Maryland: Volume 2, 1830-1839

*Methodist Records of Baltimore City, Maryland: Volume 3, 1840-1850
(East City Station)*

More Maryland Deponents, 1716-1799

*More Marylanders to Carolina: Migration of Marylanders to
North Carolina and South Carolina prior to 1800*

More Marylanders to Kentucky, 1778-1828

Outpensioners of Harford County, Maryland, 1856-1896

Presbyterian Records of Baltimore City, Maryland, 1765-1840

Quaker Records of Baltimore and Harford Counties, Maryland, 1801-1825

Quaker Records of Northern Maryland, 1716-1800

Quaker Records of Southern Maryland, 1658-1800

Revolutionary Patriots of Anne Arundel County, Maryland

Revolutionary Patriots of Baltimore Town and Baltimore County, 1775-1783

Revolutionary Patriots of Calvert and St. Mary's Counties, Maryland, 1775-1783

Revolutionary Patriots of Caroline County, Maryland, 1775-1783

Revolutionary Patriots of Cecil County, Maryland

Revolutionary Patriots of Charles County, Maryland, 1775-1783

Revolutionary Patriots of Delaware, 1775-1783

Revolutionary Patriots of Dorchester County, Maryland, 1775-1783

Revolutionary Patriots of Frederick County, Maryland, 1775-1783

Revolutionary Patriots of Harford County, Maryland, 1775-1783

Revolutionary Patriots of Kent and Queen Anne's Counties

Revolutionary Patriots of Lancaster County, Pennsylvania

Revolutionary Patriots of Maryland, 1775-1783: A Supplement

Revolutionary Patriots of Maryland, 1775-1783: Second Supplement

Revolutionary Patriots of Montgomery County, Maryland, 1776-1783

Revolutionary Patriots of Prince George's County, Maryland, 1775-1783

Revolutionary Patriots of Talbot County, Maryland, 1775-1783

Revolutionary Patriots of Worcester and Somerset Counties, Maryland, 1775-1783

Revolutionary Patriots of Washington County, Maryland, 1776-1783

*St. George's (Old Spesutia) Parish, Harford County, Maryland:
Church and Cemetery Records, 1820-1920*

St. John's and St. George's Parish Registers, 1696-1851

Survey Field Book of David and William Clark in Harford County, Maryland, 1770-1812

The Crenshaws of Kentucky, 1800-1995

The Delaware Militia in the War of 1812

*Union Chapel United Methodist Church Cemetery Tombstone Inscriptions,
Wilna, Harford County, Maryland*

www.ingramcontent.com/pod-product-compliance
Lightning Source LLC
Chambersburg PA
CBHW080251170426
43192CB00014BA/2641